Ethics and International Politics

Studies in International Relations

Charles W. Kegley, Jr.,
and Donald J. Puchala, General Editors

Ethics and International Politics

Luigi Bonanate

Translated by John Irving

University of South Carolina Press

First published in the United States by the
University of South Carolina Press

Printed in Great Britain

99 98 97 96 95   5 4 3 2 1

First published in the UK by Polity Press
in association with Blackwell Publishers

First published in Italy as *Etica e politica internazionale*
© Giulio Einaudi editore, Turin 1992

Library of Congress Cataloging-in-Publication Data

Bonanate, Luigi.
    [Etica e politica internazionale.   English]
    Ethics and international politics / Luigi Bonanate : translated by
John Irving.
        p.   cm. — (Studies in international relations)
    Includes index.
    ISBN 1–57003–076–6 (hb : alk. paper)
    1. International relations—Moral and ethical aspects.   I. Title.
II. Series: Studies in international relations (Columbia, S.C.)
JX1395.B62613   1996
172'.4—dc20   95–13017

Contents

Preface

The subject of this book is encapsulated in the question, 'Can ethical theory be applied to international relations?' Since my personal answer is an affirmative one, it follows that I adopt an original approach to analyse the state, a subject which exists only in so far as it belongs to a broader, richer reality – that of all other states. Since the ethical principles I discuss have been elaborated mainly with reference to individuals, it is necessary to clarify that the application by analogy to states of the logical and interpretative categories deducible from the conduct of individuals can only go so far. The state is intrinsically different from the individual, which means that its analysis diverges significantly too. The most important difference is that, whereas it is normal for any individual to possess rights as well as duties, this is not the case of the state. For centuries we have believed that, outside its borders, the state has nothing but rights. In the pages that follow, I attempt to show that it is more important to concentrate on its duties (without of course annulling its rights). This means that the state has responsibilities *vis-à-vis* a variety of subjects; not only its own nationals but also other states, which it must respect to the measure in which it wishes to be respected by them, and the citizens of other states, whom it cannot consider less worthy human beings than its own. This is the point around which the argument rotates, the point that demands original consideration. There is no difference, in ethical terms, between a British citizen and an Italian citizen, either before British law or before Italian law or before the law of a third state. Even if normative systems change, the intrinsic nature of the individual cannot. This means that each state has the duty to concern itself equally with all the citizens of the world, except of course when practical differences attenuate this constraint for reasons of material distance and international integration and collaboration. The most important consequence of this formulation is that every state has a duty to 'intervene' even outside its own borders to safeguard the elementary rights of individuals, whatever their state of

origin. Among the examples to which this conclusion is applicable is of
course the situation in the former Yugoslavia, and the international
community's theoretical duty to intervene to put an end to the scandalous violations of human rights that have taken place there.

It is not easy to argue a thesis of this kind, particularly in view of the
obvious complexity and delicacy of its practical implications. How can
such an operation be organized without infringing the sovereignty of
the state in question? Yet the fact that we are conscious of the immense
complexity of a given programme does not exempt us from recognizing
its justice – if of course we believe in it. Its implementation, which
involves problems of a logical, practical nature, is a different matter
again. I feel that it is necessary, in any case, to construct an international ethical theory as a reference point for measuring the shifts from
the norm which real conditions compel upon statesmen (and also upon
moralists). Either that, or we let things take their own course, dispensing not only with intervention but also with moral judgement. This,
in my view, would be an intolerable shunning of responsibility. The
huge distance which divides the ideal from the real cannot of course
be underestimated: the crux of the matter is invariably the state, whose
sociability still cannot be considered as *spontaneous*. Some use the fact
to argue that any attempt to 'moralize' its conduct is untenable. Besides
being extremely hard to refute, this type of objection raises points of
fundamental importance. It is, first of all, the reason why I have addressed the problem of international ethics from the political scientist's
standpoint, not the philosopher's – although I have based my argument
on the results of philosophical as opposed to political research. The
premise I have drawn from my political studies concerns what seems to
me to be the abstract view which philosophers have of international
political reality. They continue to regard states as autonomous, self-
contained entities, monads with only two options open to them: either
they remain as they are (in which case, it is impossible to apply any
ethical principle to them), or they join together in a purely cosmopolitan
world society (in which case, the problem would automatically cancel
itself out, and the urgent need for moral judgement with it). My position
lies halfway between the two – or, at least, runs in a parallel line to
them. What seems important to me is that we construct principles of
analysis enabling us to judge states as they are today; namely, subjects
typified by a kind of sociability that is not the sociability of individuals.
The state's sociability is specific to statehood. A state's relations with all
other states are not based solely on hatred and hostility. For most of the
time it collaborates, trades and deals, and hence coexists harmoniously
with them. The intensity of international intercourse allows states to

experience a sort of interdependence analogous to that which leads individuals to establish rules of coexistence: what ensues is a law of nations (average obedience to which is normally greater than the obedience which states receive from their nationals), international politics (in which there is more peace than war), an international society (which is moving ever more rapidly towards planetary unification) and international culture (in which ideas are circulating with increasing freedom). That this gives life to a reality equal to that of states there can be no doubt: but, seen as a whole, all these various aspects create a network of relations, so close-knit as to be analysable even from an ethical point of view. The coexistence of states and their citizens provides a wealth of material for observation which cannot be reduced schematically to the alternative of peace or war. This is the field of research of international ethics. Just as a legal system does not lose its nature simply because it has no power of coercion, so an ethical system may be constructed and discussed even if its assessments are not valid *erga omnes*, and if statesmen do not not always (or hardly ever) draw inspiration from it. If we accept this viewpoint, the development of an ethical theory of international life appears as an extremely important and original task to which, only a few years ago, no attention was devoted at all. If we learn to 'think morally' in the international political realm, this might teach us to 'act morally' in the future.

For Italian readers I honestly believe that the publication of *Etica e politica internazionale* was something of a novelty. For here in Italy the issues it addresses are discussed only rarely. English-speaking readers find themselves in an entirely different position. Over the last decade or so, they have grown accustomed to discussing the ethical dimension of international affairs, thanks to the publication of numerous works of the highest scientific order addressing the question both on an international scale and with reference to single aspects. Not surprisingly, in my study I refer almost exclusively to British and American studies. A recent book such as *Traditions of International Ethics*, edited by T. Nardin and D. R. Mapel (Cambridge, 1992), would probably have struggled to find a publisher in Italy, and certainly, in view of the Italian reading public's scant interest in the subject, would have found no publisher prepared to translate it. Italian readers would be dumbstruck to hear talk of a 'tradition' (a corpus of centuries of research, characterized by classics, schools of thought, original proposals and a specialized debate) of reflection on international ethics! Although I sought in the Italian edition to be as updated as possible, three recent books (published more or less at the same time as mine) seem to me emblematic of the different positions on international ethics prevailing in the English-speaking world.

They are: *Ethics for a Shrinking World* by G. Elfstrom (London, 1990);
The Place of Morality in Foreign Policy by F. Oppenheim (Lexington,
1991); and *An Ethic of Responsibility in International Relations* by
D. Warner (Boulder, 1991). The first sets out from an explicitly utilitarian position, the second is rigidly realist and the third is strongly
deontological. Elfstrom recognizes the ethical necessities normally expounded by Kantian-type deontologists, but believes that it is possible
only rarely, and in a very limited way, for the reasons of universalism
to prevail over those of even the most universalistic utilitarianism. In his
book he finds a series of empirical applications which invariably fail to
meet the reader's expectations: his formulation, alas, does not allow us
to go further than the material inapplicability of the principle of the
greatest good for the greatest number. I realize that the choice that has
to be made by anyone with the power to direct the policy of his country
is a dramatic one. But I would like to point out that even when he does
not make his country intervene in another state's affairs, the statesman
makes a choice; just as he also makes a choice when he sends his fellow
citizens to die in battle. But if Elfstrom recognizes that there is an
ethical component to international life, Oppenheim strongly denies that
ethical rules can be applied to foreign policy decisions. The realist formulation he adopts is totally in tune with the one H. Morgenthau
proposed 40 years ago in his famous 'Six Principles of Political Realism', listed in the first chapter of his *Politics Among Nations* (New York,
1949). For Oppenheim, the statesman finds himself in the same situation as the cashier in a bank who has to cope with a gang of robbers:
he knows that, even if he prevents the robbery, in all probability he will
be killed. The only criterion cashier and statesman can appeal to is the
instrumental rationality imposed by their being condemned to live in a
situation of extremely grave danger – that is, of ineliminable *anarchy*.

Anyone acquainted with the issues of international political theory
knows how central the word 'anarchy' is to the debate, and how
(negatively) it influences discussions on morality. It is obvious in fact
that no one in an anarchic realm can be expected to make morality
prevail over self-defence. This is one point that needs to be clarified:
only if there is no anarchy is it possible to discuss ethics. The proof of
the *non-existence* of anarchy may be sought at two different levels, one
abstract and theoretical, the other concrete and empirical. Arguments
of the first type are discussed in the pages that follow. Empirical-type
arguments, which are part and parcel of the political analysis, are
reasonably easy to identify in international political history over the last
few decades. That the United States and the former Soviet Union each
had a project of international order whence their policies drew inspiration

seems to me virtually irrefutable. They even made it materialize in their effective policies. Even now that one of the pillars of bipolarism has crumbled, factors of integration, collaboration, sharing, bargaining and compromise still prevail over conflictual, disruptive factors throughout the world. That the crisis of the eastern European world and the contemporary slackening of ideological tensions have provoked situations of contraction and even episodes of chauvinism, racism and egoism, is also true, although this seems to me a sign of disconcertion rather than of anarchy. On the entire question, the third book I mentioned, Warner's, takes a position which I share almost completely. Warner even sets out by claiming that, 'there can be no international relations without ethics' (p. 6). Although I do not fully accept his argument (especially the headstrong way in which he addresses exclusively the problems of the legitimacy or illegitimacy of acts performed by states, and responsibility and sanctions for illegitimate acts), my position tends to be closer to his than to Elfstrom's or Oppenheim's.

There is one point on which the latter two authors, whose positions are otherwise extreme, agree, and which leaves me in some doubt. Both focus their attention on the conduct of individuals, on the basis of the otherwise wholly acceptable conclusion that it is effectively people who act, and it is hence with people that we must deal. But they look only to the individual as actor, not to the individual as recipient (the viewpoint which seems to me most interesting). Theirs is a subjective dimension that I have not analysed substantially, seeking rather to identify elements that might define the responsibilities of states as such (as they are and as they act), well aware of the importance of the 'agent-structure' link to which international relations theory is currently devoting so much attention through the lens of the debate on scientific realism. The difference between individual and state is in other words relevant to my argument in so far as the second has sufficient tools to defend its rights and reject its duties, while for the individual as recipient the situation is diametrically opposite: it is much harder for individuals to elude their duties than to achieve freedom. It is from this asymmetry that my argument for the protection of human rights originates. States are artificial, by no means everlasting structures: in the space of their existence, instead, individuals expect equal treament from anyone, wherever they happen to be. It seems to me possible to note signs of progress in this direction if we consider, for example, the development (despite some difficulty) of international criminal law agreements, whereby the treatment of the individual before the law is becoming uniform today, regardless of the country in which he finds himself. This debate leads us towards the problem of international justice, both distributive and restorative. Without wishing to deny the complexity of the problem, I believe that its discussion offers an excellent opportunity for bringing domestic and international political analysis together at last (hence narrowing the gap that divides the respective academic communities). How can a state which behaves unjustly abroad be just at home? Vice versa, how can a state respect human rights on a world level and not within its own boundaries? Or, finally, how can a state be democratic in its domestic policy and undemocratic in its relations with other states? The problems regarding the state as a moral subject are even greater. The debate which followed the publication of the Italian edition of this book dwelt on some of these aspects. One observation that was commonly made was that my image of states is too abstract or ingenuous. In short, the gist of the criticism was that states have necessities, preoccupations and responsibilities that they cannot be deprived of by 'moral' interventions from the outside. What about their sovereignty, after all? Obviously, I have no arguments against the present *raison d'être* of states as they are. But it is precisely because of this 'ineliminability' of theirs that I feel, first and foremost, that their morality needs urgently to be questioned: it would be wrong to wait for states to disappear – if they ever do disappear – to point out that their conduct was immoral. Secondly, I believe that it is vital to stress that, although they justify their actions invariably and exclusively in terms of security, prudence, safeguarding of the national interest and so on, they always choose their behaviour from a variety of alternatives. The decisions they take always have a content of an evaluational order. More precisely, any choice corresponds to an order of preference, which is perceived by political and public opinion in terms of its public value, of its defence of given principles. To think of states over the last five centuries or so, and for as long as they exist in the future, as 'ineliminable' (indifferent) reference points and accept that their conduct is comparable to that of a 'billiard ball' (that is, neither reflective nor spontaneous but exclusively reactive) is to shun one's own intellectual responsibilities. In this way, the individual is left totally disarmed, unable to express any judgement whatsoever on the very state which can, if it wishes, order him to die for his country!

My argument, I must confess, is more prescriptive than descriptive and analytical, although I do use description and analysis to show the relevance of the normative aspects that I construct, especially in the last two chapters, dedicated to international justice and the moral assessment of wars. With regard to the first point, I wish to stress that the question of justice has to be framed on at least two levels; that of the redistribution of wealth and goods (the aspect I have devoted most space to), and that of the defence and promotion of human rights, which, in turn, leads us to evaluate the need, in given cases, for humanitarian external interventions. As for the second point, I have to make a self-criticism. In the pages that follow, I perhaps fail to devote sufficient attention to the relationship between ethics and war. There are two reasons for this. First, it is a classical issue: the history of the study of the morality of war and, more generally, of 'just war' is already extremely rich, and I make reference to its principal ideas. Secondly, it seems to me that the question of war is relatively less pressing than in the past; neither because there are no longer wars nor because I regard war as obsolete, but simply in as much as the state of the international system today suggests that forthcoming political events will rotate, in the main, around prevalently non-violent issues. There are other problems now in which, once more, ethical and political problems meet and merge. Perhaps the key issue in the immediate future will be the renewed clash between nationalism and internationalism, patriotism and cosmopolitanism. To use a word that is fashionable these days (though in a wider meaning than T. H. Marshall's), the question of *citizenship* has extended to international questions, such as migration, the movement of vast masses of citizens from the poorest and most backward countries to the richest and most welcoming. This is happening in a scenario in which the pride of belonging – to a homeland, to a region – is growing increasingly widespread. Hence the dispute between justice – which cannot be asserted without acceptance of some universalistic principle, however limited it may be – and the consolidation of state identity and the *vive la difference* attitude (which is capable of spawning racism). As the European Community prepares to abolish legal boundaries, other ideal, hence more important, boundaries are coming into being. I touch on some of these topics in my book. I confess though, that were I to rewrite it, I would stress them even more. For they seem to me emblematic of the contemporary international situation – that is, a sort of aftermath of a war that was, fortunately, never fought between west and east. And as in the aftermath of any war, it is now necessary to address the immense problem of rearranging and adjusting political and social relations.

I wish to make one final consideration about the international ethical consequences of the grand transformation that began in 1989. Ethical problems were virtually ignored in the bipolar international system, teetering continuously as it did on the brink of nuclear catastrophe. For many people then it sounded grotesque to speak of ethics as opposed to survival. But today the drastic attenuation of international tension not only *allows*, but also *forces* us to turn our attention to the moral problems of international coexistence. After a great revolution, such as the one the international system underwent after the fall of the Berlin Wall, it is necessary to consolidate and perpetuate its fruits. We have an enormous, mindboggling job ahead of us, but, in view of my stubborn confidence in progress, I sincerely believe that we are up to the task.

One final note: since I wrote this book many things have of course changed on the international scene. The Soviet Union, for example, no longer exists at all! I thus beg the reader of the English edition to bear this and other material changes in mind, when judging my point of view. Although some of my factual references no longer apply, I honestly feel that my argument is as relevant as ever.

Acknowledgements

Some pages of this book – just a few – have already been published as initial attempts to analyse a problem I had long seen emerging, but had never dared address. I refer in particular to chapter 2, section 3, which reproduces part of my essay in *Relazioni internazionali*, 52: 8 (1989); and to part of chapter 3, section 3, which is taken from 'Contrattualismo e politica internazionale', in *Studi politici. In onore di Luigi Firpo*, edited by S. Rota Ghibaudi and F. Barcia (Milan: Angeli, 1990).

The journey I have chosen to embark upon is an unusual one for an Italian scholar of international relations. I would never have dreamed of undertaking it had my attention not been drawn to some of the fundamental but relatively neglected aspects of the issue during my experience in the 'Teoria politica' movement. This was an academically and culturally heterogeneous group in which I learnt that curiosity for issues cultivated and explored by friends and colleagues alike may widen one's own outlook to an extraordinary degree and (I hope) improve the quality of one's work. Although, as they say, the responsibility for what I have written is mine and mine alone, I wish to thank all those who have, in their own way, been responsible for attracting my curiosity.

Since this book is, basically, concerned with the idea of progress (of moral progress which, judging at least from the brevity of its course to date, should be possible in the future), I wish to dedicate it to the generation which preceded me and (as a symbol of continuity) to the generation to come. That is, to my father and to my sons.

Introduction

An inexorable law, framed by no government, with no court to interpret it, and no sheriff to enforce it, has made us members of the body politic of the world. Interdependence is the rule of modern life. International relations are the warp and woof of the modern community. It is when we examine the nature of those relations that the true irony of the situation is revealed. They are relations between human beings, for in the world of human sciences, there are no relations between things: but they are not human relations. They may perhaps be most accurately described as pre-human. They have come into existence through the accidents and chances of economic development, not through the conscious choice of the human beings concerned.

A. Zimmern, *The Study of International Relations*

The aim of this book is not doctrinaire. It is not my intention to discuss the birth and development of studies on the ethics of international relations, although I do recognize that their history is interesting and that it might be useful to reconstruct it before it grows too complex. All of its principal bibliographical references are to be found in any case in the pages that follow. One point is worth stressing: although the literature on ethics and politics is virtually unlimited, while that on ethics and international politics is scant, virtually nothing exists to connect the two, to address the problem of the relationship between the domestic and international dimensions of ethics. The need to reflect upon this conundrum re-emerged with renewed drama and urgency at the beginning of 1991, first of all with the Persian Gulf crisis, which may have hindered the potentially peaceful redefinition of the map of world power. The situation was further aggravated by the escalation of the crisis in the former Yugoslavia (when visions of the events preceding the First World War inevitably came to mind), and the abortive coup attempt in the former Soviet Union, followed by the break-up of state unity, a sacrificial offering to an idea of nationhood which, taken to its extreme consequences or simply misunderstood, may spawn horrible bloodbaths. I shall thus seek at least to catalogue the questions raised by the advent of ethics to international analysis, which has become systematic over the last decade or so. Such questions have undermined the deep-rooted prejudice according to which the boundaries of ethics coincided with those of the state,[1] and which made no reflection on the state's conduct in its relations with other states and its responsibility to all the citizens who 'belong' to them.[2] What I would like to stress is that the state is one and one only: it is always the same, internally and externally. If, in the first case, it expresses values, draws inspiration from principles and makes ideological choices that affect millions of citizens, the same must apply in the second as well. The distinction or separation between domestic and international politics can thus only be used for technical purposes to study tangibly different situations, not incommunicable moral worlds. In very general terms, we might seek to analyse a state's levels of coherence, to clarify whether it has the duty to make its actions comply with fixed principles and rules, in its dealings both with its nationals and with the citizens of other states (resident within its own borders or in their own countries), and directly with other states.[3]

I cannot provide a systematic, exhaustive ethical theory of international relations. All I can do is to make a passionate plea for the acceptance of this dimension of reality in the citadel of knowledge. My attempt is justified by the certainty that nothing of the contemporary world can be fully understood unless it is framed in a global, international perspective. So who are the specialists whose job it is to cultivate this field of study? Electively, it is the task of moral philosophers and students of international relations. Many of them have already begun to approach it systematically, but, alas, also unilaterally – each from the standpoint of his own discipline, denying that there might be another side to the coin. Thus far, their efforts have been viewed with much scepticism by their respective scientific communities. Philosophers and political scientists ought to mix more, to converge on a common ground of reflection and research. This has yet to happen, with the result that philosophers generally fail to grasp the peculiarity of the international logic, while political scientists lack philosophical tools to apply to relations between states. The most glaring example of the need to bridge this gap is the sorry state of studies on warfare: philosophers judge war *per se* (especially in the context of just war doctrines), whereas political scientists analyse it as an epiphenomenon of the international system.

Philosophers risk losing sight of the idea that war is not something autonomous. The only way to understand it is in the context of the political relations whence it originates and which it produces. Political scientists realize that war is not a mere accident of international life but a traumatic rending of its fabric: in so far as it is neither inevitable nor natural, it fully deserves to be the object of assessments of a moral order. This book aims to encourage the integration of the two views. It offers on approval to philosophers the proposition that international politics is no longer considered exclusively a realm of anarchy and self-defence, but that it may be charted, albeit schematically, as a set of analytic principles founded on the concept of political order. Not only is it possible to make an ethical judgement on this concept and thus ruffle collective indifference to the nature of international politics; we are also compelled to acknowledge its influence on our daily lives.

In the pages that follow I address some of the central aspects of the problem which, it is important to stress, is inextricably linked to the spheres of war and peace (as events in the early months of 1991 have demonstrated). In chapter 1 I acknowledge the difficulty of such a task, especially in view of the history of relations between ethics and politics in the domestic life of states, tracing the limits within which I intend to build my argument for a reflection on international justice. Each chapter is divided into four parts, hopefully evoking something of the splendid sonata-form of Haydn's symphonies. In chapter 2, I seek to demonstrate that it is legitimate to extend the ethical problem to international relations. Chapter 3 outlines the chief characteristics of contemporary international political life: I use them to show why it is interesting to apply the moral argument to states (and the debate on the nature of nuclear war and the mutations which the possibility of its breaking out have generated in the fabric of international life emphasize the fact). In an attempt to demonstrate that states have both rights and duties (and perhaps more of the latter than of the former), I discuss what I call the 'anarchic prejudice', proposing in its place a principle of order for relations between states, capable of acknowledging the international variety as a fully-fledged form of *politics* (chapter 4). May changes of this magnitude be subsumed in some of the explanatory models already put forward? I try to answer the question in chapter 5, which looks to the history of philosophy for clues on how to delineate a world different from all past worlds: the discussion is based mainly on the war–peace relationship, the most fundamental in international life. Finally, in chapter 6, the one containing most propositions (and with chapter 7, the Conclusion, the most normative), I seek to identify the subjects of moral action and the minimum principles they have to observe, developing ideas for a theory of international justice. In this way I hope, at the very least, to demonstrate the relevance of the ethical analysis of international relations, fully aware that:

> To view the world in this light does not commit us to any particular values or standards. It does not tell us precisely of what morality consists. It does not provide us with a moral theory. But it provides the perspective in which moral questions can arise and in which moral theory can make sense.[4]

In the light of which, I make an empirical attempt to apply the principles of international justice to the Gulf war.

One preliminary *psychological* question needs to be neutralized right from the outset. The same categories we usually use for individuals or citizens are spontaneously applied to states. The process is facilitated by our habit of calling states 'by name', thus personifying them (the same mechanism is at work when the name of a statesman is used to replace that of the country he represents). But when we discover, as we invariably do, that these categories are unsuitable, we automatically deduce that the international realm is not different from the domestic one, but more backward, sometimes even primitive and intractable. Without questioning whether this deduction is right or not,[5] it is worthwhile making the effort to think of states as states and not as individuals. If we fail to find in states the features we find in individuals, it is not necessarily because, unlike the latter, they are amoral entities, but simply because their nature is something else again. The constant referral of the international dimension to the domestic one (and vice versa) may be extremely useful as an analogy, but is ultimately grotesque, if it is made imitatively or, worse still, mimetically. It is thus possible to avoid reaching the oversimplistic conclusion that international morality can exist solely in so far as it is the product of the (subjective) domestic moralities of different states; as if the sum-total of single individual moralities were public morality. In this case too, states would be considered as individuals, and it would thus be possible to speak in terms of a cosmopolitan ethic. This would be more than acceptable in itself, but it would not erase the problem as it stands at present – a problem, that is, not of the ethics of a future world, but of our own.

Not that I wish the scope of my analysis to be confined exclusively to the dimension of international relations,[6] quite simply because what we are dealing with here are fundamental problems common to all humanity. No special claims can be staked on them: they are the special preserve of no one! Having said that, it should be added that if we lack the original international sensitiveness to accustom us to global views of reality, we shall be unable to grasp their scope. In a certain sense, this means that we should *all* become experts on international relations! For the immensity of the issues involved – from peace to the protection of health (in the broad, profound sense that we have only recently begun to comprehend), from the diffusion of acceptable standards of living everywhere for everyone to the development of democracy – demands the elaboration of new *conceptions of the world*.[7] The problem today is to evaluate, fully and originally, all the various aspects of the world we are talking about. In so far as it has only recently achieved effective, global unity, it requires not only a policy but also an economy, a technology or a legal system – not to mention a philosophy. Will we have the wherewithal to grasp the extraordinary novelty of the situation created by the unification of the planet? For the first time in history there is a real, effective connection between all the events that happen, wherever they happen.[8] Although, on the surface, the Persian Gulf conflict would seem to have altered this situation somewhat, the very fact that world opinion virtually in its entirety, including most Islamic opinion, has emphatically taken the same side seems to reassert it. This is not to celebrate the rhetoric of interdependence, a generally meaningless term, but to appreciate the merging of diverse dimensions of reality. To cite one example, the world drug system entails not only social and medical problems, but economic, political and even military problems as well. More generally speaking, the tendency for conflict to decrease in the world (historical serial analysis would highlight the fact without any difficulty) and eco-awareness on a planetary scale are but two signs of this major historical turnaround. The sheer boundlessness of life in the coming millennium may be incomparable with that of all past millennia. Our conceptions of the world have to take stock of this possibility. In short, morality can no longer have a single interior dimension, nor can it remain local. Both state and planet will be objects of morality from now on.

It should be added that this is a book about philosophical matters written by a non-philosopher, and as such is not intended for specialists. If, as G. Anders remarked in the years in which the first great ethical debate was raging on the atomic bomb, there are 'no specialists in the end-of-the world branch of philosophy', we must *all* consider ourselves specialists in the conservation-and-transformation-of-the-world branch.

1

States and Morality

Is it not true to say that the issue of the rights of man, brought
to the attention of sovereigns by the 1789 *Déclaration*, is more
topical than ever today? Is this not, together with peace and international justice, one of the great issues towards which peoples
and governments are being irresistibly drawn, whether they like it
or not? National declarations were the basic premise for the birth
of modern democracies. Has not the universal *Déclaration* of the
rights of man proved to be the basic premise for the democrati-
sation of the international system? And has this not, in turn, brought
about the demise of the traditional balance of power, whereby
peace is invariably a truce between two wars, and the beginning
of a new era of permanent peace with other options besides war
alone?

N. Bobbio, *L'età dei diritti*

1 THE ARGUMENT

Is it possible for us to judge international politics? Is the question worth
asking anyway? If we take as our guide the responses offered in the
history of western culture to an analogous doubt (is it possible to judge
politics as a whole?), then any attempt to extend to international relations
an idea which is unfeasible *per se* even on a more general plane would,
admittedly, appear to be utterly senseless. Politics is assessed in terms
of success or failure, not of good or evil, of fairness or unfairness, of
justice or injustice. In short, it is judged in ideological, not moral, terms.
Yet, although the conclusion almost invariably reached is that any moral
judgement in politics is undemonstrable, (although the fact that it is
pronounced at all is not deemed unjustifiable),[1] the debate on the morality
of domestic politics has known virtually no respite. That on the morality of international politics, on the other hand, has hardly got under
way at all.[2] The question is only ever raised in times of conflict, when

condemnations of enemy behaviour are made by the score. What better proof of the existence of 'moral judgements' than the fact that they are actually formulated? One might of course add that, at international level, moral considerations are rendered superfluous by a much more peremptory form of judgement: more precisely, by the recourse to arms (which, except in exceptional circumstances, has long been abandoned in domestic politics). Whereas in the debate on the relationship between ethics and politics on the domestic scene, the positions are extremely diversified (but do, nevertheless, exist),[3] at international level the issue inevitably rules out the debate itself, almost as if international politics were inevitably – and necessarily – immoral (as opposed to arguably or simply amoral). The sole directive[4] worth its salt here would appear to be that of defence against, and victory over, the enemy,[5] of the over-powering and domination of the vanquished, beaten opponent. This is the practical consequence of political realism, the theory seemingly most in keeping with international affairs. The most famous and influential champion of this approach was H. J. Morgenthau.[6] It would appear though, that doubts rack even those who, acknowledging the scientific foundations of international political analysis,[7] are prepared to counter the charge of immoralism. Refuting the equation of political realism with immorality, Morgenthau even attempted to reverse the terms of the question. Far from believing that the realist state is responsible for immoral policies, he asserted that it is the only form of state which actually complies with the moral obligation to pursue the national in-terest. And, so his reasoning goes, if that leads to the use of force or recourse to armed violence, the reason for this lies not in the inherent evil of such a state but in two totally 'objective' facts: in natural human aggressiveness or blood lust on the one hand,[8] and in the absence of an integrated international community on the other. As a result,

> the attainment of a modicum of order and the realization of *a minimum of moral values* are predicated upon the existence of national communi-ties capable of preserving order and realizing moral values within the limits of their power.[9]

At which point, the ways of the debate on ethics and domestic and international politics diverge. This 'minimum of moral values' seems achievable exclusively within the state, not among states. In the state, some form of integration exists: among states it is impossible to note anything of the sort. The real immorality, therefore, is arguably ascrib-able to the statesman who passes over the difference and pretends to act on the international stage according to the principles of domestic politics.[10] Any search among the writings of those philosophers who have discussed the ethics-politics nexus for applications, or even only exemplifications, relating to the international political realm would be in vain. In short, the impossibility of an absolute foundation[11] for political morality has spawned the relativism, pluralism or definitive autonomy of politics from morality, not disaffection with the issue. Does this 'failure' mean that we haven't to extend the ethical problem to the relations of states? Is the untenability of an absolute foundation a good enough reason for not discussing theories of international political obligation or principles of international justice? Let us suppose (as I do in the final chapter) that international justice depends on the safeguarding of the human being. Would we deduce from the lack of an absolute foundation for human rights,[12] that it is useless to talk about them, or even to continue to promote or protect them? On the contrary, wouldn't we seek at least to clarify the arguments adopted in support of each justification, the specific contents to be attributed to single rights and so on?

2 INTERNATIONAL RIGHTS AND DUTIES

This latter point in particular can help us demonstrate the relevance of our arguments on ethics in international politics. By way of an example, it is worth considering the relationship between all the various bills of rights of the past and the Universal Declaration proclaimed by the General Assembly of the United Nations in 1948. The former consist of all the fundamental principles whose observance or otherwise is potentially one of the first objects of international political judgement. The sum of all national bills of rights (assuming, that is, that each state has included their basic principles in some way in its constitution) does not *per se* add up to the Universal Declaration, simply because not all states ascribe the same value to individuals. There is also another much more significant difference: the Universal Declaration enunciates the inalienable rights of human beings everywhere, addressing a series of 'negative' orders to states: the latter 'cannot' enslave, torture or unlawfully arrest any individual.[13] To each right enunciated for individuals corresponds (or should correspond) a duty for states, which, nonetheless, ceases to exist at state boundaries. News of a violation of human rights in Chile does not allow, or still less, compel the Italian government (or Italian citizens) to intervene to put a stop to it. For each sovereign state, in turn, has the inviolable right to respect for its own prerogatives. Perhaps we sometimes fail to dedicate sufficient attention to one of the main consequences of all of this: namely that the 'universal' rights of citizens are planetary, whereas the corresponding 'universal' rights of states are, instead, national, statist and restricted, although it is reasonable to believe that a 'condensed nucleus of values and criteria universally accepted by all states' has now been developed.[14]

Citizens wherever they are have both rights and duties: states however have (or are supposed to have) rights and duties only in the domestic sphere, whereas in external relationships they have rights but not duties.[15] The resulting dissymmetry helps us understand why domestic and international political theory have diverged. Our cultural tradition is full of assertions of the separateness of ethics and politics – of the realm of political action (judgement of its success or otherwise) and that of moral judgement (justification or criticism of political action).[16] Yet debates have always raged about the best possible forms of government, the nature of political obligation, social justice and democratic principles – in short, about the ideal society. Although they have grown increasingly profound, complex and sophisticated, they have never appealed to considerations of an international nature. Perhaps this has happened because the duties of states are supposedly unfindable.

This is one way of explaining the untenability of the extension by analogy of 'domestic-based' analysis to international relations: the rights and duties of individuals are 'universal', whereas the state's only duties are 'local' – *vis-à-vis* foreign citizens, whenever they enter its territory. With regard to its own citizens, the state has, at most, the duty to protect them when their rights are violated on some other state's territory. Yet if the rights of citizens are truly 'universal', then we are forced to deduce that it is possible to excuse a state which infringes the boundaries of another to run to the rescue of the locals – whether to free them from a bloodthirsty regime or to save them from starvation or to prevent an ecological catastrophe.[17] On what criteria can we base our assessment of this kind of conduct? How is it possible to extend the conceptual framework and the theoretical debate that have developed round the state to relations between states, in which only one of the two pillars of the moral argument – that of rights without duties – is left standing?

In other words, if something is 'unfindable', either it does not exist or it is too well hidden. If the second possibility were true (and assuming, hypothetically, that there is something to discover), we would simply have to organize our search better to understand the origins of the prejudice that first opened the gap between domestic and international political ethics.[18] In the first realm, the situation we find is well-structured and consolidated. No actor is excluded from the game, and there is a rule for every stage in it. At which point, comparison with the international realm is most revealing: the only rules states have are the ones they assign themselves, or which they are willing to agree upon with other states. Thus far, the difference is great, but not excessively so. Yet if, among states, no body exists to resolve divergences over rules, simply because no state can be obliged to do anything, except by superior force (materially, not formally, speaking), it is difficult to imagine any justification for the realm of international politics. One spontaneously translates all this into the conclusion that international politics inevitably[19] reveals itself to be unfair, whenever a controversy arises between two states. From here to leaving the international political dimension to its own devices, the step is of course very brief. As Hobbes pointed out, 'It is an old saying, That *all lawes are silent in the time of warre*, and it is a true one, not onely if we speak of the *civill*, but also of the *naturall lawes*' (*De cive*, V, 2, pp. 85–6); applied to states, natural law 'may be called *that of Nations*, but vulgarly it is termed the *Right of Nations*' (*De cive*, XIV, 4, p. 171); natural law, in turn, is applied to states (which, 'once instituted doe put on the personall properties of men', ibid.), so that 'the same Law, that dictateth to men that have no Civil Government what they ought to do and what to avoyd in regard of one another, dictateth the same to Common-wealths . . . there being no Court of Naturall Justice' (*Leviathan*, ch. 30, p. 244). In the anarchic context, 'that condition which is called Warre' (*Leviathan*, ch. 13, p. 88) in which states find themselves, 'this is also consequent; that nothing can be Unjust. The notions of Right and Wrong, Justice and Injustice have there no place' (ibid., p. 90).[20]

The conclusion that ethical reflection on international politics is impossible originates in the culture which has been responsible for seeking a foundation for the modern state: its success has gone hand in hand with the evolution of this way of organizing political life. A simplifying conception of international politics has ensued. In a kingdom in which 'nothing can be unjust', everything is possible: statesmen have no (moral and political) responsibility other than *salus popoli*; their action will never be immoral. I wish here to address this particular consideration, which is obviously of fundamental importance to the type of problem I intend to discuss. First of all, I would like to explore a series of commonsense ideas which imply the point of view, to test whether they may in some way widen our ethical perspective. The first concerns the incoherence that we ought supposedly to recognize between domestic and international politics, when, for example, we see that many states implement notably divergent, if not opposite, domestic and foreign policies. No one questions the British democratic tradition, but, at the same time, it is impossible to forget that for centuries its foreign policy was colonialist, racist and ultimately imperialist. In this case, it would be arduous to argue in favour of a justification based on the state of necessity! An analogous contradiction faces anyone wishing to compare US domestic policy in the sixties and the policy adopted in the same period in Vietnam. Was defending the West against the alleged advance of communism a good reason? A host of examples might be cited, but a third one at least seems to me necessary to explain the gist of my polemic. Statesmen very often change their opinions about one another (as do states about other states). Hence Saddam Hussein, supported by the western world for the duration of his war against Khomeini's Iran, was subsequently condemned for his attack on Kuwait. Something very similar has occurred in attitudes to the Syria of Assad (another ruler widely regarded as a dictator), against whom western states started to reduce their hostility when they realized that he was gradually moving away from the Soviet Union (well before 1989!), and that Syria might somehow play a helpful role in normalizing the situation in Lebanon and was opposed to Saddam Hussein's Iraq. Even Qadhafi, long condemned as the funder, and sometimes the instigator, of the majority of terrorist outrages over the last two years, is allowed to return to the international fold, when he shares the same enemy as the West. What can these examples teach us?

A first answer to the question, one coherent with the realist school of thought, would exploit the lesson contained in my examples to support the argument that any moral judgement in politics is untenable. States deal with anybody according to needs and circumstances: they are in no position to make subtle distinctions about the uprightness of their interlocutors. Only one thing counts and that is the end, and it is possible to achieve that end by accepting compromises. The latter are entered into only too willingly if they can be useful in realizing the nation's interest, if they can help to achieve victory. Be that as it may, it is possible to draw another, radically opposite, lesson from the self-same examples. It may be that statesmen consciously accept conceptual compromises, judging them useful or, better still, morally wholesome, precisely in so far as they seek to safeguard the interest of their nation. But what is this if not an admission that statesmen have a notion of good and evil of their own, and hence act politically according to principles? In the case of British colonialism we might thus conclude that it was considered proper to build the wellbeing of British citizens over the ruins of thousands of people born in far-off lands. In the case of the indiscriminate violence perpetrated by the United States in Vietnam, it might be argued that a GI's life was worth so much more than that of a member of the Vietcong as to justify the use of any means to protect the first and end the second. Moving on to the third case, it would be easy to argue that alliances have always been broken and that all states have found themselves compelled by circumstance to enter into compromises at one time or another, or to make the best of things in their dealings with other states which they neither admired nor trusted. Even those who defend it, however, must surely admit that the acceptance of a moral compromise implies the existence, not the absence, of morals. When someone admits to bad behaviour, or to not always assigning the same value to human life, or to being prepared to stoop to pacts with the devil, doesn't he follow moral yardsticks, the very ones that are supposedly impossible? More explicitly still, the justification made in examples such as those cited is very simple. It reads like this: 'since others act in an evil way, it is absolutely necessary, for purely and exclusively defensive reasons, to behave like them – or even worse than them!' Even the inherently good state ends up acting badly (consciously maybe, but 'involuntarily' and irresistibly). More precisely, since other states are evil (or, for the purposes of the argument, let us say 'immoral'), the 'moral' state is forced at the very least to behave 'amorally', and, if need be (in war, for example), 'immorally'. If this is true, then politics (or at least international politics) is no mere technique which any statesman can apply by the same standards: on the contrary, it implies moral judgements on political problems. Choosing to be an ally of Nazi Germany, as Stalin's Soviet Union did in 1939, is more than a mere technical operation.

Morality, which was chased from the main door of the neutrality of politics in general, on the basis of the distinction between the worlds of ethics and politics, has thus returned through the window of the judgements *continuously* formulated in political life! One might also add that in this reintegration process, international morality brings with it domestic morality, as becomes evident if we reflect that it is always statesmen, who also have a political role in the life of their country, who take the decisions that not only have weight internationally, but also affect their fellow citizens, electors and subjects. The standard of international conduct might even prove a useful device for controlling domestic conduct. Are we still to consider democratic to all intents and purposes the state which causes the indiscriminate death of thousands of individuals, solely because they belong to another race or follow a different ideology?

Originally introduced by the doctrine of natural law, a prejudice has developed and been consolidated which has separated the two spheres of politics – domestic and international – in terms of a single, fundamental dichotomy: order versus anarchy, organization versus chaos, peace versus violence. Among the many consequences of this fracture is the one which interests us here: that between rights and duties, acknowledged as being equally essential in domestic politics (in which it is, indeed, the *sine qua non* of basic consensus), and rent asunder and dismembered in international politics (in the context of which each state claims rights and denies duties).

3   STATE AND STATES

Political activity takes place in two realms – the domestic and the international. Very roughly speaking, they are distinguishable by the fact that, in the first, there is interaction between individuals and, in the second, between states. In the first, every form of unlawful physical violence is banned, while, in the second, hardly any form of recourse to violence may be considered illegal, since there are only a very few, very vague general rules to regulate the question. How does one respond to this? Again, very roughly speaking, one might affirm that, in the first case, it is possible to identify order – and whether it is fair or unfair, good or bad, is an entirely different matter. In the second, there is no order at all, since it is impossible to distinguish between the enforcement of rules and the overriding superiority of physical (military) force. Add to this the fact that, in the first case, subjective or individual rights enjoy outside protection, thus guaranteeing neutral judgement, while in the second all rights (assuming they exist) are exclusively those of self-interest, so that everyone fends for himself, within the limits of his power.

One might therefore conclude that life is safer in the first context than in the second, that the reason for the difference may depend on the different stages of development of the two. For a long time, possibly for millennia, relations between individuals were very similar to relations between states. Progressively – perhaps because it was simply unbearable, perhaps due to the development of forms of social integration which have accompanied the shift from clan to tribe to village to city-state to state – the situation has evolved to its present condition. Ever since states as we know them today appeared on the scene (roughly speaking, since the sixteenth century), their development too has progressed through a series of different stages. Who would deny that differences exist between Europe in 1648, at the end of the devastating Thirty Years' War, and Europe in 1945, victim of another, still vaster conflict?

One might reasonably observe, first and foremost, that international relations had grown more intense and continuous, more complex and integrated, albeit acknowledging that, in the meantime, the techniques of war had also grown more violent and destructive. In short, a form of civilization had taken place in international relations as well. Large-scale international conflict had grown more complex in terms of numbers of forces deployed and geographical dimension, but also progressively less frequent. It gave rise to forms of reorganization of interstate relations which tended to consolidate the differences of rank that had crystallized (between victors and vanquished, for example). All of which might lead one to the conclusion that, if the state (and its citizens with it) has emerged from anarchy and the society of states has not, the gap between the two situations has progressively narrowed, albeit slowly since it is possible to perceive signs in international life at least vaguely similar to those of the domestic civilization of states.[21] Finally, assuming that the consolidated order within the state provides the opportunity for any inhabitant to express judgements and evaluations on the quality of its domestic life (by taking part in political or ideological debates, but also making a stand on principles, on form of government, on democracy, on socialism and so on), it may be possible to single out the foundations upon which each state is based, and hence discuss them, expressing preferences for certain forms of political order, and opposition to others. Let us ask ourselves, therefore, whether something analogous may not happen in states as a whole, viewing them as a unique or unitary system, if not an actual society. Among other considerations, we might highlight the absence in this latter scenario of a minimum basis of shared or imposed values (values which give rise to the material formation of a state),[22] without which one would be confronted not only with a virtually unmanageable plurality of principles, but also, in all probability, with a fundamental conflict of principles, resolvable only by a call to arms (war, that is). Within the state, on the other hand, we would find a pluralism with insurmountable limits; namely, agreement on basic principles, thanks to which the multiplicity of possible positions and circumstances would be preserved within the terms of the survival of the system itself. Are traces of this minimum cohesion threshold (which might be considered as the set of values shared by the community) to be found in international life?

Their presence is a *sine qua non* for any argument on international values. The first of these might, at first sight, be that of peace,[23] which is, after all, a basic, unifying value.[24] The immediate objection one might make is that the specific (historical-political) content of peace might be judged unacceptable by some. The second, more general objection is that certain states might (and some already have) reject this value, irrespective of its content, preferring a permanent, absolute model of conflict. This is what Hitler's Germany did, and what an Islamic state might do in its 'holy war' against the infidel. It thus transpires that the semblance of symmetry we thought we had discovered has melted away. Are we then to dispense with all non-passionate judgements on the war in Vietnam or Hitler's warmongering? Have the reasons which forced Roosevelt into war the same value as the Nazi dictator's? This point is of such importance it is worth taking a step backwards to remind ourselves that the two realms – domestic and international – are clearly distinct, and hence to ask whether the value system embodied by Hitler (and which he implemented in his warmongering) in the Germany of the Third Reich seems to us to be justifiable.[25] In all probability, albeit conscious that it is impossible to provide an absolute foundation for political values (and hence to reject some of them), we would agree that the most repugnant aspect of the Nazi value system is the principle of natural inequality among individuals: that – worse still, from our standpoint – tolerance towards this principle for pluralism's sake might backfire against us, since, were it to actually materialize, it would seek to annihilate all opposition, exterminating anyone unwilling to accept the idea of inequality! Principles such as that of Nazism would be deleterious for any society in the long term, and it is on this basis that they can and must be rejected. Yet we might also agree at this point that, if Nazi warmongering had these ends, it would be easy to understand the reasons of all those who opposed it. Immediately, however, we would have to ask ourselves whether, having come this far, we ought not to recognize the moral duty to intervene against Nazi Germany in peacetime too – not only in retaliation to its treacherous acts of aggression. First, we would have to acknowledge that this question is tantamount to an implicit admission that international politics may be subject to moral judgements. Secondly, we might add that a policy of deliberate, conscious and systematic racial extermination deserves to be condemned, persuading anyone informed of it that it is his moral duty to act to make the policy cease. One might also object that western states, at least at the time of the Munich Conference (September 1938), already had sufficient proof of the standard of Hitler's policies and morality, yet they welcomed him to the negotiating table as one of their own. If I might express a subjective value judgement, I would observe that, irrespective of any political error they may have been committing by choosing an appeasement policy, they behaved feebly, even stooping to moral compromise. But didn't they do so precisely to achieve peace – a much more highly prized good at the international level, though not morally superior *per se*?

I would be only too glad to leave aside this problem of the conflict of values were it not for the fact that it lies at the very heart of our topic. In international politics it appears under the guise of the ideological dispute between opposed power blocs. Everyday experience continuously presents us with conflicts of a moral nature. Indeed, it might be argued that, without conflict, there would be no morality either.[26] Furthermore, the idea that emerged above (if there are values in international life, it may be possible to catalogue them) inevitably fuels debate. An example is the conflict mentioned above between the ideals of peace and conflict. The international realm presents yet another complication: on the one hand, peace seems to constitute, more than a fully-fledged value, a precondition for the realization or pursuit of any other value, while, on the other, a 'just war' might be preferable to an 'unjust peace'. On the international scene, alas, there is nothing subtle about conflict: its logic is one of peremptory, hence almost invariably dramatic, alternatives. One might tentatively add that peace is not a value in itself, but only when it is accompanied by a special quality, its being *just*. What I mean is not that every real peace may easily comply with this condition, but that the condition which justifies a war could not, in this case, be the mere subjective reason of a state defending its natural interest, but the unjustness of international relations. It could of course be argued that war is always justified by the simple fact that we have little conception, if any at all, of international justice. Yet it is one thing to assert that there is no justice, another to conclude that it cannot exist. A rough theory of international justice is thus needed to provide a minimum basis for a feasible, workable discussion of values in international life.

4   NATIONAL INTEREST, INTERNATIONAL MORALITY

The main idea put forward in this book is that a moral theory of international life *is* possible, if the duties of states are established and reconciled in accordance with the rules of justice[27] inferable from one fundamental obligation; namely, the treatment of all individuals on an egalitarian basis, irrespective not only of race, sex, culture and social extraction but, more important still, of citizenship or nationality. Traditionalists have always deemed an international ethic impossible. Today the stimulus to reverse this way of thinking comes from renewed awareness of the fact that the stands made by states on the international scene – albeit inextricably geared to the safeguarding of national interests – are almost invariably dictated, indeed justified, by choices of a moral nature. Italy entered the First World War subverting its system of alliances to achieve what its rulers judged to be the national interest – the redrawing of some of its borders. The United States intervened in Korea to halt the expansion of world communism, and later repeated the move in Vietnam and El Salvador. For a long time the Soviet Union supported movements and/or governments in various parts of the world which promised to realize socialism. The states of western Europe which in 1957 decided to establish and increasingly incentivate new forms of integration did so to improve relations among their citizens. Ideologists reason in the same terms when they affirm that a capitalist world system founded on *laissez-faire* is the one that will ensure the highest standards of living, as do utopians who, in striving to promote perpetual peace, point to a higher form of social-political organization. Examples of this type might be cited almost *ad infinitum*, from sixteenth-century Spanish and Portuguese imperial expansionism in the Americas, to the policies of the Papal States and the Vatican, to Islam's desire to free the world of the infidel.

Yet the element which unhinges traditional justifications of statist action is the fragility of the pillar upon which the theory of the state's relation with other states rests. It consists of the idea that sovereignty knows no limits, or rather that the state, in substance, has nothing but rights (in the external sphere), while its only duties are pactional. If international life involved states and states alone, we might accept their legal relations system's being built on the idea that the abstract right of each to all has its sole limit in the analogous right of other subjects (or, more generally, that rights and duties are equal). Only when they are legally recognized are states prepared to enter into relations regulated by 'limited' rights – founded, that is, on the reciprocal respect of the rights of each. As far as a state's relations with its citizens are concerned, the traditional arrangement sees each state as having obligations towards its own, but not to those of other states.[28]

In reality, things are not quite as simple as that. In fact, states do not only have reciprocal rights (and the duties which ensue from the pacts they undersign), but also duties (exclusively duties, I would argue) towards all citizens. In short, they have duties towards the whole human race. The subjects in question are not the two dualities, state–citizens and state–state. A third type of relationship ought to be added:[29] that between states and humanity, which all states without exception are duty-bound to treat in the same *just* way. One might even go so far as to argue that, whereas individuals have rights and duties towards their own state, but also towards other states,[30] states – which have rights and duties towards other states – have only *duties* towards the citizens of all the countries in the world.[31] It is in this asymmetry that the premise for workably applying the moral argument to international relations resides. International relations, after all, are not the exclusive preserve of contacts between the legal inventions that are states, but rather the set of relations which, via the state, citizens everywhere in the world enter into peacefully whenever they trade and travel, and conflictually whenever they exploit, fight or kill one another. Why on earth should all this be considered *unimportant*?

The rights and duties in question are of course moral and not positive, nor are they legally regulated. This does not mean, however, that rights cannot give rise to duties. Does it make sense, though, that, in their special mutual relationship, states and citizens are separated, the former on the duty side and the latter on the rights side?[32] The linkage of right and duty is easily recognizable when subjects have the same nature.[33] But is that possible with states, on the one hand, and individuals, on the other? The question is all the more apt if we consider that states, in their direct relations with individuals, have *only* or *exclusively* duties, while individuals, symmetrically, have only rights. One tends to wonder whether it is states which serve individuals or vice versa. Such conjecture, however, leads us away from our main point, which deserves to be analysed in its specificity, not – at least *prima facie* – in its obviousness. We have argued that the US government is duty-bound to treat Vietnamese citizens the same way as it treats US citizens: that much is unlikely to raise objections. But will the other consideration – that of 'the rights without duties' of citizens towards the community of states (and excluding the minimum duties discussed above) – be just as acceptable, if it is applied to the Vietnamese citizen who effectively has nothing to ask of the US government other than respect for his fundamental rights?

It is of course difficult to offer simple, sensible answers to questions like this. After all, respect for human rights may vary widely from country to country. Thinking back to Pol Pot's regime in Cambodia or Pinochet's in Chile or the racial policy of South Africa, one holds out few hopes for the universalization of human rights, without considering that ideological divergence and so-called 'religions of state' may exacerbate contradictions further. Nevertheless, it is just as difficult to find arguments against an affirmative reply to the question above. The Vietnamese *has* the same birthright as an American: he cannot be treated differently. The sky he is born under cannot change a human being. Although it would be wrong to forget that, in practice, things are different,[34] the nature of the problem does not change. In certain respects, *mutatis mutandis*, the problem is comparable to that of the promotion of democracy inside states. Incidentally, almost everyone takes the furtherance of democracy as a value (and not only as a procedure), but it is the result of the most diverse, contrasting and often non-democratic methods. The promotion of human rights and the democratization of international life are, in turn, two great avenues along which principles of justice might be, if not disseminated directly, at least backed and supported, since 'human rights, democracy and peace are three necessary stages in the same historical movement: without recognized and protected human rights, there is no democracy; without democracy, the minimum conditions for the pacific solution of conflicts do not exist.'[35]

The image of international politics which thus emerges may of course appear naïve or excessively optimistic: but it purports to lead to a theory of international politics with normative aspects, and in some way pledged to fostering wider knowledge of the mechanisms of international life, making it increasingly an everyday, fixed component of our analysis of reality. The problems on the agenda of international ethics are immense in size and scope. Any initial flaws in the argument might be compensated by innovative results later. The challenge we have to face is thus a considerable one. Transformations in international politics are admittedly rarer than those in domestic life but are, when they occur, much more disturbing and often more dramatic. For a long time, we were discouraged by the sheer obscurity of international politics, which discouraged us from analysing the subject theoretically. Now that selfsame obscurity encourages us to address the problems of international life, stripping them of the secrecy and reserve imposed by the foreign offices of the past, and to acknowledge their importance to our daily lives. In short, it persuades us to uncover and understand their most recondite mechanisms.

Something which we often find astonishing about international political analysis is the simplicity of its interpretations, the banality of its explanations, its lack of a professional idiom. Perhaps no other language in the social sciences is so packed with metaphors and mechanistic references, which, evocative as they may be, nonetheless point to limited autonomy of reflection. The image of 'equilibrium' comes from physics, wars 'break out' as if they were compressed gases, the state of international relations is 'tense' or else its 'climate' is 'unstrained'.[36] Most explanatory models indulge themselves in the most blatant causal mechanism (think of the analysis of the 'causes' of wars).[37] Our reflection on the foundations of relations between states may help us to consolidate a specialized language as a token of increased awareness of the importance of these problems.

2

The International Ethical and Political Space

Even before Ceaucescu's corpse was cold, western politicians were being quoted in the press on how they regretted they hadn't been severer towards such a cruel dictatorship – of which they had been the guests only months previously. For his part, our foreign minister called for new ideas to be developed on the 'right of interference'. It is in the name of this same right of interference that the great liberal, democratic America has, not without difficulty, meted well deserved punishment on the Panamanian dictator, General Noriega. All of which is fine. The Chinese students of Tienanmen Square have now realized, alas, that such virtuous sentiments would not have been applied to their country. France has recently approved public funding for an important Citröen group project in China, but refused to sell patrol boats to Taipei at the first raising of an eyebrow by Beijing. The United States have just authorized the sale of three satellites to Deng Xiaoping, and Great Britain has followed suit with military radar equipment. All the world's peoples lucky enough to be familiar with the subtlety of western thought will have grasped that holier-than-thou indignation and the right to interfere do not apply to dead or precarious dictators.
Pierre Bernard-Reymond, Letter to *Le Monde*,
10 February 1990.

1   THE ARGUMENT

The doubts expressed in this letter to the French daily *Le Monde* are doubts which strike anyone who pauses to reflect upon the logic underpinning the effective relations between states. On occasion, 'normal' social, commercial and ideological relations, and not just warlike ones, become a cause for concern, if not for scandal, only to be forgotten due to their apparent intractability. Is it possible to overcome this obstacle and formulate judgements on international politics? Judging by the history of our culture in the past, the answer would be a resounding 'no'! Yet, on second thoughts, it is not so easy to justify the ethical fracture we thus legitimate between citizens, society and institutions, according to whether they are on this side of the border or that. After all, how could a state which acts *immorally* towards other states – and hence its citizens – act *morally* at home? Three quarters of a century ago, a British idealist philosopher asked himself whether the state might be considered a *moral agent* and, after answering in the affirmative, went on to argue that even if one reaches the conclusion that the state in its absoluteness has no duties but to itself, this would not rule out that

> the state has a duty to itself in respect of its behaviour to other states; and we might even suspect that we are vexing ourselves with a mere question of words, since in any case *a moral agent cannot have a duty to another which is not also a duty to itself.*[1]

Although perception of this problem was at least contemporary with the birth of modern international relations, it was almost universally neglected until very recently. This was because it was widely believed that survival itself was a big enough worry for states, and that any form of abstract morality might have ruinous, hence unjust consequences for states wishing to comply with it. Nevertheless, a partial but incontrovertible pacification of international life has made itself increasingly felt in the popular consciousness over the last decade or so (a consequence of the widespread sensation that the quasi-impossibility of atomic war has effectively materialized). It has, moreover, elicited deep dissatisfaction with the lack of criteria for judging the actions of states among scholars of international politics, previously accustomed solely to strategic calculations, military studies and evaluations of the balance of power. For the idea that in a now prevalently peaceful context (at least in relation to the danger of *great wars*), the conception of the ethical neutrality of the state's action is no longer acceptable is growing widespread.

The sole aim of this book is to offer arguments to cure this malaise, to unravel this paradox. Even the contemporary history of international relations seems to reflect the importance of the issue. If we consider the problems most commonly addressed in the major specialized reviews, read by the world's academic community in its entirety, it is easy to see that a shift has occurred: the peace–war nexus, previously a central issue, has now been replaced by topics relating to the 'civil' dimension, such as; the role of ideologies in international analysis; the importance of the stabilizing function of the leading powers; international regime theory; discussion of the democratic nature of international life; or reformulation of an international system theory, no longer founded on war but on participation and pluralism (one might also note, conversely, that there has been a drastic decrease in the number of articles on the international crisis, on the balance of terror and on the strategic theory in general).[2] Particularly conspicuous is the proliferation of articles referring directly or indirectly to the ethical dimension of international life (as my bibliography demonstrates). The academic community's about-face is merely a reaction against the importance which international relations theory long assigned to the concepts of nationhood, statehood and sovereignty, in the light of which research was reduced to a repetitive, frustrating admission of the unchangeability of the standards of conduct of international life. For too long the latter was viewed exclusively in terms of its deeply rooted and disturbing problems: war, revolution, the atomic bomb, the destruction of mankind. Far be it from me to belittle the magnitude of such threats, but there can be no doubt that the reality of international relations today (and, I am tempted to say, always) also consists of a multiplicity of other contacts, problems and relations (be they economic, social or cultural – or, in a word, civil) which have progressively woven a pattern of everyday life which does not fit the rigid framework of traditional theory. It is by no means a coincidence that one of the books which has enjoyed the greatest success in the last few years is dedicated to the birth of a sort of political economics of international relations.[3] This is but one of many examples of the development of analysis of economic interdependence, seen not as a mere financial relationship, but as an essay in coexistence and cooperation between states. Extensive research has developed,[4] while a lively theoretical debate is raging, principally as a result of the publication of a book by K. Waltz.[5] The subtitle of one recent collection of essays is 'Postmodern Readings of World Politics': its 'Preface' refers to the influence of the European philosophical and intellectual traditions stemming from post-modernism and post-structuralism, going so far as to question the Enlightenment foundation of international relations.[6] The transformation of the cultural fabric of international analysis[7] has allowed political theory to dedicate greater attention to relations between states – something which, for entirely different reasons, Thomas Hobbes was able to overlook altogether three and a half centuries ago. The various chapters of this book (each of which commences with a presentation of the argument to be put forward) address, in a kind of problematic progression, areas in which ethics might be applied to international relations. Let us launch ourselves, therefore, into a polemical attack on the awe which the sacral prerogatives of the sovereign state have invariably provoked.[8]

2   AGAINST A PREJUDICE

It was not only the simplicity and primitiveness of international life in the mid-eighteenth century that allowed Hume to assert that, 'we must necessarily give a greater indulgence to a prince or minister, who deceives another; than to a private gentleman who breaks his word of honour.'[9] Previously, contractarian theory had been even more explicit.

> Concerning the Offices of one Sovereign to another, which are comprehended in the Law, which is commonly called the *Law of Nations*, I need not say anything in this place; because the Law of Nations, and the Law of Nature, is the same thing. And every Sovereign hath the same Right, in procuring the safety of his people, that any particular man can have, in procuring his own safety.[10]

Contemporary realism is not all that dissimilar:

> The interests of the national society for which government has to concern itself are basically those of its military security, the integrity of its political life and the well-being of its people. These needs have no moral quality. They arise from the very existence of the national state in question and from the *status* of national sovereignty it enjoys.[11]

How is it possible to argue such a view? R. Niebuhr, one of the masters of contemporary realism, positive 'that a sharp distinction must be drawn between the moral and social behaviour of individuals and of social groups', offers the following theoretical justification (actually, the only one I know of): 'Since there can be no ethical action without self-criticism and no self-criticism without the rational capacity of self-transcendence, it is natural that natural attitudes can hardly approximate the ethical.'[12]

That states are not duty-bound to judge themselves (I am not of course referring to statesmen, but generically to societies or public opinion) is such a widespread prejudice that, as happens when popular wisdom has its say, the saying

> *Our country, right or wrong*

has entered common parlance, arousing almost spontaneous, universal patriotic sentiment. The slogan was coined by one Stephen Decatur[13] in the course, it seems, of a toast which he made in Norfolk, Virginia, in 1816. Of the two ideas it evokes (patriotic loyalty/blind obedience), no great store is set these days by the second, a figurative, elliptical expression of the unfailing and uncritical obedience of citizens and, even more so, soldiers, to the superior decisions of their leaders: its tone smacks too much of Hollywood! The same cannot be said of the emphatic first notion.[14] Yet the idea here is not to *absolve* the state, or, rather, *one's own* state (tantamount to the simple, more or less conscious application of a benevolent judgement), but to rule out the possibility of its activity being subject to ethical assessment by others than itself.[15]

It is my explicit aim to refute this thesis, and I do so by arguing that the state can in no way regard itself as being free from obligations simply because it is sovereign. The fact that there are no superior authorities cannot be used willy-nilly to justify a situation in which absolute indifference reigns: the fact that there is no one to condemn my behaviour does not mean that I am not subject to moral judgement or censure. I am fully aware of the richness and authoritativeness of the tradition which has opposed this formulation. Images of international anarchy and reason of state proclaim respectively the impossibility and the uselessness of expressing moral judgements on the conduct of the state which (irrespective of, or without regard for, the quality of its rulers) acts for the good of people, doing what it can and what it must, and, by its very nature, operates for the exclusive benefit of the population which it represents and guides. All of which obviously turns the state into an amoral entity unsubjectable to moral judgement. In the pages that follow, I argue instead that, in such an eventuality, we would be guilty of shunning our moral prerogatives, and that, *in the nature of things*, there is no insurmountable impediment to the application of moral judgement. The content of such judgement is, of course, an altogether different matter. I do not conceal the fact that my argument contains normative aspects, for it is my purpose to demonstrate that certain internationally significant actions are *better* than others, and that national interest cannot always and inevitably be the law of the life of the state.

If things were as I say they are, it would mean that we have been very slow in constructing an ethics of international life and, personally, I am convinced that this is so. Why, therefore, should something that has been overruled for centuries become possible, peremptorily and without a care, at the present time? And why, moreover, should a single dimension of human life, politics, be judged in one case and neutralized in the other?[16] Let us ask ourselves, first of all, where this prejudice comes from. Synthetically, its principal cause may be sought in the backward-ness of collective sensibility, which for centuries regarded international life as being somehow intermittent, like a volcano which passes from periods of eruption (wars) to others of inactivity (peace). This view is an ingenuous one: it was progressively diluted until World War II, when all forms of separation of the two facets – domestic and international – of the nature of the state were eventually erased. The Holocaust and the bombs of Hiroshima and Nagasaki are proof of – and enduring monuments to – the fact. Once the war was over, however, once its traces had been cleared away and its misdemeanours forgotten (like a football pitch after the the whistle has gone), life seemed to resume from where it had left off before the conflict began.

Is this the way of the world? Do wars have no other purpose than to destroy, devastate and kill? In war, death and violence are not ends but means – means for the conquest of power. It is hence impossible to approach any understanding of, let alone judgement on, war, unless one grasps the aim to which it tends, as opposed to the aim which provoked it. What needs to be understood is the political order which the out-come of war produces, not the end for which war breaks out in the first place.[17] In this way, it is possible to see how, and to what extent, the outcome of war determines the structure of subsequent international political life. Victors and vanquished participate on an unequal footing, as the outcome of conflict makes extraordinarily and inflexibly plain. Conversely, the arrogance of the image of international life founded on equilibrium obscures such awareness, suggesting that the birth of a new arrangement at the war's end is a question which concerns those players who resume the great game of free equilibrium. The analysis of war's role in the explanation of international relations demands close reflec-tion upon two aspects: (1) judgement on international life; (2) judgement on war.

(1) 'International life is anarchic, hence unjust': it is of this postulate, or prejudice, that the history of international relations theory is an offshoot. As it is obviously impossible to argue that international life is *normally* just, all one can do is appeal to the source of such injustice – to anarchy, that is. Unless it is the hypothesis of chaos we are referring to, the anarchy we find is a symptom of a lack of law or jurisdiction: but the definition applies only in part to the international realm, in-ternational law being customary and pactional, and anything but in-effective (except, of course, in some cases – invariably the most important ones!). Generally speaking, in their reciprocal relations, states have always found themselves on an unequal footing in terms of power, resources,

prestige and alliances. How can one help deducing that all of this gives rise, albeit in limited periods defined by a state of peace, to generally effective rules of conduct, whose violation is sanctioned not by a judge but by another state? The effectiveness of the rules imposed by some states on many others thus produces a normative framework designed to govern subsequent political relations. It is inappropriate, therefore, to describe this situation as anarchic. So why argue then that it must necessarily be unjust?[18]

Realist theory (which boasts an extremely rich historical heritage, peopled by the likes of Machiavelli and Hobbes and, more recently, Niebuhr and Morgenthau)[19] denies that the state is anything other than *force*, and deduces, therefore, that the same is true in equal measure of states taken as a whole. This consequence implies admission of the state's natural and unquestionable right to act (here I use 'state' in the formal, legal meaning of the term, referring, that is, to specific territorial forms of organization which, as such, have natural autonomy). How can we demonstrate the state's 'natural right' to exercise its force? History of course tells us that, at some point in its development, humanity expressed a preference for organization into states: but this gives no state the eternal divine right to exist. One might argue that the state has by nature a right to anything at all, limited solely – *de facto* and not by right – by the analogous claims of all other existing states. But one would have to have a most singular conception of the state to do so.[20] One would have to have a conception similar to Croce's, for example, according to which, in practice, 'as necessary forms in which historical life moves, states resemble the so-called forces of nature', which are thus indifferent to any judgement, hence 'states, in so far as they struggle one against another, are not ethical but economic individuals.'[21] But do all states possess such individuality? In 1816, 23 states were members of the international community. In 1919 the number had risen to 49, in 1959 to 89 and, two years later, to 111. How is it possible – especially in the eyes of populations which were long denied a 'birthright' (to set themselves up, that is, as sovereign entities) – to justify the fact that the 23 states in 1816 comprised, infringing their rights, the 111 of 150 years later? There are no states *in nature*: they are the artificial product of the political history of humanity at a certain stage in its development. On the basis of what principle, therefore, may states resemble *forces of nature*? The fact is that the single state would not even exist without all the others. Each derives from the separation of a given territory from the rest of the world.

Indifference to the *relativity* of the state (which is at the base of realist thinking, and hence of statist doctrine)[22] is directly reflected in assessment of the nature of war. If states are forces imposed by nature, it is a mere coincidence that they are 'perpetually embroiled in a life struggle for survival and prosperity',[23] that war is nothing other than 'an earthquake or some other telluric upheaval',[24] and that it is no more subject to moral judgement than they are. But is it possible to trace war's inevitability to its 'naturalness'? How are we to homologate natural and social inevitability? All the earthquakes that had to take place have of course taken place, but we cannot say – for we cannot know – the same thing about wars. We know the conditions of earthquakes, but we know neither their reasons nor their ends. Are we to say, likewise, that wars are without reason? There are, as is well known, many doctrines to justify and/or explain wars. There are ideological reasons, economic reasons and psychological reasons. Yet they have all been soundly confuted. The only formulation which seemingly makes itself inconfutable, relates wars simply to the existence of states, seeing the former as the sole vital law of the latter. Plainly, if there were no states, there would be no war in the sense in which we traditionally understand it. But there are states[25] – in the broad sense of the term they have existed for almost half a millennium – and there are wars.[26] Before we ask ourselves whether – and if so, how – wars may be avoided (as federalism does when it simplistically pretends to solve the problem by abolishing the sovereign state), we must first question the state–war relationship today, or, to be more precise, as it has developed over the last five centuries. Are we to claim that each of the wars that have broken out in that period of time was inevitable; that the reason behind it was mysterious and impenetrable,[27] or that it depended exclusively upon thirst for power?[28]

(2)   It goes without saying that if we accept a formulation of this type no criticism of war is tenable and no judgement can be formulated – quite simply because there would be nothing whatsoever to express a judgement upon. Against nature we can do nothing. It is hardly necessary to point out here that it is precisely this renunciation which explains why the facts of international life have been barred from the moral universe. In this universe, based on bare necessity, the sole priority is to end up on the winning side! But if we have no ethical criteria to judge war, how can we refute the Nietzschean folly that 'it is good war which sanctifies any cause',[29] and not the other way around? This point is more than mildly polemical, and deserves deeper reflection. It is necessary to study the conditions which make war *justifiable* (or *unjustifiable* – which amounts to the same thing in my argument), and which hence highlight its politico-cultural nature as opposed to the

presumed naturalness referred to above. If it is to be an object of assessment, war must have a meaning, which must be sought not among its causes (that is, the events which take place before the war breaks out), but among its effects: not where war comes from but what it leads to.

Volume 8 of Clausewitz's *On War* (the unity and date of writing of which have been the subject of great controversy) allows us at least to establish that the author had a clear perception of the need to separate the ends achieved *through* war from those reached *in* war.[30] Aron has rightly called attention to Clausewitz's distinction between the use of the word *Ziel*, referring to the ends *in* war, and that of *Zweck*, referring to the ends *of* war.[31] It is also worth stressing Clausewitz's systematic positioning of the specification. He discusses it in volume 8, chapter 6, the one in which he examines and justifies his most celebrated precept ('War is merely the continuation of policy by other means', volume 1, chapter 1, section 24). Which means that the arguments presented were central to Clausewitz's overall conception of war. Thus, after demonstrating 'The effect of political aim on the military objective' (chapter 6, section a, p. 603), Clausewitz analyses the proposition that 'War is an instrument of policy' (chapter 6, section b, p. 605), which illustrates the reasons why war cannot be an object of autonomous consideration, since it 'is simply the continuation of political intercourse *with the addition of other means*' (my italics), given that it 'does not suspend political intercourse'.[32] War cannot be understood except in the broader context of the political reasons (*Zweck*) which guide the aims (*Ziel*) of military actions. It is at this point that Clausewitz uses a metaphor that has since become famous (albeit rarely discussed or commented upon): 'Is war not just another expression of their [i.e. governments'] thoughts, another form of speech or writing?' (ibid.).

Clausewitz thus clearly perceived that the meaning of war was not to be sought in its military content, which is just another form of expression – a technical device, that is – which acquires meaning only when its grammar is enlightened by a logic of its own, by a syntax.[33] The meaning of war is to be sought instead, in the political determination that supports it: 'Policy is the guiding intelligence and war only the instrument, and not vice versa.'[34] Thus, the object of prevalent and priority attention will not be the way in which war is conducted – not *jus in bello*, to express the concept in legal language – but its end, the intention with respect to which war is instrumental. This is why I wish to focus not on how war breaks out, or how war comes about, but on what its aims are: not, in other words, on *jus ad bellum* but on *jus post bellum*.[35] Yes, this is what we need to know about wars: it is on this point that it will be possible to make assessments, to formulate judgements.[36] All this has to be sought, though, not in the subjective justifications for war, which all states relentlessly advance, but in its consequences: that is, in the nature of the postwar arrangements determined by the victors.[37] Although it is not true that 'anything goes' in war, the state of necessity is capable of warping the moral conscience of anybody – or almost anybody. Things change once the war is over: an order has been constituted and rules have been imposed on all parties to the conflict. The nature of the peace thus determined is the true object of our attention, since, in the meantime, some states will have imposed themselves over others, and the content of international relations subsequent to conflict may have been affected. After all, if this were not the case, armed conflict would serve no purpose. Which is not to leave war to its own devices, but rather to stress that – irrespective of any judgement on conduct in war – it will be possible, in any case, to express judgements on what happens in the aftermath, when states are no longer at war.

3   THE LIMITS OF SOVEREIGNTY

The ethics of international relations and the schizophrenia of domestic and international politics owe their topical interest today to a single common denominator, the central element of which is the very idea of sovereignty. On the one hand, the idea is no longer glorified as it used to be: either that or its absoluteness has been modified by the extraordinary growth in economic and cultural integration (although many differences and disparities still exist, the unification of the world into a single system is now *fait accompli*). It is now recognized, moreover, that sovereignty may be subject to limitations: for, normal prerogatives apart, the situation whereby a very few states have a near-monopoly on nuclear weapons has produced a sort of stratification of power, and inevitably also of sovereignty. In addition, in the light of the history of nuclear politics, the fact that the arms of mass destruction have had a great influence on the recourse or otherwise to war – due to the risk they entail of dragging humanity into a maelstrom of catastrophe[38] – it is possible to understand the reasons which have spurred a postponement of the terror of nuclear war and, consequently, a reflection on its morality and, even more so, on its use as a deterrent.[39] On the other hand, in such conditions, the distinction between domestic and international politics – in my view, inherently unjustifiable in any circumstance and at any time – appears less indisputable, and indeed, distinctly implausible in a world as unified as the present one. Suffice it to consider the fusion of the two dimensions in the handling of ecological problems[40] to fully appreciate the need to reconcile *internal* and *external*, domestic and international politics. The growth of international peace has done the rest. As the international realm has grown less anarchic, so reflection upon it has begun to develop, inevitably combining with political state theory to generate international political theory as well.

One cannot hide the fact that revision of the concept of sovereignty has valuational implications, and leads to extremely important consequences. The problem is addressed in the concluding pages of 'Der Wande der Souveranitatsbegriffes',[41] in which Kelsen studies the contrast between the two fundamental formulations – subjectivist and objectivist – of the relations between domestic and international law. In his analysis, Kelsen highlights another contrast, that between imperialism and pacifism. He derives the subjectivist hypothesis, which proclaims the primacy of domestic law, from the emergence of the legal formulation on the basis of which state sovereignty is absolutely intangible;[42] while to the objectivist hypothesis he traces the model

of a universal legal order, of the theory – based on the objectivity of law – of the primacy of international law under which are comprised, in supreme unity, in the totality of *civitas maxima unica sovrana*, the legal systems of single states.[43]

The subjectivist formulation gives rise to the primacy of both domestic law and domestic policy. Indeed, according to Kelsen, it leads directly 'to the affirmation of the pure power viewpoint', which celebrates the insuperability of sovereignty. What international law can exist in a realm in which the other states exist exclusively as 'biased legal systems', and only in so far as they are recognized by one's own state? Where there is no law, how can there be justice?[44]

Why is the objectivist conception, according to which international law is logically superior to domestic rights, pacifist? The reason – and here the wheel turns full circle – resides in the temporary, artificial nature of the state described above: 'Only provisionally, and by no means forever, does humanity split into states which, after all, are formed in a more or less arbitrary fashion.'[45] The centrality of the idea of sovereignty is thus reappraised and restored to its provisional historical context. Yet contemporary international politics is made up of (albeit limited) *sovereign* states: it is in the light of this particular characteristic that it is necessary to address the question of international ethics, dispensing with the unconditional nature of sovereignty. However, it is also necessary to bear in mind that this implies appealing to another intractable dimension of the theory of the state – the latter's relationship with the *nation* category (all the more so, since, in this realm, the expression 'nation-state' is often used). The relationship is an explosive one in view of the split it may cleave between the two terms. Only rarely do 'nation' and 'state' succeed in actually coinciding, in conformity with what is one of the great ideals of any form of patriotism. There can be no doubt that the demand for national independence is a historically progressive objective. It served first in Europe and then in the rest of the world as a means of erasing colonialism in all its forms, and it is as yet impossible to say whether it has exhausted its task. But to identify the nature of the state with that of the nation is an entirely different matter. Nothing, in theory, prevents us from thinking that unity of race, culture, tradition, language and habits may coexist with other similar unities.[46] However outrageous it may sound, nothing would prevent a state from extending its laws to more than one nation within its boundaries, or a nation from being distributed over more than one state.[47]

It is worth observing here – *en passant* since my prime interest is the ethics *of* or *for* states and not of individuals – that Kelsen's hierarchical formulation prompts the consideration that all states *should* assign the same contents to human rights, since these fundamental principles are written into general international law. Moving in reverse from domestic to international law, we might find instead that the diverse domestic legal systems do not reserve equal treatment to fundamental rights – nor could they accept any interference in this particular sphere. Hence S. Hoffman's almost rhetorical question ('can one make of human rights the priority of priorities, as if foreign policy were nothing but the execution by a state of its legal and moral obligations?'), far from prompting a negative response such as the one he proposes ('human rights are neither the only possible goal of a foreign policy, nor even the only possible moral goal of a non-Machiavellian foreign policy'),[48] might be answered affirmatively in so far as an individual, *as such*, has the same rights wherever he is born. We thus comprehend why it is possible for Kelsen's legal internationalism to be defined as pacifist. By debunking sovereignty, it reduces the disruptive scope of nationalism and proposes, without further explanation, a technical, non-ideal image of the state. Plainly, as long as the state is seen as an unrivalled authority and other states exist exclusively in so far as they are 'recognized' by that authority, international life cannot be considered anything other than a sum of reciprocal recognitions (always unilaterally established, and hence revocable); that is, as something provisional, intermittent and indeterminate, without the subjectivist intervention of a state's will. Here, then, we have a strongly state-centric view of international relations, which inevitably resorts to the theoretical apparatus of political realism and the yardstick of power as the sole criterion for assessing states. It is to counter such arrogance that the international polemic of federalist thinking has developed; alas, with its uncompromising criticism of the myth of the power-state, it has ultimately juxtaposed one ideology (however preferable it may be) to another. The development of a political theory for international relations might well have followed a different, more rapid, course, if it had been based on recognition of the specific nature of international life, whose material substratum is not an anarchic congeries of sovereign authorities, but a sort of society[49] whose diverse elements are nonetheless associated by the pursuit (albeit conducted in conflicting ways) of analogous and, indeed, common ends, as is the case of survival or the defence and conservation of humanity's collective goods.[50]

The implausibility of a common authority extending over and above states has always been considered a compulsory preliminary question for any conception of order, without which international politics has been left to its own devices as a realm of the imponderable and, in a certain sense, of the unknowable. At best, it has been entrusted to straightforward factual description and, at worst, to outbursts of irrational, primitive passion. The only judgement currently formulated on international life is the one which distinguishes between 'good guys' and bad, our allies and our enemies, good and evil. But the fact that, despite all, we continue to formulate judgements on the international realm – as when we condemn the war sparked by Nazism, or reject the justifications made for US intervention in Vietnam, or protest against Israeli neo-colonialism in the Middle East, or judge the war between Iran and Iraq unjust on both sides – at least explains the topicality of the issue: the pursuit of a common foundation which these albeit scanty judgements must necessarily share – unless of course we acknowledge that their formulation depends exclusively on whether we were born Nazis or not, on whether we are Jewish or Palestinian, American, Iranian or Iraqi or whatever![51]

The same formulation must be applied to the idea of nationhood, without a radical reassessment of which any future plan for the organization of international relations risks being unfeasible. This is not only (though the fact merits some attention) because the last two wars, the greatest ever, were fuelled by the idea,[52] but chiefly because of its abstractness today. If the drive towards nationhood is (and this, as I have already said, is possible) historically progressive until liberation from a situation of subservience has been achieved, it ought to lose its ebullience when the state is formed (and reunited with the nation).

From that moment on, the problem will no longer be the celebration of one's nation or power, but the creation of a state that works. A perfect example of the way in which this idea might evolve is the transformation undergone by the boundary concept. The latter has long since been left standing by the material logic of relations between states,[53] as is demonstrated by the curious and little known fact that the vast majority of African state boundaries have remained virtually unchanged since the day they were defined. And no boundary in the world has ever been drawn with as much artfulness as that adopted by the countries which colonized Africa! It follows that, 'The assumption that there are "natural frontiers" which can somehow be delimited on the basis of topography and which would therefore be less arbitrary than the current African borders is much more problematic than is normally assumed.'[54] Without wishing to regard this evolution in African political life as a definitive model (and without overstressing that 'the recent national and international history of Black Africa challenges more than it supports some of the major postulates of international relations theory'),[55] there can be no doubt that the case of Africa is an exemplary one, especially if we take stock of the number of times the common idea of nationhood, the clan or the tribe has been violated on African soil. That the idea of nationhood is re-emerging now, at the end of the twentieth century, as a consequence (or is it a cause?) of the crumbling of the Soviet empire, can be nothing other than a pathetic, dangerous legacy from the past: for we today live in an age in which problems have boundless dimensions. Be that as it may, the simple material discovery that frontiers have disappeared or been shifted, is in itself a trifling matter with no moral scope at all. What does have vast moral scope – as I shall seek to demonstrate below (chapter 6, section 2) – is the moment in which state and society come round to reappraisal of their relationship with human beings – citizens and foreigners, friends and enemies, allies and neutrals.

4   TOWARDS A NEW CONCEPTION OF INTERNATIONAL POLITICS

The pre-condition for any discussion of the ethics of international relations is a general theory of international politics in which the peculiarity of relations between states provides the basis for any subsequent assessment of their conduct. What exactly are international relations anyway? To define them, we must begin from the concept of the international system, by which we mean the sum-total of contacts between states (be they commercial or cultural, friendly or conflictual), taken as an autonomous dominion with its own specific rules of functioning, hence of analysis. There would be nothing new or useful about the idea that relations between states give rise to a system, were it not for the fact that it enables us to consider the hierarchical nature of the diverse relations according to the hypothesis that not everything which happens on the international scene is equally relevant. For example, the INF treaty on the dismantling of Euromissiles signed by Reagan and Gorbachev on 8 December 1987 cannot be considered on the same plane as a trade protocol between Italy and Algeria. One might even go so far as to consider disparity a founding concept of internationalist analysis: 'natural'[56] and 'artificial', but not perpetual and unmodifiable, disparity.[57] One might go even further still, arguing that the aim of any empirical analysis of international relations is to determine the system of variations within the international hierarchy. If we reserve first place in the chain to the idea of the inevitability of international relations (which is simply the logical consequence of the single state as the monopolistic appropriation of a territory),[58] it follows that states as a whole are arranged in an order (hence with stratifications) created by the natural and artificial disparities mentioned. Plainly, the only way this hypothesis can be verified is by confrontation, the consequence of which will be either the submission of the least privileged to the strongest, or conflict – war. But war, in turn, is not made up merely of military operations (and victory *per se* is but a verification, an encashment of securities).[59] If it were, there would be no need to fight at all! It is the 'Scale of the military objective and of the effort to be made'[60] which defines both the scope of the conflict and, as a result of its outcome, the framework of relations between all the states which, having continued politics by other means, have fought the war.

Unless we argue that international life is a perpetual war 'of everyone against everyone', we are forced to acknowledge that each war has to be assigned a role of its own: otherwise, it simply appears incomprehensible. Yet it is possible to identify a war's role exclusively by observing its outcome – in practice, the establishing of a system of hierarchical order among the states that have fought it. It is illusory to believe – as the balance of power model suggests – that after a war, international life resumes in the same way that, following a long illness or an earthquake, life returns to normal, and what has been destroyed is reconstructed. Life after war is, for those who have experienced it,[61] incomparable to life before it. The signs of war are indelible:[62] politics (which has continued throughout the war) identifies them and shapes them into a forced framework of peace,[63] which then sets about the task of organizing the new international system – an original political fabric woven from new relations of disparity between states.

The only way of recognizing this model – a veritable war system[64] – is of course through empirical analysis or, more precisely, historiographic inspection, which, if it is to refer to reality, needs to be supplemented by tools of empirical translation. It will be necessary, first of all, to demonstrate that wars are not all equal; that is, that only some of them perform the constitutive function whereby a new system of international order comes into being.[65] It will then be necessary to periodize international systems. This will allow us to define them and identify any originality they may possess, which in turn will help us to determine the uniqueness of each single system (of its rules of functioning, in other words), or of its own characteristic, original regime.[66] But if an international system, defined in terms of a historical period, possesses a regime, it follows that it is acquainted with a certain regularity of conduct which consequently becomes predictable in so far as it corresponds to the politico-historical conditions under which each actor plays his part. The analogy between the logic of political regimes applied to analysis of the domestic political system and the same type of analysis applied to the international system, would be workable if it were possible to identify in that system a legal authority, the possessor of the monopoly of legitimate force. Although this is clearly not the way things stand, the nature of international disparities generates something very much like it, in the sense that some states (the dominant states, the great powers, the ones that have won the most recent constitutive war) are effectively enabled to act and intervene throughout the system. In this way, their power is akin to that of undisputed authorities, self-appointed guardians of an established order born of violence and conserved by the threat of new violence.

In this model, one fundamental, dynamic element is missing: that of a transformation theory concerned with the possibilities the system of order possesses of modifying itself over time. In schematic terms, one may believe that there can be *change* in the international system only when some new large-scale war upsets the pre-existing order. In theory, that is how it would be if the system ran smoothly; if, that is, its order were totally, absolutely and exclusively successful – and if, I might add, the nature of states were the same as that of their citizens. Yet the analogy obviously cannot go as far as that.[67] In view of the historical succession of international systems to date, we might be inclined to sketch the following abstract hypothesis: at the heart of each system is conflict, and the question is; will the losers seek revenge? Hence, the reasons for war in the future are already to be found *in nuce* in the imposed peace of the past. This, alas, is only one of many possibilities: there may be divergences and differentiations within the winning coalition; attacks may be brought by emerging, innovative states; upheavals inside one or more states may cause wide-ranging redefinitions of political relations – including the single state's relationship with international power. What will be the consequences of these possible transformations, which originate both in the international realm, with modified mutual relations between states, and the domestic realm, with changes in political regimes or relative power (be it economic, political, strategical or cultural) of single states?

These are the questions facing international political theory today. Inevitably no answers are forthcoming, as the idea that international politics deserves to be considered on a par with politics as such – and hence subject to the same degree of analysis and research as domestic politics – has yet to be universally espoused. This of course neither means that there is no international research, nor that it is impossible to theorize on international relations.[68] It simply reveals that the journey *towards* an international relations theory is a long and tiresome one, both because of the inherent nature of the enterprise and of the scepticism which surrounds it. In attempting to outline a possible programme of research into international relations, I fully realize that it would be wrong to propose the application of moral judgement to issues of little or no substance. At this point, however, it seems to me that the principles of analysis presented offer an impressive series of topics for serious reflection. Moral judgements may, in fact, be formulated:

1   on the wars that have been, rejecting the consideration that in war all principle is set aside. Who would be prepared to argue, for example, that the war conducted by Roosevelt was the same as that conducted by Hitler?[69]

2   on wars that have not been, but which are the object of totalitarian posturing – like nuclear war, which has even given rise to ritual codes of conduct such as the strategy of deterrence;

3   on the way in which the strongest state or states that have won wars wield their power – as when they dispatch an expedition force to an 'allied' country to restore order there, or when they seek to conquer a new ally – and, more generally, on how they influence the normal progress of international life;

4   on the standard of the general regime of the international system which results: the international system upheld by the 'Concert of great powers' in the 30 years following the Congress of Vienna of

1815 was certainly less respectful of the principle of nationhood than the contemporary international system; while the international system in the age of Louis XIV contained not a sign of the embryos of democratization which seem to be emerging in the present one;

5　on the nature of existing political regimes and on the comparison of their merits, on the basis of which states may purport to export their own models; or on when countries are boycotted because their domestic regime is unacceptable (as in the case of South Africa and its segregation policy); or also on when economic aid is promised or granted to countries which set up a regime more consonant with that of the donor state;

6　on the standard of international life in general; with regard to human rights, for example, one of the guidelines of US foreign policy in the second half of the seventies; with regard to the forms in which the vast international trade network is organized, seen from both the economic and productive, and cultural or social viewpoints; with regard to the collective problems of humanity, such as the handling of the ecological situation, raw materials supplies or the exploitation of space;

7　on peace and its conditions: whether its conservation depends on submission or on free acceptance; whether every type of peace is acceptable *per se*, and whether its diffusion can modify the *standards* of conduct of the actors of international life;

8　on international justice, taken as the sum-total of those principles by which every state would, under conditions of equality and reciprocity, be willing to abide;

9　on international order, finally, acknowledged as a *sine qua non* for harmony and for the continuous, complex and inevitable exchange which gives rise to the duty of mutual respect as an elementary rule for survival and coexistence, both for states and for individuals, both in reciprocal relations within the two classes of moral subjects, and in their real and effective encounters – as is the case in international life.

Ever since states have existed, the idea that each of them may share values with others has seemed untenable. How else could we explain why the earth's inhabitants have split up into separate, different states, if not by the fact that their value systems are incompatible? Is it not true to say that conflict between them has always been caused by the clash of ideal-political models? (The United States had no designs to conquer the Third Reich: it was the Nazis' idea of politics, not a lust for power, which forced the United States to contribute to the war effort against

Germany.) Little wonder that we rarely ask ourselves whether a state may perchance act on the basis of some principle: it ought to have no other principle than power. Hence the traditional belief that the state has *rights* but not *duties*. But international life is not only a *war of everyone against everyone*: long periods of peace have existed and do exist. In the meantime, have states been guided solely by chance and fear? Now that it has, at last, been recognized that the earth has but one destiny (determined, as it is, by the possibility of almost instantaneous nuclear destruction), there is widespread awareness that international life is (and was) much richer and more complex than images of war (or war-mongering?) had ever led to believe. It is one thing to argue that states are not, by their very nature, bound by any mutual constraint (and hence that any ethical argument is untenable), it is another to admit that they pursue profit rather than justness (which does not preclude moral judgement).

It would, however, be oversimplistic to argue that the entry of ethics into international relations is merely a result of material progress and interdependence – something, that is, that can give content to values and judgements, but not determine their existence. Although the passing of time has influenced the intensity and substance of relations between states, we cannot overlook the view which argues that, since the seventeenth century, a system of international legal rules designed to regulate international relations has taken root and flourished. Irrespective of the contents thereof, how can we fail to recognize that, already in 1648, states saw themselves as constituting a community (albeit intermittent and incomplete), and that the issue of laws alone was proof of the fact? Values have evidently changed, deriving, in turn, from the success of one power rather than another. What has not changed are the reasons which govern the elaboration of the rules necessary to discuss values themselves – to judge them, compare them and, ultimately, to counter them. Individuals have joined together into families, families into states, and states into an international community. It is the latter, therefore, which is the subject of *universal morality*, both because it enjoys a material primacy over more limited local (state) normative systems, and because it encompasses the entire planet. (Universal morality is not, in these terms, a sort of sum-total of state and cosmopolitan morality – one that is state-oriented as opposed to humanity-oriented – but rather the ideal venue for basic judgements on international life, with regard to both states *and* citizens.)

We know a lot about ethics *vis-à-vis* individuals, nothing about ethics *vis-à-vis* states.[70] Good and evil, justice and injustice cannot be 'local': they must be global and general. Why on earth should what a state considers good for its citizens not be good for the citizens of other states as well? Is it that the evil committed against the citizens of another state is no longer evil because that state is a long way away? The first question we must ask therefore, is whether states, to quote Molière, 'have been speaking prose without knowing it': in other words, whether they are always and invariably inspired by values. This would be easy to demonstrate by simply analysing the stands of statesmen who, whenever they have to justify their recourse to force, resort to values, at once condemning those of their adversary. More than of the presence or otherwise of justice in international politics, we ought really to speak of its justification, which is normally made by invoking the national interest and the good of the nation, rather than some universal conception of justice. Although we will be unable, in this way, to arrive at a system of ethics, and to define the best type of international politics, we will at least demonstrate the importance of committing effort to a dimension, that of the (international) political realm, which, despite its dramatic vitality, has been neglected for too long. At which point, it is almost banal to stress the centrality of the topic for the future of mankind. Why should we resign ourselves to the 'moral inferiority of international politics'?[71] Why shouldn't we debate the point?

3

The Ambiguous Nature of Peace

It's plain to me that wars have changed. . . . This is a situation in which [there has been] a quantitative change, a change, that is, in which the advantage of aggression over defence – of attack over defence – has shifted, in which this quantitative change is for all the world like a change in quality, a change in the nature of the world.

J. R. Oppenheimer, *Letters and Recollections*

1 THE ARGUMENT

The nuclear era is one enormous paradox. It founds peace on the threat of war, order on the fear of anarchy, equilibrium on the most glaring inequalities. The clash between the two great social-ideological models has long been based on a sort of joint agreement: the capitalist system has outlived its imperialist destiny, and the socialist system has been forced to repudiate its international objectives. In largely unforeseen and unforeseeable ways, the nuclear era even seems to have affected the destiny of the social manifestation that is war: it has undermined the most authoritative ethological or sociological explanations for war, dispelling every certainty about its constant presence in the history of humanity. I do not wish of course to declare that war's time is up: one cannot help sensing, however, that some sort of grand transformation is currently under way, sweeping war further and further to the edge (and not only in a geographical sense) of international life. Whether this is simply a cyclical phenomenon, or something more than that, it is impossible to say. But it appears increasingly likely that the atomic bomb has made all its power felt, not by actually exploding, but by triggering a qualitative revolution in the nature of war. We thus arrive at the ultimate, most important paradox. For 30 years, opponents of the armaments policy demanded qualitative change, arguing that nuclear weapon production had to be stopped precisely because any war fought with such weapons would provoke the extinction (albeit not immediate) of mankind. This argument was always rejected by the very statesmen who now have the job of managing the change that has evidently taken place anyway, given that the current 'crisis' of war seems to derive from the near impossibility (relatively speaking) of the traditional recourse to violence. Be that as it may, there is still a long way to go before it will be possible to declare that humanity is entering an era of peace!

2   THE MORALITY OF DETERRENCE AND THE PRACTICAL PROBLEM OF PEACE

Faced by the prospect of a war to end wars, capable of totally destroying humanity, even those spontaneously inclined to think that war is just one of the many accidents that can happen to humanity – hence inevitable or, better still, inevitably recurrent – are forced to review their position. This is basically because, for the last half-century, the situation has been as precarious as it has been consolidated. None of the attempts to justify war elaborated over the centuries envisaged the hypothesis of the final war: such an eventuality was utterly unimaginable in the past.[1] But it is not only the inadequacy of justifications for war that is at stake here. More generally, it is necessary to come to terms with the novelty of the situation which came into being after 6 August 1945, inducing a global rethink of the place war occupies in reality. At first, the US atom bomb was of course justified as an attempt to pre-empt an analogous German project, and later as a means of saving a large number of American lives.[2] The Manhattan project heralded an extraordinary, not to say monstrous, breakthrough, though few people had time to realize the fact then.[3] It is relatively immaterial these days to establish how aware Truman and his advisers were of what they were doing in late July 1945: in wartime, politicians perhaps more than anybody else mislay their sense of morality. Of much greater importance to us today are the effects of nuclear weapons on political life in the meantime; not only in terms of the unification of international affairs on a planetary scale (for the first time in history and with the common denominator of the prospect of universal disaster), and their anomalous reorganization into armed and vigilant government by just two states on behalf of all the rest. No, what interests us most here is that states were deprived of their preferred means of resolving controversies – war![4]

The task of finding the ideal configuration for an international system permanently on the brink of disaster thus slipped out of politicians' hands, and was resolved, paradoxically, by strategists. Here was a brand-new professional category, a product of the nuclear era. Previously, strategists had been responsible at most for winning or losing wars, never for maintaining the *balance of terror*, the abnormal new technique for conserving peace by continuously threatening war. It is thus the very idea of war that has changed profoundly. A total war fought with nuclear arms and at the same fever pitch as World War II would certainly mark the end of civilization as we know it, and of the process of continuous development which has characterized state-centric, capitalist societies since the sixteenth century.[5] Whether strategic theory has the capacity to dominate such enormous problems or not, there can be no doubt that the phenomenon it is grappling with is without historical precedents. The atom bomb is a scientific discovery which has exercised an extraordinary influence not so much on techniques of warfare as on the theory of the causes of wars, not to mention the philosophy of history, which is invariably concerned with the meaning of wars.[6]

The philosophical and, subsequently, the political and ideological debate on this astounding innovation has enjoyed not one heyday but two. Each began with the publication of a work that was to trigger lively debate: *The Future of Mankind* by K. Jaspers[7] and *Just and Unjust Wars* by M. Walzer.[8] The first deals with the clash between capitalism and communism, the second with one country's right to intervene in another. Looming in the background of the first is the Cold War, in that of the second the war in Vietnam. The two problems they pose have remained unsolved to this day. In the first case, is the risk of a 'final' war the gravest risk of all? In the second, does a great power conserve the right to intervene in the domestic affairs of another country (especially if that country is a long way away and cannot create immediate danger near to home)? Rolling the two questions into one, is the war era over? Nobody is blind to the fact that, by their very nature, these problems are packed with aspects which relate to the value of life (which Jaspers contrasts with the value of liberty) and the quality of life (which Walzer portrays in terms of the safeguarding of legally constituted governments). Given that nuclear war plainly had to be avoided, and that the reasons which invariably lead humanity into war remained nonetheless the same, nuclear arms were eventually transformed into a sort of bizarre agent of international social control. They avoided wars by threatening them, ensuring international order with the menace of escalation. From Jaspers to Walzer, thinking on nuclear war revolved around a type of conduct, which was at first imagined in theory, then assumed by heads of state in practice. Plainly, in so far as it is the product of lucid human willpower, strategy demands to be judged. And if we cannot judge human conduct, what can we judge?

The conduct in question, that of deterrence, was shaped round the threat of atomic destruction and organized so that the danger of war made peace possible. Seldom in history has such an abstract logic materialized into fact.[9] Today we must assess it, not in terms of its *success*, but in terms of its *morality*; not so much because its success is now *fait accompli*, but because it fails to help us find an answer to the following, vitally important question. Is a strategy which threatens the greatest evil (war) to achieve good (peace), acceptable? Only an ethical theory can resolve this contradiction: but if it is to do so, it must yet again address the 'ends – means' relationship. For many, many years the solution was found in the 'state of necessity', as if the very urgency of the problem precluded reflection upon it. That this was the case seems to be confirmed by an odd coincidence: it was precisely, and only, at the moment in which the emergency ended (when the threat of nuclear terror had diminished considerably) that a most lively philosophical debate arose on 'the morality of deterrence'[10] – almost as if it is only possible to judge *ex post*, after the *moral* question has been resolved. If we add to this one of the fundamental conclusions in the doctrine that has debated this issue philosophically (namely that deterrence is basically justifiable as long as it is not an end unto itself but 'an element in a broader policy whose principal aim is at once to avoid nuclear conflict and to foster processes of "cooperation" for a peaceful solution to international controversies',[11] it becomes clear that this type of rationalization defies 'assessment'. Who would argue today that deterrence has been a failure?

Even if the merit of peace at the highest level in the last half-century belongs to the strategy of deterrence, this is only one aspect of the problem. It concerns fact, not value. And even in this limited context, is it possible to demonstrate that peace has been created by deterrence? The argument that there have effectively been no wars between the two main power blocs is irrelevant: for how is it possible to demonstrate that they would have broken out, if things had been different? The facts are that the nuclear breakthrough was addressed and analysed with the utmost care, that this gave rise to a series of strategic devices which were applied by both parties to the conflict, and that all internationalist analyses since have confined themselves to those devices. Not that the moral question can be said to be resolved simply because the inventor of the strategy of deterrence *did not know* what its outcome would be, and hence was able to elude (although he should not have done so) moral problems by concerning himself exclusively with his brainchild's success. Yet some people did recognize the problem. In 1964, speaking of the studies of the deterrence theory's 'big three' (Kahn, Kissinger and Schelling), A. Rapoport exclaimed, 'I readily absolve the strategists of charges of paranoia. A much more appropriate term for this type of thinking is psychopathic and, that is, utterly devoid of moral sense!'[12]

Alas, the doubt remains that, yet again, the problem was never actually posed, since political theory at the time was positive that deterrence was the sole assurance of survival, and as such required no justification. The logical corollary of this formulation – if the intensity of deterrence is reduced, then world stability will be reduced too – is untenable. It is useful therefore to devote more attention to the political nature of the extremity argument:[13] have *extreme* situations occurred over the last fifty years? Before I answer the question, I wish to point out that here we are faced with facts, not assessments. When was the last time either of the two great powers behaved in such a way as to persuade the other that it was in a 'state of necessity'? Was it during the Korean War, or in 1956 during the Suez crisis, or the invasion of Hungary? During the war in Vietnam, or in 1968 in Czechoslovakia? During the Middle-East crisis, or the invasion of Afghanistan? Only one episode appears to actually fit the forecasts of the logic of deterrence and that is the 1962 Cuban missile crisis. Judging from the way it was handled, however, this crisis seems to have been more affected than effective, manoeuvred with greater lucidity than we normally associate with a 'backs-to-the-wall' state of mind. Nor should we forget that, technically, the language of deterrence was used most by the United States in a situation in which there was nothing to suggest that the Soviet Union intended to use Cuba as a base for an attack on them.

So if the situation was not extreme, how come the two great powers agreed to implement the strategy of deterrence? The anomaly of the situation, in my view, is that, oddly, the problem of nuclear war was addressed *as such* and not in terms of its *instrumental* function. For example, by considering (nuclear) war as an extreme eventuality, the philosophical debate on the 'quality' of the atomic bomb[14] has failed to question whether any of this was of political significance: if, that is, nuclear war could be interpreted effectively as a situation of reciprocal aggression among those who had the possibility of setting it off (as if war had, in a certain sense, emerged from its Clausewitzian context and stopped being a political instrument).[15] It is true that if atomic war had broken out, it would have killed politics. But, in the meantime, the consequence had been mistaken for the cause! Why did this happen? Why not discuss it in an ethical context?

The answer to this methodological doubt is, in my view, as simple as it is fundamental. If it were to emerge that the policy of deterrence was not a 'necessity', but merely one of the many options open, and that it was chosen as a means of political control over allies and adversaries alike, then the right cum duty to formulate moral judgements on the conduct of governments in their reciprocal relations would be assured. If terror was not the sole motive of men of state, then they deceived their fellow citizens and those of the rest of the world as well. Wouldn't they deserve to be judged for their action? If they mistook ends for means, or, advanced justifications to disguise their effective ends, how can we continue to argue that the international realm is a pure state of nature in which the only free choice available is that of survival? Actually, this immoral (not amoral!) 'lapse' is, it seems to me, only slightly more reprehensible than the complacency of scholars who, with very few exceptions,[16] accepted the official version of this clash between the two worlds uncritically. This is not of course a suitable context for detailed criticism of the ideology of deterrence. Nevertheless, in order to introduce the alternative – an ethic of peace – it is necessary at least to stress how deceitful deterrence proved to be. In fact, it allowed the two states in a position to exploit the threat of nuclear war to dominate the international scene and build two empires,[17] which subsequently 'passed the parcel' of guaranteed survival one to the other. To support the thesis, it is enough to recall that the course followed from July 1945 was not the only one practicable. Following the famous Alamogordo experiment, the United States could have put their new weapon to different uses. Likewise, even after they had dropped it, they might have decided to foster a policy of international atomic energy control.[18] The Soviet Union might have refused to follow suit. The possibilities are endless!

What I wish to convey here is the paradoxical nature of a political strategy which envisaged the heftiest investment ever made in history for one aim and one aim alone: to build objects designed to serve no purpose whatsoever![19] This consideration is not based on a conspiracy theory: it simply unmasks what was really an ideology, not a necessity, a political choice dictated neither by chance nor by the evil of the adversary, but by a common will to implement a plan for world domination.[20] This, *in nuce*, is the constitutive logic of wars. Put a different way, the government designs pursued by the dominant powers might be considered a veritable *peace plan*. Paradoxical as it may seem, deterrence worked, and the geographical distribution of trouble spots changed. They were now concentrated at the edge of the international system, in areas which had not been involved in World War II,[21] and which were hence outside the range of application of the deterrence strategy. In short, the prize at stake was not worth the nuclear risk! As a result, the borderline between war and peace now seems dangerously thin, but this is an inevitable consequence of a policy which threatens war to achieve peace instead of promoting peace to avoid war.[22]

As subtle strategic rationality totally subverted values, so peace theories were disregarded, supplanted by the 'prudential' advice of strategists. Nonetheless, one still wonders whether it is not possible to give peace a positive content. Here I refer to peace not so much as a spiritual dimension,[23] but as a dimension of international political life. Instead of basing peace on threat, tension and unpredictability, it might be possible, slowly but surely, to make a conception of *just peace* materialize. This idea might, in the abstract, be developed on two different levels: that of the individual and that of the state. I wish to concern myself exclusively with the second, simply because international peace is a direct function of the will of states, although the latter, in turn, are merely representatives of their social substrata. In order to address this long neglected, delicate question, I shall make symmetrical use of the theory which has sought to justify war. Is it not possible to justify peace by the same argument?

Following the arrangement proposed by N. Bobbio,[24] let us consider four different justifications for peace: (1) as defence; (2) as a lesser evil; (3) as a necessary evil; (4) as a good.

(1)   Paradoxical as this procedure may seem, it is possible, in theory, to imagine a peace deriving from a defensive formulation. For example, a state might prefer the conservation of peace to reprisal against wrongdoing, provided of course that the latter is not mortal. The position which the British philosopher Thomas Hill Green expounded in his lectures to the founders-to-be of the 'idealist' movement which was to give life to the League of Nations ('the destruction of life in war is always an evil, whoever is responsible for it')[25] was espoused by the likes of L. Woolf according to whom, 'it is darkness, doubt and ignorance which breed fear, and fear which breeds war.'[26] A defensive attitude cannot by its very nature be cowardly *and* warlike. The (moral) idea of refusal to attack also has communicative impact: it disappoints the hopes of the potential enemy, who thus has no war preparations to denounce! That this formulation is by no means unattractive is demonstrated also by more recent reflection on 'strategic' applications of non-violent thought through so-called 'defensive defence' (the organizing, that is, of territorial commandos whose purpose is confined to making invasion extremely difficult).[27]

On the one hand, the formulation may appear conservative, since in practice it prefers the preservation of the status quo even to a hypothetically just war: on the other, besides presenting itself merely as a first step (and, as such, at once identical and opposite to a minimal just war doctrine), it also rejects the only type of peace which international politics is capable of offering, founded on the technology of nuclear war,[28] and hence even less acceptable than the unilateralist approach. The latter is prepared to expose itself to the risk of enemy aggression unarmed[29], while even its more moderate gradualist versions subordinate their every step to enemy reciprocity.[30]

(2) Is it possible to argue that peace is a lesser evil? That peace may not – *per se* – be a good becomes immediately evident if we take a historical view of any war. When the fighting ends, one of the states involved (the loser) will certainly consider peace an evil, albeit lesser with respect to its own annihilation. Germany, divided in two at the end of World War II, found herself in this predicament. For Italy, the so-called 'mutilated' peace at the end of the World War I in 1918 was much preferable to the defeat it had risked suffering only a year earlier. Similar lines of reasoning were elaborated by the Egyptians at the end of the Six Day War and by the Israelis at the end of the Yom Kippur War.

It may be possible to justify this conception of peace more effectively by thinking in terms of the eventuality of war as opposed to a war already fought: to situations, that is, in which, in view of the risks involved, a state prefers to suffer an injustice rather than embark upon a war. This was the attitude – alas, doomed to the bitterest disappointment – of France and Great Britain during the Munich conference in 1938, and Serbia might also have adopted it in 1914. And this was precisely the point Norman Angell was making when he argued that, in war, not even victory pays, since it always costs more than it yields.[31]

(3) It is in addressing the nuclear hypothesis that we can apply our reversal of the justifications for war most symmetrically. More than as a lesser evil, the peace which derives directly from nuclear paralysis cannot be considered other than a *necessary* evil![32] Adding just one more argument to the many already existing in favour of a state of peace, however unsatisfactory it may be, I wish to point out the magnitude of the danger of the so-called 'nuclear winter'.[33] It would not only cause harmful glaciation in territories subjected to nuclear bombing, but would also extend its devastating effects to parts of the world previously unaffected, since the movement of the immense toxic cloud raised by bombing would provoke a progressive lowering of the earth's

temperature. How is it possible not to consider peace, however unsatisfactory or unjust it might be, preferable to a justice which would drag populations and countries totally extraneous to the conflict into the same maelstrom? No restoration of rights exists to atone for the crime committed against the southern hemisphere, for example, which would presumably be extraneous to a war between nuclear states.

(4) The arguments in favour of peace as a good are the most obvious and predictable – which does not mean that they are without value. Here in particular we must question whether it is possible to think only in terms of a residual version of peace in the contemporary world, as was the case with the three previous interpretations. Or is this peace somehow preferable to all other alternatives? To argue as much, it is necessary to briefly shelve the nightmare of nuclear catastrophe (we shall be returning to it in the next section), to avoid which any alternative seems to become acceptable and preferable. If it is to constitute a good, peace must be preferable, *ceteris paribus*, to every other alternative, not imposed by external, strategic conditions. It is in response to the just war theory's sharpest criticism of this last formulation (that is, if a war can be considered just by both parties to it, this frustrates any effort to justify it) that the *just peace* hypothesis reveals all its force. There is nothing to prevent a just peace for all parties from being achieved (which is not the case of a just war). I am forced to admit of course that this has never actually happened in history (or at least since national states have existed), simply because the nature of the peace experienced by the international system has always depended on the outcome of a war; that is, on an event which separated victors from vanquished, permitting the former to impose the terms that suited them upon the latter. In short, peace to date has always been *unjust*.[34] The best way to defend its reasons – more effective than the tendentially moralistic defences with which the history of the problem is scattered – is to demonstrate the extent to which (once more symmetrically) it performs the functions which war (were it to be judged a necessary evil) fails to do. It is of course easy to argue that peace may effectively contribute to the *moral* or *civil* or even *technical* progress of humanity. It is plain to see that today there are other routes to moral, civil or technical progress[35] than those of courage in the face of danger, of the melting-pot of races and customs which come into contact with one another in wartime, or of the allocation of immense financial resources to scientific research. The contemporary debate on the crisis of the very idea of progress is sure to acknowledge that the age of progress has, with all its alleged flaws, produced at least one benefit: it has unified the

many diverse societies of the world, blending values, cultures and knowledge. Internationalization is no longer fuelled by the 'driving force' of progress, which may have performed some function when the world was still unaware of its own limits, but which has lost all its attraction in this, a world which stakes its boundaries in space.

How much do we actually know about peace? It is usually conceived negatively in relation to war,[36] sometimes merely as a post-war event, the situation *de facto* established once the war is *over*. It is no coincidence therefore that, despite the immense commitment of the founders of *peace research*,[37] we continue to think of peace as a fact rather than a value *per se*. All of this must, however, be referred specifically to international life or, better still, to international relations, the sphere to which the practical problem of peace rightly belongs. At this level, we ascertain, first and foremost, that the history of peace – as yet unwritten! – has always been extremely restricted. In the period between 1815 and the present day, a total of only about 25 years has passed without new wars being fought! The problem is of course more complicated than the bare figures reveal. Suffice it to think that peace is the subject of the most bizarre geographical calculations. It would appear that peace *is* worth more in some areas than in others. The war in Vietnam did not upset the stability of the international system, whereas a war between the two Germanies would have done so immediately. In an age of global interdependence such as the present one,[38] can peace be made in piecemeal fashion? In order to emerge from this contradiction, it is necessary to specify that, on the one hand, everyone would welcome an increase in the quantity of peace as a material fact: on the other, though, however great the quantity of peace may be, its only inherent value is instrumental – it serves a purpose! Let us conclude then that the diffusion of peace in the world is a prerequisite for detailed discussion of the use that can be made of it, of ways in which it can be used better, and that the hierarchization of peace corresponds substantially to its various possible forms: the *peace cum truce* (or interval, or suspension, as in the Thirty Years War); *traditional peace* (the simple absence of hostility), which, albeit preferable to war, is virtually neutral from the ethical point of view, since it does not arise from an out-and-out desire for peace; the *peace of terror*, quantitatively superior to the traditional form, but more totalitarian still; and finally, *just peace* or *satisfactory peace*,[39] the best version imaginable, and also the most unlikely to materialize, for if it is to be achieved, it is necessary for 'the quality of international relations to change radically, for the era of suspicion to end and that of security to begin'.[40]

It is not difficult to see how the four types of peace described above correspond symmetrically to the four justifications for war:

Justification	*Typology*
war of defence	peace cum truce
as a lesser evil	traditional peace
as a necessary evil	peace of terror
as a good	just peace

Applying by analogy the criteria adopted by Bobbio to assess the relationship between the *feasibility* and *effectiveness* of the various forms of pacifism,[41] we observe once more that, albeit highly feasible, defensive peace is neither effective nor particularly incisive. Conversely, peace as a good is extremely difficult to attain, but provides a settlement which is just and satisfactory for all the parties to it. Historically, the first three justifications for war and types of peace have revealed themselves on numerous occasions,[42] while the fourth pair has never materialized to date. Is this because it is practically *impossible*? And can historical evolution of international politics shed light on the matter? One final question: has the extraordinary modification of conditions of (nuclear) war affected conditions of peace as well?

3 ETHICAL INDIFFERENCE AND EMERGENCY

If it is true – as Arnaldo Momigliano once observed – that books and reports on war are a downright calamity,[43] it is just as true that, by its very nature, war apparently makes any conclusive reflection on itself impossible. No less than Aristotle observed that, 'peace . . . is the end of war'.[44] All the ambiguity of this bond between war and peace transpires from the words Plato puts in the mouth of Clinia of Crete: 'For "peace", as the term is commonly employed, is nothing more than a name, the truth being that every State is, by a law of nature, engaged perpetually in an informal war with every other State.'[45] This was most likely the origin of the tradition which has always pessimistically considered war a reality unto itself and peace as a mere residual, albeit non-negative, element. And if the semantics of the word 'war' have spread much further than that of the word 'peace' (we speak of pre-war, post-war or Cold War, to name but three common compounds: we do not use the word 'peace' with the same frequency), the age-old evocation of the peace-war combination – in Tolstoy as in R. Aron's *Paix et guerre entre les nations*, to cite two examples – seems to imply that the two are inextricably bound in an incessant and preordained sequence. Yet anyone observing their many different facets is racked by doubt. First, there is the question of their reciprocal relationship: when one is present the other is absent – or do they also occupy intermediate positions? Is it a question of states (of peace or of war) or of actions? Are the two different by nature? After all, peace is a situation and war an action.

To these doubts and to the many others that might be advanced, the advent of the atomic age has brought with it another fundamental, even more dramatic one: the war-peace chain must be broken, so has war really become 'impossible' and peace 'inevitable'?[46] And what kind of peace are we talking about anyway? In other words, may the world in which we live be considered predominantly peaceful or incurably war-like? Which is there most of – peace or war? Never as in the last half century have the two been so inextricably linked. The extension of areas of peace has been countered by an increase in limited, local conflicts.[47] The speed in the development of weapon arsenals and military potential has been matched by increased caution in their use. International tension – the USA–USSR relationship, for example – seems to be regulated by the same law. There is neither true friendship nor undying hostility; provisional agreement accompanies permanent threat. There is neither peace nor war.

It is even possible to question the terms of this compromise, as if they were so schematic as to leave room for something in between, something *different*: 'a peace that is not peace, a war that is not a war.'[48] Which is why, if they are not to prove 'calamitous', studies on war should seek, first and foremost, to justify the permanent and irremediable contradiction that exists between threats of war and peace agreements, between explosions of uncontrollable violence and displays of good will. *Tertium non datur* says the Latin adage, but it is precisely to the exploration of a third, middle passage, an alternative to the drastic option between war and peace, that I would now like to lend my attention. One of my aims in doing so is to unmask the hypocrisy which ultimately bars the moral argument from the international political context, as if domestic politics were invariably superior. Is it not true to say that, in states too, political life is *apparently* neither moral nor immoral, and that economic development is neither good nor evil, and so on? As if the realization of every principle had given rise to culturally uncertain, wavering and unpredictable models.

The two trends – the first accidental, the second permanent – seem to converge in the device designed to provide world peace: reciprocal deterrence, which is founded, as we all know, on the exchange of credible threats of mutual destruction. From the fifties, this situation was so original it was adjudged by philosophers and political scientists alike to be without historical precedents. The atom bomb, it was agreed, was *qualitatively* incomparable to any of the weapons of the past. Two very different, indeed opposite, analyses of this view developed. One was reassuring, the other catastrophic. It is hardly necessary to recall that the first was espoused mainly by the world's politicians, whereas the second found followers exclusively among minorities whose aim it was to debunk nuclear politics and mobilize the masses against this new totalitarian form of dominion. The first postulated a form of heterogenesis of ends ('how evil may give rise to good'),[49] developing under the wing of a providential conception of history. The second observed, pessimistically, that since man has never stopped using his discoveries, if humanity were unable to refrain from its habit of making war, total destruction would prove inevitable.

Now fortified by over 40 years' experience, the supporters of both positions possess the arguments to demonstrate the correctness of their respective forecasts. Yet, since the politics of deterrence continues to linger in the background of any political-international scenario, and since nuclear war has still to break out, I wish first to establish the kind of judgement that can be made of such a consolidated situation. Secondly, I intend to argue, and to demonstrate, that this situation has, nevertheless, regulated a sort of *mutation*[50] of the rules of international political life. And this mutation serves, in my view, as a sort of litmus paper for the reliability of the projections on the future elaborated by cyclical models of history.

The nuclear age can be summed up by pairs of opposite 'neither-nor' negations. While, on the one hand, threat-based politics is conspicuously immoral, on the other, the threat of war is considered preferable to war itself. For the last ten years or so, an intense academic debate has raged around this dilemma. It may not be a coincidence that it only began 30 years after humanity's entry into the atomic era; almost as if the nuclear issue had only then emerged from a preliminary, purely strategic stage (the nightmare of survival at all costs) as a general moral problem concerning everyone. It is now a problem concerning not only politicians, but above all, the masses, who are, after all, the principal recipients of the politics of deterrence. The results of this debate (which I am now about to sum up in brief) will, I hope, demonstrate that humanity would effectively appear to be experiencing a second, *new* phase in its nuclear history. The first scholar to frame the problem in the terms that interest us here (posing the question: how can we judge a situation of peace which relies on the threat of war?) was M. Walzer. His argument – a utilitarian one, if we accept the distinction made by Hardin and Mearsheimer[51] – is basically that of the 'lesser evil': since 'supreme emergency' is now a permanent condition, 'We threaten evil in order not to do it, and the doing of it would be so terrible that the threat seems in comparison to be morally defensible.'[52] Not surprisingly, most other analyses also revolve round this position. Even the extremely heated debate over the drafting of the US bishops' pastoral letter in 1983 ended up, albeit reluctantly, by espousing this approach.[53] Clearly, at the heart of the matter is the notion of emergency. This is why both T. Nagel,[54] in general terms, and R. Dworkin and T. Nardin[55] discuss the notion of 'extremity', denying that its conditions exist in the nuclear issue.[56] While it is by no means easy to unravel the knot in one go, the conclusions of another analysis of the same problem (albeit favourable to the use of the notion of 'extremity') provides at least some hints on how to illustrate the consequences of the path followed. (Of course I take for granted here that the position to be discussed is the prevalent one whereby threat is admissible as long as it does not materialize into action.) After discussing the arguments in favour of and against the thesis of the ethical admissibility of threat, R. Tucker concludes: 'What is the alternative to deterrence with its threat to do evil?'[57] His answer is that there is none, and hence that the only possibility is acceptance – if need be, resigned acceptance – of the status quo. Long live the weapons of world destruction, just as long as they are never used!

The judgement which follows is, it seems, flawless: nuclear weapons perform their task by not being used, and deterrence is at the height of its glory as a general theory of political action. The paradoxical nature of the situation thus reaches absolute proportions. It is quite literally impossible to distinguish reality from fiction or peace from war, to discern whether peace is due to a sincere pacifist urge or a dizzy rush to build (or pretend to build?) new bombs. There is only one way of escaping from the trap sprung on us by the weight of events, and of finding not only a moral but also a logical justification for it. This is to believe that the development of the debate and the conclusions it has reached offer evidence (albeit extrinsic evidence) of the fact that humanity has left the first stage in its nuclear evolution behind. International life has entered a dimension in which *politics* has prevailed (perhaps definitively) over force, in the sense that international relations cannot be considered refractory to constraint, a dominion of the absolute liberty of sovereign states *superiorem non recognoscentes*, but a realm which has begun to have its own political order on the basis of which binding decisions for the community are taken, an exact reproduction of Easton's *authoritative allocation of values*. Hence nuclear war has never broken out, not so much by chance or because counterpoised threats have averted it, but – though not prevalently – because international political reality is now *something else* with respect to the past or, to use more traditional terms, because the age of *pure* reason of state has come to an end.[58] I shall not judge whether this is a good thing or a bad thing. Allow me simply to say that states, all states, are adjusting their every decision to the present rules of the game, and that they no longer allow disputes to be resolved by war. (Nor have I forgotten that no true authority, separate and *super partes*, exists in the international realm.)

If, therefore, the international system is a political one, in as much as its decisions are effectively binding on states as a whole, and that there is a 'space for politics' in the international realm as well, what is going to replace the classic anarchic model? My own suggestion, which merely attempts to broaden the horizons of an idea which is the object of great interest in international research today, is to view relations between states as if a set of 'principles, norms, rules and decision-making procedures on which the expectations [of the diverse international actors] converge'[59] had developed among them: in other words, as a regime. The regime of an international system hinges on the content allocated to its various organizational principles by the will of the most powerful states; or rather, of those which, through their superiority in war, have won the power *to control* the system.[60] It is thus possible to justify the suggestion that the contemporary international system originates in the *mutation* engendered by deterrence politics which, now tantamount to a symbol of everything associated with the nuclear era, was responsible in the first place for changing the relationship between state and war. Here, at last, we have the justification for the 'neither peace nor war' formula whose dubitative nature continues to reflect the inevitable tentativeness of an analysis such as the present one.

Born to account for the rules of the game, which were accepted (not necessarily approved) and respected only when applied to given 'issue areas', such as the regulation of international river waters, the sale of cars, the price of crude oil, gold, cereals and countless other collective goods, the regime logic has gradually extended to an ever increasing number of problematic sectors. It has, moreover, generated regimes for nuclear armaments and non-proliferation. To give some idea of this view's innovative scope, it has even been demonstrated that, through the so called 'hegemonic stability theory',[61] it might mark a theoretical turnaround in internationalist analysis. The theory rests on the belief that the presence of a hegemonic actor (or actors) in the international system produces advantageous results not only for itself, but also for all the others, since its capacity to determine the regime which regulates the distribution of virtually all goods provides benefits for the community of states.

Whether the hegemonic stability theory may be accepted or not depends basically on its implicitly ideological aspects which, on the one hand, seek to justify the hegemonic role of the United States,[62] and, on the other, to conjure up a static, unmodifiable international system. The fact remains, nonetheless, that it is grounded in the hypothesis that international life today is characterized chiefly by order: not spontaneous but negotiated order, in which the upper hand achieved by some political parties over others is clearly visible. How can this world image – if not idyllic, at least reassuring – be reconciled with that of the violence which we see periodically breaking out in trouble spots everywhere? To understand such a world, both at war and at peace, is no easy matter, and there are no shortcuts to comprehension. It is, however, possible to overcome the difficulties involved by analogy. Think of the formation of the modern state, of the wearisome process of the concentration, reduction and final elimination of autonomous power centres to make way for giant state-controlled combinations.[63] To understand contemporary global reality, it is more instructive to think in terms of order than of anarchy, since there is more of the first than of the second.[64] This order has imposed itself on most of the world in direct proportion (and this is no coincidence) to the level of socioeconomic development in the various countries, and in inverse proportion in the least developed countries, which are usually the ones that have achieved independence most recently or have been most ravaged by imperialist exploitation. The extension of the general order to the fringes of the system (to its periphery) continues to be a stress factor: re-echoing as it does from the boundaries of the empire, it risks jeopardizing the latter's solidity. It is also true, however, that the possessors of power will, at the same time, develop actions to reduce, slowly but progressively, the number of these marginal situations as well. Whether they succeed or not is an entirely different matter. (How is it possible, after all, to correlate the local gravity of an event to its possible global consequences? How many events cause immediate panic only to appear much less serious when viewed with detached hindsight? And how many others, seemingly less significant, end up having incalculable consequences on the ones to follow?)

4 THE HETEROGENESIS OF MEANS

An extraordinary chain of events in different countries (especially in the socialist and Islamic worlds) has had a tremendous impact on the international scene. As we come to terms with the change in the international climate, including the decrease in the number of wars in progress round the world, as we applaud the ending of the tension between the United States and the Soviet Union (which, for the first time in the history of their world dominance have dismantled their military bases – and not only because they had grown obsolescent)[65], we are failing to fully appreciate the pre-condition for all of this: the 'ending' of the age of the balance of nuclear power, and hence of the irremediable ideological differences around which the international system was structured. The 'Cold War' internationally and the 'communist dilemma' domestically – these have been the key preoccupations of any political debate in the course of the last half century. On the international as on the domestic plane, the east-west divide had an ideological content: containment helped to produce the roll back which was the sole means of curbing Soviet expansion. Among other things, voting for bourgeois (liberal-democrat) political parties was seen as a way of safeguarding the principles of western democracy which communist parties were seeking to undermine. It was thus that domestic and international politics eventually joined together in a form of unforeseen (and as such, unjustifiable) unity. It is in this sense that recent history has been inextricably enmeshed in the web of *revolution* – domestic or international, endogenous or exogenous, it makes no difference. Think, for example, of the anti-communist mania of US rulers in the fifties and sixties; of the Latin American question in the era of the Cuban model; of the 'holy war' against communism in Vietnam; of (para-revolutionary) domestic and expressly international terrorism. Domestic and international politics once used to meet (or clash) on this terrain too. Now, however, a great deal has changed on the world political scene. The Soviet Union and China are no longer the leading lights of the world revolution, nor have others come forward to take their place. What has happened to all the localistic (Latin American models, for example), Third World and neutralistic surrogates of the past? Who still remembers Nehru?

Is the transformed image we now see before us clearer, more comprehensible than the one before? Or isn't it more obscure, harder to decipher? My argument is that political reality, in turn, has undergone an unprecedented *revolution*,[66] as a result of an instrumental change in the relationship between politics conducted within the state and politics conducted between states. I believe that this has led to a *mutation* in politics which, far from complicating the picture, may actually have simplified it. This is not necessarily a value judgement. In the history of painting, the abstract revolution was the culmination of a process which had set out from primitive drawing in pursuit of perfect reproduction of the visual image. Once that had been achieved, the impressionist movement revealed its 'falsity', and cubism and informalism proceeded to kill it. Likewise, now that it has reached its climax (that is, it has exhausted its heuristic capacities), the perceptive ('visual') approach to politics is now entering a 'revolutionary' phase. Whether this phase is abstract or cubist is immaterial: the true analogy is that, like great early twentieth-century painters, this type of approach is now in search of new instruments to depict a subject which has been modified so much as to be unportrayable using traditional methods. Whoever would imagine that such great upheavals in tradition could arise exclusively from modifications in feeling (of ways of seeing)? Haven't we to face the fact that since, for some reason, reality has changed, so interpretations of it must change as well? More than the *end of ideologies*, shouldn't we question the advent of a new ideology which, like a sort of 'false consciousness', has been disseminated all over the world? But ideologies are not nature, they are culture. We must thus seek to understand their origins, to assess their impact and their success. Such great upheavals can be neither coincidental nor sudden, although it is possible that none of us grasped their warning signals, which were probably concealed behind humanity's somewhat unconscious entry into the nuclear era. Even before discussing the impact of the atomic bomb on history, anyone who regards it as overstating the case to pin all the blame on war must remember that war is the vastest, most totalizing phenomenon that human communities ever have to address. Its importance is so great that there are, theoretically, no limits to its impact. (Let me also add that I shall not deal here with the strategic dimension of the nuclear era: it will simply remain in the background as an example of the technology which came into being then. What does interest me are its political and anthropological implications in the present way of judging war, be it nuclear or classic, hence also the logic of international political life.)

The first element which affords us a glimpse of the change that has taken place is that the international system theories elaborated between the fifties and the early eighties are now proving inapplicable. I agree that it is somewhat ungenerous to expect to find an immediate correspondence between theoretical models and the complexity of reality (which often transforms models into rough copies of itself!). But it is not so much analyses of bipolar and multipolar *form* that are going through a crisis (virtually or completely inapplicable as they are) as those analyses of the *nature* of the international system which make special reference to the central importance of its heterogeneity,[67] symbolized by the ongoing battle between capitalism and socialism and embodied in competition between the United States and the Soviet Union.

No modern war has had an ideological matrix. Each has been fought between great powers – *competitors* in the sense assigned to the term by economic theory[68] – in the course of territorial conquest and the economic exploitation of an increasingly wide, open world. That this situation should consequently generate first the doctrine of the primacy of foreign over domestic policy, then that of imperialism, is but further proof of the fact. In other words, the war proneness of the modern world did not derive from incurable ideological hatred, from irreconcilably contrasting models. It was but the celebration of the bourgeois myth of the invisible hand which translates, in turn, into the interpretative key of the *balance of power*. It is no coincidence that the latter allows anyone to ally with anyone, an arrangement that would appear to be unfeasible in situations in which states are separated by sharp disagreements of principle.

In the contemporary world, the nature of war has changed so much, it can no longer be fought for the same reasons and in the same ways as in the past. Conflict has become *permanent* and *ideological*. (If violence has not vanished altogether, it is not because the above is untrue, but for two different motives: one is extrinsic and concerns the colonial and post-colonial wars which are liquidating a world now dated; the other is intrinsic and refers to the geographical location of war which, since it cannot be fought directly, is now farmed out to other states, allies and subjects.)[69] Not that this has made the dispute uncontrollable. On the contrary, precisely the explosive, totalizing conjunction of war and ideology has produced first *paralysis*, and then *mutation* in the functioning of international life. No one can doubt that the period historically classifiable as the 'Cold War' in its first phase, and as the 'balance of terror' in the second, saw the heightening of a sort of determinism of international politics over domestic politics in virtually every state (although it was perhaps only perceived much later). Any destabilization of regimes (especially those in the central area – Europe) was viewed as a catastrophe to be averted at all costs. It was deemed preferable to leave a (live) hostage in enemy hands than to risk the death of all concerned.[70] It was thus that the domestic problems of single states were liable to be elevated to world significance. This in turn gave rise to the process of *globalization* (inductively, the covariance of two entities cannot always be explained by the influence of one over the other – there may be a third which explains them both), somewhat ingenuously used to explain the development of human, social and interstate communications and contacts in the same period.[71] What is most important here is to note that never before in the history of the modern world had states felt endangered as a result of a change in regime in some far-off corner of the planet. Such an important development must have important reasons. One might conclude on an emphatic note by saying that through globalization humanity was entering the age of *conservation*, now a *sine qua non* for survival.

The question of survival in the atomic age thus surmounted every obstacle and broke every barrier, including national boundaries. In this way – again, for the first time in history – a sort of *unification* was recorded between domestic and international politics. Now any event anywhere was a matter for the whole world. A sort of diabolic heterogenesis – of *means*, not of *ends* – turned what had been conceived as a simple instrument of victory in battle into the symbol of a new way of conducting politics on the brink. If this really does correspond to the latest evolution in the international system, the description needs to be turned into some sort of explanation. One of the many books dealing with so-called *postmodernism* includes a penetrating observation (the author speaks, as scholars of postmodernism tend to do, about architecture, but the idea may be extended to other fields) on the rift that has allegedly opened up in our present way of viewing reality. It is, it argues, the result of a 'mutation in the object', as yet unaccompanied by an equivalent mutation in the subject. Nor do we possess the perceptive means to harmonize with this hyperspace.[72] 'International politics' as an object has *mutated* too, but we have not.

Do we have material proof of the transformation that has taken place? The number of wars in the world has dropped drastically, the (national and international) revolutionary factor has disappeared altogether and interest in the ideological debate has waned. Is it possible to suggest the cause of all this? (Or perhaps it has been replaced by the widespread ecological anxiety which derives from awareness not only that the degradation of the environment may be fatal, but also that everyone, states and citizens alike,[73] must *collaborate* if it is to be halted.) The atom bomb was the great vector of the process of world unification: perhaps our 'addiction' to it has, in turn, brought about a *mutation* in our expectation of war: that is, if this particular 'driving force' of history has ceased to function, the very nature of political life must have mutated,[74] and a mutation must have taken place in the nature of war as well. Following its experience of the potential of nuclear weapons, war has, in a certain sense, become impossible. For 40 years, the relative impossibility of war provided strategic theorists with food for thought. Arguably, what escaped them was that all this could not have happened without accompanying social modifications to the very perception of war. As if, by abolishing war, humanity was ultimately being deprived of one of its own existential elements.[75]

What are the possible consequences of the mutation in war's role for the nature of international politics? If we consider the singularity of a situation whereby for the first time in history, *means* had modified an *end*,[76] we can appreciate the abnormality of what ensued. For not only has the once irremediable dispute between different worlds been appeased, but those same worlds have now also entered a phase of harmony in which they have allied (or, rather, united) to conserve the unitary, 'de-ideologized', postmodern world of today. If it is true that for centuries war was at the centre of international political analysis, one might be excused for wondering whether, now that war – or at least, catastrophic nuclear war – has disappeared, international analysis will disappear too. The answer is, of course, no. It, in turn, will be compelled to adjust to the disappearance of the element which made the contemporary world something akin to the Hobbesian state of nature.[77] The reason why the contemporary world has been able to survive the bomb, even without a *tertium super partes*,[78] thus becomes clear. International politics must *emerge* from its state of nature to come to terms with the mutation of war! The heterogenesis of means thus completes its course, modifying the traditional *end* of international politics – the conquest of power.

As in nature, mutation entails a variation which, in turn, entails a substitution. The variation which concerns us here is humanity's embarking upon a less warlike era, and the substitution is its passage from anarchy to order. Proof of the process is that the balance of terror, which, according to strategic theory, pivots on uncertainty, reciprocal insecurity, improvisation and instability, has now become certain, secure, permanent and stable! That the bomb has changed the world is in itself neither a good nor an evil: it is a fact. But, in the light of this conclusion, is it not necessary to modify the traditional condemnation of the monstrosity of nuclear war? No, it is not! On the contrary, without 'mourning' war,[79] the new situation allows fewer wars to break out, and, in all probability, those that do will be extremely limited and circumscribed for at least as long as the two great powers are on hand. It would be wrong to forget that the mutation which has taken place was undoubtedly caused by a form of totalitarianism that we have had to accept in exchange for the conservation of life,[80] and that this can in no way be considered a good thing. But the most important consequence is what might be imagined as the *conclusion* of the war cycle (which has nothing to do with the possible *extinction* of war). War seems, that is, to have exhausted all its possibilities. After seeing its capabilities increase alarmingly, it tottered on the edge of self-destruction with the advent of the atom bomb: once its importance had reached a peak, it withdrew from the scene. Warfare has been replaced by order founded on threat. From now on war can only repeat itself: hasn't it already said all it has to say?

4

Duties of States and Ends of Politics

And still for two years the immense human entity called France –
of which even from a purely material point of view one can only
feel the tremendous beauty if one perceives the cohesion of millions of individuals who, like cellules of various forms, fill it like
so many little interior polygons up to the extreme limits of its
perimeter, and if one saw it on the same scale as infusoria or
cellules see a human body, that is to say, as big as Mont Blanc –
was facing a tremendous collective battle with that other immense
conglomerate of individuals which is Germany.

M. Proust, *Time Regained*

1 THE ARGUMENT

The fact that the relational life of states is not a natural necessity but
the consequence of a historical event – the formation of nation-states –
explains the relatively limited attention devoted to the nature of the
relationship which is established between one state and the whole of the
rest of the world. With respect to the latter, the single state is nothing
more than a *subtraction*, since 'borders are always artificial because
states are not natural creations'.[1] This is the reason why every state has
always maintained that, outside its own authority, no other could be
valid, thus generating the unconditional authority model. Plainly, these
two premises could not give rise to a formulation of international analysis founded on a principle of *sociableness*, as interindividual relations
analysis did. Not that general principles of international law did not
develop,[2] or that the so-called international community formula[3] was
devoid of significance. But the anarchic model, which was justified not
only by facts but also by the sovereignty theory, fitted the reality of
relations between states much more faithfully.

International anarchy thus became the preferred interpretative key
to international relations. This caused international theory to age

prematurely, passively accepting the exclusiveness of the anarchic formulation without questioning whether the nature of relations between
states might not reside in something other than reciprocal hostility or
diffidence. It thus failed to grasp the straightforward eventuality that
the principle of anarchy might conceal some form of ideological deri-
vation. Isn't it possible that 'the anarchy problematique might come to
be understood, not as a necessary condition that the realistic conduct of
politics must take to be beyond question, but as an arbitrary political
construction that is always in the process of being imposed'?[4] In other
words, by resigning ourselves to the international anarchy model, aren't
we offering the best possible justification for power politics?[5] The same
question might be asked of the way in which the anarchic formulation
prevents any element of an ideological nature from entering the analytical
framework. It is not only in the contemporary world that we note the
far-reaching phenomenon of the creation and organization of international consensus on an ideological basis (such as that set into motion
by the two sides which 'fought' the Cold War). Didn't the 'congress
system' of the post-Napoleonic Concert of Europe perform the same
function? The barring of any reference to political (not, of course, natural)
order helps to remove all ideological argument from the international
realm. Yet how many times have we heard talk of imperialism or conservative foreign policies or 'international policing' by this or that state?
Isn't the annulment of ideological connotations one way of preventing
a clash between ideal values and images of preferred worlds developing
in international politics as part of the power struggle? And is international
politics exclusively a continuing no-holds-barred struggle with no rules
and no leeway for bargaining? Why should human rights policies run
into an insurmountable limit at state boundaries consecrated to guarantee the reserved dominion that has so often been used to protect the
most inhuman repressive policies? Can all this realistically lie beyond
the interest (not to mention assessment) of international theory?

2   POLITICAL THEORY AND INTERNATIONAL ANARCHY

The backwardness of international political analysis, in itself and in
relation to domestic political analysis, is generally explained in two
ways – one of substance, the other of method. The first is grounded in
reality: it says that international life is violent, incoercible and uncontrollable. The second instead derives from the transfer by analogy of the
tools elaborated for reflection on domestic politics to international

politics. In short, the fact that domestic political analysis is obviously much better developed than that of the 'outside world' has been used as *proof* of the effective intractability of international politics.

These are the premises most commonly exploited by those who question the relevance of international relations theory. The most authoritative voice in this respect is that of Hobbes, and it is no coincidence that he was the first political philosopher to seek to justify the foundation of the state when it assumed its modern structure. Reduced to its simplest terms, the Hobbesian argument may be summarized as follows: unlike individuals, who have left the state of nature to enter civil society, states are destined to remain in a condition regulated exclusively by the law of nature, which no authority on earth can enforce.

If things were really as simple as that, there would be no need for international relations theory at all, and still less for an ethic to judge them by. Estimates of strength and convenience, of whether to apply the ethic or not and under what conditions, would suffice to quench our thirst for knowledge and comprehension. There is a very short gap between this and the image of international life as *bellum omnium contra omnes*, so short it is very often bridged. This does not mean, however, that the image is a satisfactory one for those who seek to trace international life to some rudimentary explanation in an attempt to express more than just *de facto* judgements on it. It is impossible, on the one hand, to believe that Hitler may be judged[6] for killing millions of German Jews (his fellow citizens, hence a problem of domestic politics) and, therefore, condemned; and then acquitted – or, more precisely, not tried at all – because his was simply one way of intepreting his country's national interests (world war, hence an international problem).

The idea that the laws of nature[7] are the only limit on states is transformed in practice into the admission that no limit can be placed on them, that international politics is unalterably primitive and that the core of relations between states is 'the recourse to the Elementary which in the relations between great powers is fundamental.'[8]

Although war as such is undoubtedly the most monstrous, unjustifiable thing humanity has ever invented, there can be no doubt either that the logic of international political life typical of the end of the second millennium cannot be reconstructed by appealing to its 'elementariness': where the reference is not insufficient it is misleading and ideological.[9] Were we to ask the heads of state or foreign ministers of the countries active in the world today for their opinions on this point, hardly any of them would reply that he believes he is moving in a state of nature!

The incomparability of a Hobbesian image and a contemporary image of international life might be easily resolved by observing that the very nature of the second is the result of almost four centuries of substantial modification, and that an interpretation that was valid in the seventeenth century is no longer adequate in the twentieth. Yet there would still be a contradiction between the unmodifiable anarchy of international life and the progress that has arguably been achieved in the course of time. There is a great deal of evidence to suggest that international relations theory needs to be completely re-elaborated. It is possible to observe in at least two ways that scholars of the subject have a somehat fuzzy conception of the word 'theory'. Some of them believe that theory (in international relations) is merely a synonym of ideology, while others, more drastically, think that there is no need for theory at all. A good example of the first position is the great dispute on methodology which was sparked in the milieu of international relations by a polemical essay by H. Bull, a scholar who had previously concerned himself chiefly with the arms race. Albeit referring in his title to the subject which interests us here (*International Theory*),[10] Bull, like his interlocutors and even some adversaries,[11] actually speaks only of *approaches* to international relations (whether their study should be based on the precepts of the classics of political philosophy or international law, or on the most mathematically sophisticated quantitative research). Although this is of course an important topic, of the greatest interest to professionals in the field, it refers to a pre-theoretical or rather propaedeutical stage in the construction of theory without, in any way, performing all the tasks of theory proper.

The best example of the second case, still relatively neglected in a specialist context, is that of an essay by M. Wight with the telling title *Why Is There No International Theory?*.[12] The very definitions he proposes make it clear that Wight's intention is to address the question we are discussing here: 'If political theory is the tradition of speculation about the state, then international theory may be supposed to be a tradition of speculation about the society of states, or the family of nations, or the international community' (p. 18). I shall not dwell on the way in which Wight develops his anti-theoretical argument,[13] save to say that he leaves little room for optimism – 'I think it is possible to argue that international theory is typified not only by its slenderness but also by its intellectual and moral poverty' (p. 20). I wish instead to move directly to Wight's proposal, summed up in the equation: domestic politics is to international politics as political theory is to historical interpretation. The reason for this is supposedly that it is possible to theorize about domestic politics, which concerns the best possible way of living, but it is impossible to construct a survival theory (p. 33).

Thus the first term in the first expression of the equation should be linked to the first term in the second: that is, it is possible to elaborate political theory on politics. If, instead, we link the second term in each equation, international politics and historical interpretation, it transpires that no theory is possible on international politics for the simple reason that everything there is to be understood is already explained by history. Although Wight elaborates his formulation with extreme, perhaps excessive, boldness, it cannot be said to be particularly original. It has been reiterated and reproposed from Hobbes downwards, and a good many scholars have evidently found it convincing in view of the undoubted 'slenderness', as Wight puts it, of existing theory. The problem is that this inevitable 'slenderness' is mercilessly blamed on international relations by those who postulate their uselessness. This is not the place to present a general international relations theory (although that would be the best way of refuting Wight's preliminary question factually and not with mere positions of principle), but it might be useful to discuss the appropriateness or otherwise of international life as an object of political theory. (Whether this is possible is another matter.) Wouldn't it be old hat to set out from the anarchy discussion? Although there has been a wealth of reflection on the subject,[14] it may suffice to observe that faithful application of the international anarchic image ultimately prompts an exaggeratedly negative judgement on international life[15] – to the extent that one wonders how humanity has managed to continue in this realm for so long.

Albeit heterogeneous, international system theories agree that it is necessary to go beyond the unconditional nature of the anarchic image, although most of them do continue, in contrast with the hierarchical image of the state, to define international systems as 'anarchic [and] decentralized'.[16] There can be no doubt though that all those who use the expression, 'international system', acknowledge not only that international politics may be studied as one of the social sciences, but also that theories may be propounded to explain international events. The most significant example of this trend (although it admittedly goes too far when it prescribes rules of conduct for states) is a study by M. Kaplan[17] which identifies every possible type of international system, suggesting applicable models and distinguishing between those that have occurred in history and those that have not. The sharpest difference between the two realms of politics (domestic and international) seems to be that the recourse to war is excluded from the first and included in the second. Without questioning this disparity, I would like to show that it does not necessarily lead to the conclusion that it is possible to theorize only on realms subject to normative systems, and not on those characterized by a regime of self-defence. My argument makes use of an empirical observation and consequently suggests that a correction be made to system logic. What better proof do we have of the existence of actual, tangible order than the disaster which ensues when its break-up leads to war? The fact is that, as states acknowledge no authority superior to their own, so, generally speaking, over long, historical periods, they live and act as if some 'sociable' fabric actually existed. This is what transpires if we observe the accords that states undersign; the dynamics of international conferences and the high-power discussions held at them are a carbon-copy of those visible in the political life of a state. Who would deny, after all, that the two main power blocs did, in the 40 years they lasted, establish and consolidate rules of procedure designed to foster mutual compatibility? Not that I care to make the world appear better than it actually is: I merely wish to highlight that 'normal' political life exists on an international scale too, and that the international system theory deals with a reality that is not wholly anarchic. Hence the growing interdependence typical of the contemporary world may be fitted into an interpretative framework which, far from explaining why a certain system of international relations is conserved (its permanence is a condition, not an end!), seeks to show why relations are what they are. In short, although reality *per se* is not a system, one can attempt to interpret it as if it were – just as a fact cannot be explained by another fact but by a hypothesis. This is the logic of the international system. The latter is not a real entity in the sense that it does not exist materially – it is not a synonym of 'all the states in the world', but it does produce systems of hypothesis based on the original proposition. It is the framework of the relations which exist between states at any given moment in history which determines their actions.

The deductive course of international system theory is founded on the 'constitutive' effect which some wars have on international order. It imagines, that is, that understanding of the logic of international politics cannot be based on an image of wars, great and small alike, simply as proof of human stupidity and the uncontrollability of passion. It replaces this with the hypothesis that not all wars are equal, that some have an 'ordering' function, in so far as their outcome leads to a relatively hierarchical reorganization of international relations (in which, that is, not everyone can do everything, as would be the case in the anarchic logic). This is true both when it is possible to glimpse the embryo of diffuse or distributed authority among the states that win this particular type of war (so this is the purpose of wars!), and when a framework emerges in which each state, according to the position it occupied in the previous war (victor or vanquished, friend or enemy of the winners), must play the binding role assigned to it. (And in this way, an order will be determined by the obligation to obey the rules of the game thus consolidated, which only a new great 'constitutive' war may alter and redefine.)

This alternative, all-encompassing interpretation of international life, radically opposed to the anarchic paradigm and variations thereof, is capable of responding to all or almost all the problems inherent in relations between states. It proposes what amounts to a Copernican revolution in international relations theory in the original, self-sufficient way in which it attributes to the same empiric material a meaning totally different from that suggested by the anarchic paradigm. It reminds one of what happened to the theory which guided Wassily Kandinsky in his pursuit of a non-superficial, straightforward, photographic way of capturing the meaning of the images of reality which our eye registers. No one would doubt that violins or guitars are not materially made the way Picasso or Braque painted them, but it is possible to argue that these artists' interpretations capture a meaning that is deeper than – or at least as true as – descriptive, passive repetition.[18]

Reality and the reproduction thereof cannot coincide unless every link between them is erased. Hence my confutation of the innate (spontaneous) prejudice according to which international relations only have one level of analysis – the objective level which results from the egoistic action of states moving in an anarchic realm. Doesn't this view preclude the detachment that has to exist between the objectiveness of interpretative structures and subjectiveness of the conduct to which such structures refer? If we are inspired by an anarchic conception, we find nothing but anarchic conduct. If we accept instead that just as there are different ways of 'seeing' the same object, so, in their actions, states follow a particular world vision, we may thus make the distinction between states which favour collaborative policies or policies inspired by principles of sociableness and/or integration, and states which effectively behave *anarchically*. Isn't this one way of describing the conduct of Iraq from 2 August 1990 (to cite a recent example)? A conception of international order does not deny that such order may be violated nor that it may be challenged and that some states act *against* its principles. (There may be various reasons for this: suffice it to think of the reasons that anarchic theories have always used to justify their refusal of the state.) The international anarchy debate has failed to take account of the distinction. What is merely one possible form of state action has thus been turned into a condition of common action by attributing to *subjective* decisions the capacity to elevate themselves to the status of an *objective* law of conduct. It might be more useful to interpret the debate as an ongoing clash between order and anarchy, between peace and protest, between happily integrated states and others that are not only unhappy but also intent on subverting the existing order. In this way, although anarchy has been demoted from its status as a 'common natural condition' to that of a simple form of action, the anarchic interpretation would acquire a much greater heuristic scope, and would be applicable to real, effective conduct and not to improbable world views. There are of course states which behave anarchically. But why should we deduce from this that the international system is a reflection of them and them alone?

3   BEYOND THE INTERNATIONAL STATE OF NATURE

International political reality is so much less known (and studied) than domestic politics that it seems only natural that we should resort to the latter to shed light on the former. Likewise, when 'we have to explore an unknown domain, to conjure up an idea of something unknown to us, a model taken from a known domain is an indispensable tool for guiding research and imagination.'[19] There are well-known, age-old antecedents to the idea that international aspects of reality may be viewed from the inside. In Plato's *Laws* (I, II, 626 b–d), when the Athenian questions whether the fact that 'every State is, by a law of nature, engaged perpetually in an informal war with every other State' is typical of other situations too, Clinia of Crete replies that this is also the right attitude for village towards village, for one house in the village towards another and for each man towards every other, and that 'all men are both publicly and privately the enemies of all.'[20] In more general terms, the same concentric logic is adopted by Aristotle: 'It is therefore manifest that the same life must be the best both for each human being individually and for states and mankind collectively.'[21]

Although the stress in both cases falls on the uniformity between different situations rather than on any actual analogy, the two arguments are important in so far as they are akin to a prerequisite for application of the individual–state analogy to the international situation. It is worth stressing here that Aristotle admits, more or less implicitly, that judgements as to which is the best kind of life may be extended to 'humanity as a whole'; which is tantamount to saying that transposition to international life cannot be ruled out *a priori*. Yet the history of the individual–state comparison (is there an affinity or not?) is an extremely lengthy one, too long to reconstruct here. I shall confine myself to a series of references designed to offer some idea of the fortune it has enjoyed. I leave Hobbes aside for the moment as I shall be devoting him more careful analysis below. My first reference is to an apparent negation of the individual–state analogy. According to Hume, 'here is the difference between kingdoms and individuals. Human nature cannot, by any means, subsist, without the association of individuals ... But nations can subsist without intercourse.'

What is important for our purposes, though, is the consideration which Hume proceeds to derive from the difference: 'the observance of justice, though useful in relations between nations is not safeguarded in them by such an impellent necessity as in relations between individuals.'[22] It thus follows that 'since the *natural* obligation to justice among states, is not so strong as among individuals, the *moral* obligation which derives from it, must necessarily partake of its weakness.'[23] Which is to acknowledge, albeit in muted tones, that ethical judgement is admissible in the international realm.

Kant's analogic formulation – 'Peoples, in as much as they are states, may be considered as single individuals' – is much better known. In a separate passage, he applies the analogy: 'For states which live together in a mutual relationship, there can be no other rational way of coming out of the natural lawless state ... than to dispense with their wild liberty as single individuals do.'[24] As long as the natural situation perseveres among states, it is impossible to make moral judgements: once the confederation has been formed, there will be morality but, by then, states will have been replaced by something midway between a world federation and a confederation.[25]

This first form of analogy is supplemented by a second – that between the state of nature and international relations – which enables us to interpret international politics,[26] and takes the argument to its logical conclusion. The argument becomes: while individuals coped with the intolerableness of the natural situation by joining together into states, states, in turn, can only join together by ceasing to be states, and are hence condemned to remain in the natural condition of anarchy. This is obviously just a synthetic reformulation of the Hobbesian position founded on the contrast between the individual and international realms:

Concerning the offices of one Sovereign to another ... I need not say any thing in this place; because the Law of Nations, and the Law of Nature, is the same thing. And every Sovereign hath the same Right, in procuring the safety of his People, that any particular man can have, in procuring his own safety.[27]

Up to the sixties, although Hobbesian studies dwelled frequently on the problem of *bellum omnium contra omnes*, they did so only in the individual context.[28] The interest for the application by analogy of Hobbesian theory to international relations has thrived in the last few years. It may be traced, if I am not mistaken, to D. P. Gauthier's appendix to his *The Logic of Leviathan*[29] in the field of philosophical interpretation, and to H. Bull in that of political interpretation. All the more curious (or, if you prefer, interesting) is that it has grown as much among philosophers as among scholars of international relations.

Regardless of whether we view the Hobbesian image (it would be wrong to speak of analysis proper) as acceptable or not, its greatest attraction – apart from the the almost sculpturesque power of the exposition – is the sheer simplicity of its deduction. Hobbes of course only addresses international relations as such marginally, and sometimes with a *negative* function to make the positive characteristics of civil society stand out all the more.[30] For the sake of something akin to systematic completeness, he draws from the theoretical model elaborated to justify the formation of the state a brief outline of what must be regarded as the international situation, which is by nature different from the domestic one. That sovereigns have no choice but to follow natural law is, for Hobbes, neither a good nor an evil: it is an inevitable fact.[31] This formulation obviously implies the parting of the individual–state parallel, since individuals may emerge from the state of nature, whereas the state is forced to stay there. There is, however, a second consequence – Hobbes's implicit identification of the causes of wars – of such great importance that international theory (scarce as it has been to date) ought to be directed more at it than at the image of international warfare. If there can be an artificial remedy (the Leviathan) for the natural *bellum omnium contra omnes* of individuals, but not for states, then the 'three principall causes of quarrell' which Hobbes sees in human nature, 'competition, diffidence, glory' (*Leviathan*, XIII), can continue to manifest themselves freely in the international realm. If man's nature were not the way it is, there would be no need for the state: if there were no states there would be no international anarchy. It is evident that, if this were the real state of affairs, nothing could be done to avoid wars.[32]

It is significant, in this respect, that one of the most sensible applications of the domestic–international analogy should have been suggested by a philosopher, one of the first exponents of the fledgling field of political-philosophical research into international ethics.

As we experience it, that society might be likened to a defective building, founded on rights; its superstructure raised, like that of the state itself, through political conflict, cooperative activity, and commercial exchange; the whole thing shaky and unstable because it lacks the rivets of authority. It is like domestic society in that men and women live at peace within it (sometimes), determining the conditions of their own existence. It is unlike domestic society in that every conflict threatens the structure as a whole with collapse.[33]

While the above remarks, especially the one on the inevitability of war, are certainly a fair summary of the Hobbesian position, it would be wrong to neglect *another* Hobbes, the one who, in *De Corpore*, written in 1655 only four years after *Leviathan*, makes a judgement on the cause of wars which would appear to be totally different from (if not incomparable with) the one we are accustomed to. Speaking of the utility of moral and civil philosophy, Hobbes observes that its principal end is to defeat ignorance. After pointing out that, 'All the calamities which human industry can avoid arise from war', he specifies that it is not some deeply rooted evil which drives men to 'massacres, desolation and lack of all things', for anybody can understand

that massacres and poverty are evil and harmful ... Therefore, the cause of civil war is that people are ignorant of the cause of wars and peace and that there are very few who have learned their responsibilities, by which peace flourishes and is preserved.[34]

This passage, more than any new view of Hobbes's relevance to international politics, justifies our insistence on the aspect of his thinking which, according to the most common interpretations, effectively denotes an analogic and not merely imitative-repetitive formulation according to prevalent interpretations.[35] Let us consider them. It was Gauthier who first stressed the basic elements from which we shall begin. After reiterating that, according to Hobbes, nations live in the state of nature, Gauthier acknowledges that the appearance of nuclear arms has ultimately made the international state of nature resemble the one which Hobbes imagined for individuals. This of course says a lot about the ability of states to override the condition: for since the security of each at once increases the insecurity of all the others, it thus aggravates the common situation. Gauthier concludes that, although he imagined that the most powerful states might collaborate to exercise joint world hegemony, Hobbes continued to judge the international situation to be more tolerable than that of individuals; that even if

'Hobbes can improve our understanding of international affairs . . . here, as elsewhere, he is but a limited guide.'[36]

H. Bull, to whom we owe the first application by analogy of Hobbesian thinking to international politics, makes a much more passionately intense analysis.[37] He resumed his own argument fifteen years later,[38] first expounding the imitative model of the interpretation of Hobbes, then confuting it. After observing that the recourse to reasoning by analogy often betrays a lack of familiarity with the object of study (p. 45), Bull counters Hobbes with the argument that 'international society is unique and owes its character to qualities that are peculiar to the situation of sovereign states' (p. 45), and then makes a direct confutation of the affirmation that states and individuals find themselves in an analogous situation. It is not true, he posits, that in the international state of nature there can be no peaceful industry or production, trade or navigation; nor is it true that states are vulnerable in the same way as individuals are, or are roughly alike as individuals are. States may be self-sufficient: individuals cannot be.

Thus, neither Gauthier nor Bull accept the analytical interpretation of Hobbesian thinking. Altogether different though, is the interpretation that might ensue from the premise that the *model* counts more than the mechanical *application* that can be made of it.[39] The Hobbesian model is, after all, obviously dependent upon the need to override the state of nature. Just as individuals perceive the intolerability of the natural condition, so do states, in so far as they experience periods comparable to the type of peace which develops among individuals who have entered civil society. Making all the due distinctions, it is possible to say therefore that the *natural law model* applies to individuals as to states.[40] The *quantum* of international order which is consolidated in the course of time is simply the result of the action of an 'international Leviathan', embodied by one or more states according to circumstances.

After being neglected for some years, the theme was relaunched in the seventies; on the one hand by C. Beitz, who rejects the analogy argument,[41] and on the other, by M. Forsyth who, albeit in limited terms, re-presents it, recalling attention to the effects the laws of nature allegedly have on the international state of nature which, he suggests, has been *modified* and is hence no longer unconditional.[42] Beitz's argument, expounded at great length, seeks mainly to confute international moral scepticism,[43] demonstrating all the reasons – including *de facto* reasons – which differentiate state and individual. Beitz concludes that,

> when the state of nature is applied to international relations, one must recognize that analytical and prescriptive interests may require different

interpretations of the state of nature. If we wish to *understand* the behavior of states, perhaps it would be helpful to view them as rational actors which respond to international circumstances on the basis of a calculation of their rational self-interest.[44]

M. Heller carries this line of argument to its logical conclusions, claiming with some force that the application to international relations of the theory which underpins *Leviathan* derives from a 'misleading analogy'.[45] His arguments are that, for states, the possibility of war is as dramatic as it is for individuals (hence they too should make an effort to realize a civil society rather than remain in the state of nature); that the state of nature is no more tolerable for states than for individuals; and finally, his strongest point, that differences in nature between states and individuals are so great as to render analogic or parallel reasoning unusable. All of which comes to a head when Heller denounces the following contradiction: 'if states are to get out of the state of nature, they must agree on the laws of nature: if states could agree on the laws of nature, there would be no need to get out of the state of nature'.[46] Hence, if states are similar to individuals, it is hard to understand why they have failed to follow the same course. If they are different, why ask them to realize something that is by nature impossible?

If this really is the way things stand[47] – and reiterating that what is at stake here is not fidelity or otherwise to Hobbes, but the relevance of an international relations theory and hence of a normative international relations theory[48] – the first problem is to clarify whether the analogy procedure is acceptable and, if it is, to show how it may be implemented. As far as the first point is concerned, one fails to see why the Hobbesian model cannot be fruitfully taken into consideration: one is tempted to question whether, as Hobbes's is a hypothetic and ideal-typical reconstruction of how individuals decide to join together in civil society, a logic founded likewise on the absolute intolerability of an unlimited state of nature can be applied not to states across the board, but to the way in which they set about achieving peace for themselves. No state has war as its end. In the period in which each lives in peace with the others, one might perhaps imagine that it has to some degree emerged from the state of nature; any periodic relapse will depend on the weakness of the regime established in relations between states, in comparison to that inside states. Yet this is precisely the difference which prompts us to reason by analogy and not repetitively! It is necessary simply to bear in mind that it is possible to withdraw from the pact of association and subordination, both to keep the heuristic procedure which follows from the analogy within suitable limits, and to avoid seeking in the second term of the analogy elements of the first that simply are not there. If the analogy as such promises to shed light on the nature of international life, it is necessary to squeeze from it anything it can offer.

The best way of avoiding the sensation that international politics, hence international political theory, is irremediably and insuperably backward is to attempt to override the anarchic image – which once more, and perhaps unfairly, we attribute to Hobbes – as an unchangeable structural principle of international relations. Without wishing to dwell on the ensuing contrast with the rich but controversial realist tradition, the reason for this is that, while the idea of anarchy conjugates with ethical indifference (in the realm of anarchy, force prevails over justness), the idea of order, regardless of its content, necessarily entails discussion of its value, hence of its ethical substance.

In view of the startling catalogues of wars which modern computer science has offered us, it may appear almost grotesque to set out from *order* (by which I mean the constitution set up at the end of a war which has produced a political order) and not from *anarchy*.[49] Which is why it may be worth remembering that even Rousseau regarded the enterprise as desperate but not impossible, as he notes in the last lines of the *Social Contract* (IV, IX). As one of his first commentators, J. L. Winderberger claimed, perhaps with excessive enthusiasm, 'the *Social Contract* postulated the *International Contract*'.[50] In actual fact, the only true lesson to be learnt from a review of interpretations of international politics by analogy is the one which sheds light on the widespread and constant misunderstanding on the basis of which analogies have been made between individuals and states, and not between the ends of domestic politics and the ends of international politics. And if it is true, in Hobbesian terms, that domestic political quarrels culminate in a domestic political order founded on contractual theory, we might argue that international politics too has as its end the bargaining of a general order valid for the entire international system.[51]

We thus come, at last, to an analogy that is more than just formal. Can the ends of international politics resemble those of domestic politics? Negative responses to this question have always been founded on the anarchy argument. International life has no standards that are equally valid for all subjects, nor does it have authorities that are commonly recognized. Instead of, or prior to, seeking positive alternatives to what might be defined as the 'natural law prejudice' in international relations, it is useful to clarify the terms of the question: first the word 'anarchy', then the concept of 'authority'. As far as the first is concerned, I wish to refer to the observations made by H. Bull and T. Nardin. Although he hailed from the British school of international realism,[52] Bull sought to intersect the elements of order and disorder which, in turn, typify the international realm, by applying the 'anarchical society' notion. Anarchical in as much as they are not subordinate to recognized authorities, states give rise, nonetheless, to a veritable 'society', which exists

> When a group of states, aware of given common interests and common values, form a society in the sense that they consider themselves linked by a common series of rules in their reciprocal relations and participate in the life of common institutions.[53]

This is not just a recent consequence of more intense interdependence: an international society began to consolidate itself as early as the Peace of Westphalia (almost in Hobbes's time!), when

> European states and the various independent political communities with which they were involved in a common international system came to perceive common interests in a structure of coexistence and co-operation and tacitly or explicitly to consent to common rules and institutions.[54]

A second example of 'overriding' of the anarchic image is T. Nardin's *Law, Morality and the Relations of States*. Discussion of this study allows me to introduce the second specification I promised with regard to authority in international life. For the time being, I do not of course wish to discuss Nardin's general thesis – that is, that distrust in international law is quite simply the result of a misplaced expectation, that it is not the job of law to achieve order and morality, but to regulate relations between states even in times of conflict.[55] I do wish, however, to examine one of the premises of the general argument. Not only does Nardin undertake to distinguish between society and anarchy (pp. 34–42), highlighting the multiplicity of meanings that may be ascribed to the two terms and the ambiguities that ensue from them, but he also argues that to address the problem of international relations we must first understand their nature. Taking for granted that states give life to a society, he asks whether that society is finalist or 'practical' (regulatory). If we accept the first model, we are inevitably led to disturbing conclusions on international morality in view of all too foreseeable contrasts between its ends, and hence on the possible realization of the ends for which the 'association' that is international society is formed (there is endless evidence of the failure of unitary projects). More careful attention to the historical development of international society highlights the existence of 'practical associations' (in which 'practical' refers to 'models of conduct') founded on 'the relationship among those who are engaged in the pursuit of different and possibly incompatible purposes, and who are associated with one another, if at all, only in respecting certain restrictions on how each may pursue his own purposes' (p. 9). If this is the way things stand, it is possible therefore to maintain that 'it is the common practices and not the shared purposes that provide the terms of international association' (p. 15). We are in this case clearly confronted by an almost total disintegration of the negative image of anarchy, and hence also by the uncomfortable realization that moral evaluations are, in any case, impossible.

That Nardin rejects the possibility of any 'original contract'[56] does not invalidate interest for his conception of international society, which he defines on the basis of 'the most fundamental practices and procedures, embodied in customary international law, that are presupposed by the particular transactions through which states bind themselves jointly to pursue certain shared purposes.'[57] If anything, the crux of the matter is: can these 'shared purposes' really exist? For what ends might international society have been constituted? The observations of the two authors discussed here provide no answer to the questions, but simply point out the prerequisites for any discussion on 'authority' in the international sphere. Authority may, obviously, be exercised exclusively in a realm which has overridden the anarchic stage. Bull shows that states obey common rules, while Nardin insists on proceduralism and the development of a common framework of rules in relations between states. We thus have the indicators to guide us in our pursuit of the *seat* of international authority – if there is one.

Does it make sense to address such a problem? Even if we accept that customs and rules are effective between states, we will not necessarily acknowledge that, between them, relations of authority have been formed through a sort of international *government*. It is precisely to resolve this doubt that it may prove useful to recall precedents that are applicable by analogy to the case in question – the Hobbesian contractarian model, for instance. In view of my specifications, the principal difference between the domestic and international realms has to do with the relative permanence or duration of order in either. The constitution created by the political movements inside what is later to be a state is, by vocation, perpetual, since once an agreement has been reached, there is no reason to question it further. But a hypothetical *international constitution* cannot expect to be so solid. This conclusion – based on fact, not on necessity – derives from the realization that the recourse to war has, relatively speaking, been easier to date in the international realm than in the domestic one. To clarify this point it is necessary to dwell not so much on the domestic constitutional as on the international order. The premise according to which international life too may arrive at some form of regulation, seems to me unquestionable. If this is the way things stand, it is necessary to single out the *constitutional principle* by which such regulation is to be inspired. The source of every international order is the outcome of the constitutive war which gave life to it in the first place. Partly in the light of the propositions of Bull and Nardin, we may now add to this the consideration that the distinguishing feature of the international realm is a sort of 'hyper-contractualism'; or, more precisely, *its vocation for continuous renegotiation of any government agreement.* Whereas the force of domestic order stems from its unquestionability, that of international order is conserved precisely because it is continuously being questioned, or, better still, because of the greater risk it runs of being subverted. The international contract, which is imposed by the winner of a war and not agreed upon by the members of the international community, is by nature less solid, in so far as it is invariably the result of a dispute which has divided victors from vanquished. Any bases for mutual consent are thus unlikely to be lasting, as they must be continually verified by the contract's guarantors, or even by the coalition which one might imagine acting as an 'International Leviathan',[58] the government of the international system.

The example which most evidently corroborates this formulation – order as a product of continuous bargaining – is the military policy of the United States and the Soviet Union over the last 40 years and more. I refer not to its technical and strategic aspects, but to its political scope (which justifies its central importance to the contemporary world), which is visible not so much in the dramatic events it forebodes, as in the sophisticated dialogue that has developed around it. Let us pretend for a moment that we know nothing of any of this, that we have no prejudices and live, as Rawls says, under a veil of ignorance. How do we explain the fact that two political subjects set out, on a cyclical basis, to agree to limit the very armaments that they are building with the express purpose of annihilating one another? An answer may of course be sought in the situation of pure anarchy and the breakneck race to find a means of flooring the enemy. But if these two enemies meet to *renegotiate* the composition of their nuclear arsenals, not hiding their progress but actually displaying it, then the anarchic image loses its impact and has to be replaced by the hypothesis that, in reality, the same two enemies have non-marginal interests in common, and that such interests may prevail over the causes of hostility. In short, the recourse to military dialogue may be a tool for verifying the solidity of the fundamental compromise on which they have built their common position of international supremacy.

That all this breeds substantial and significant differences with respect to the government agreements-compromises which parties reach inside states is self-evident. But this does not diminish the validity of the experimental analogy proposed here. On the contrary, it is precisely in cases such as this that its utility is greatest. Yet even if we extend the example of the United States–Soviet Union relationship to uncover further evidence of 'collaboration' between the two, it would still be insufficient to demonstrate that international life is as 'civil' as domestic life.

4   CITIZENS AND STATES

On the one hand, we have evidence of the existence of an international (albeit invariably despotic) order; on the other, we have the ongoing scandal of the wars which are being fought in the world today, the disturbing sight of continuous bullying and seemingly never-ending outbreaks of violence. I could of course support my argument by exploiting the internal–external analogy to observe that just as many depressing malfunctions are to be found within states: what else are terrorism, corruption, the mafia or the high crime rate, for example? Yet what I am seeking is not revenge but confirmation. In arguing that international life too may be the object of ethical judgement, I have presumed that this may be possible only if it has a constitutional arrangement of its own. I believe I have demonstrated that it has. For the motives I have explained, this position becomes all the more credible if we compare it with its traditional alternative whereby the existence of wars and other forms of violence preclude *on all counts* international life's emergence from the condition of anarchy. Yet it seems clear to me that if my argument has demonstrated that there are ways out of anarchy, then it is only fair that the inverse be acknowledged; namely, that the anarchic version of international politics is now untenable. If we prove that, in part, it no longer exists at all, this is enough to validate the argument. Thus far however, I have at most demonstrated that it is possible to judge international politics, but I have said nothing about how this may be done in practice. I shall now, therefore, make a few suggestions, advancing as a further (albeit impressionistic) piece of evidence in favour of my case the fact that many other scholars are now pursuing the same objective.[59]

The first point one might make (incidentally, a further justification of the argument's relevance) concerns the relationship which the state has, on the one hand, with citizens and, on the other, with other states. Everyone agrees that states, each with different ideological premises, must do their utmost to allow their citizens to live well, to do what they will provided it is lawful, to be safe from illness and hunger and so on. The state must, in a word, be 'just' (or alternatively, coherent with itself and its citizens). But if a state is just domestically, how can it (basing itself on the same values) be 'unjust' with other states? Can a state which recognizes the rights of minorities at home implement a colonial policy designed to oppress other nationalities? If a state is democratic (or socialist) domestically, how can it behave despotically or imperialistically towards others? R. Niebuhr argues first that 'group relations can never be as ethical as those which characterize individual relations'. Then, formulating his argument on motivations that are, to a large extent, the opposite of the ones set out above, he acknowledges that 'from the standpoint of analysing the ethics of group behaviour, it is feasible to study the ethical attitudes of nations first.'[60] I find this a most convincing statement. Reframing the case, if 'coherence'[61] between internal and external actions is a duty for the state, we have, first and foremost, a principle on which to judge foreign policy and, secondly, we transcend the traditional separation between 'moral or immoral' domestic politics and 'amoral' international politics. If a state behaves immorally abroad, it cannot be moral at home (and vice versa). The argument that the external immorality of the single state is imposed by the immorality of other states thus becomes untenable. If each state were moral *per se*, then all states would be.

A second possible development regards the relationship which exists between the international order as I have sought to describe it, and the idea of justice which must evidently precede the formulation of any ethical judgement. To appeal to the 'quantity' of international order leads us nowhere, for it allows us judgements of legality, but no judgement of what interests us most – legitimacy. The existing international order is, after all, simply a result of the bullying of states which have defeated others in war. Is it possible to discover a fundamental principle and, as in any legal system, to shape derived standards round it? The minimum principle, the right to exist, appears at first sight to be applicable, but in practice it is not. There is nothing to suggest – nor could there be – that states have the right to exist, as, one might argue, individuals have.

Attempts have been made on more than one occasion to solve this particular problem by shifting the seat of the 'state's natural rights' to its citizens. This is the cosmopolitan proposition of Beitz, according to whom:

in debates regarding foreign policy choices, it would seem preferable to dispense with the idea of national interest altogether and instead appeal directly to the rights and interests of all persons affected by the choice. . . . It is the rights and interests of persons that are of fundamental importance from the moral point of view, and it is to these considerations that the justification of principles for international relations should appeal.[62]

Scott and Carter reach much the same conclusion in a brilliant essay in which they ask whether states might not be considered moral agents. Their answer is that, in its intercourse with its citizens, the state is at most their advocate and as such is *morally* duty-bound to defend their rights.[63] The seat of morality, however, rests with individuals and lies outside the scope of the state, which is simply their representative.

The problem is a most complex one. Plainly, if we were to admit that the possessor of rights and duties, albeit filtered through the state, remains, nonetheless, the individual, then the whole castle of international morality would collapse. Humanity would thus be confronted by a great problem; namely that the full accomplishment of international morality would be unimaginable unless all states became extinct. Albeit formally unexceptionable, this conclusion is nonetheless something of an exaggeration. Would we really have to suspend all judgement until then? Would all states really be entitled to do anything at all in the meantime? Would we only be allowed to condemn the United States for their use of defoliants in the Vietnamese countryside, and not to make a (moral) judgement on their desire to dispose of Vietnam? Or on Soviet conduct in Afghanistan, and so on? As long as we talk of states as if they were individuals, this will effectively be the case. But if the natural law prejudice leads us down a cul-de-sac, aren't there alternative approaches? The only one I know of – and whose ends are certainly entirely different from my own – is Hegel's. My attention was first drawn to Hegel by M. Mori's remark that, in his view, it is 'an error to consider the state – on the basis of analogy with the individual – as an individual or person subject to legal and/or moral determinations'.[64] We may add to this Hegel's claim that between states there exists 'a *bond* wherein each counts to the rest as something absolute', and hence 'in war, war itself is characterized as something which ought to pass away',[65] and also that relations between states rest 'partly on so-called international *law*, the general principle of which is its presupposed recognition by the several states' so that 'it thus restricts the otherwise unchecked action against one another in such a way that the possibility of peace is left,'[66] one may conclude that his point of departure is totally different, characterized as it is by the centrality of the state. Yet although the portion of Hegel's thought that may be considered as a theory of international relations reaches conclusions closer to Hobbes's than to those I have tried to develop (Hegel 'denies the possibility of morality in international relations'),[67] this does not affect my conviction that – albeit not in a Hegelian direction – his observations might have traced a different path towards international relations theory.

One more formulation is possible: namely, that the state, however much it may be artificial and non-organic, does constitute nonetheless a unit with a certain historical authenticity (comprising the contingencies which have made it small or large, strong or weak, rich or poor in natural resources – all characteristics we may consider as random). It is in the light of this historical context that we must seek the moral code to judge it by. I shall pursue this code by appealing to two more examples. Let me specify first though that I shall not be following the route of positive law to avoid giving the impression that I am looking for a short cut. I shall consider just what international positive law recognizes as such (there is even a sophisticated body of law on the matter). My first example comes from paragraph 58 of *A Theory of Justice*.[68] Here Rawls asks 'how the theory of political duty applies to foreign policy. Now in order to do this it is necessary to extend the theory of justice to the law of nations' (p. 377). Rawls proceeds according to his 'original position' image, indicating the principles that would, in this way, be recognized to regulate the conflictual claims of states. They are equality ('Independent peoples organized as states have certain fundamental equal rights'), self-determination ('the right of a people to settle its own affairs without the intervention of foreign powers'), self-defence ('against attack, including the right to form defensive alliances') and lastly, the principle that treaties are to be kept ('provided they are consistent with the other principles governing the relations of states').[69]

My second example is that of the almost equally famous *Just and Unjust Wars* by M. Walzer who, after recognizing that there exists an international society of independent states, formulates an aggression theory based on the following points: international society has a law that establishes the rights of its members – above all, the rights of territorial integrity and political sovereignty; any use of force or the threat of force by one state against the territorial integrity or political sovereignty of another is a criminal act; aggression justifies either self-defence by the victim or a war fought by the victim aided by any other member of international society; nothing but aggression can justify a war of self-defence; the repulsed aggressor can also be punished.[70]

All of this is of course disappointing.[71] None of the principles explained by these two authors improves on what the Grotian tradition has been elaborating for the last three centuries. Equality, independence, self-determination and self-defence are principles to which all treatises of international law devote their first chapters these days. Alas, I fear that little can be done to dispel the disappointment. One cannot complain about the intractability of a subject in one breath, then criticize it for being backward in another! Once we have atoned for this historical backlog, all that remains for us to do is to remember that this section set out to demonstrate the relevance of international ethics. Without attempting to lay down fixed principles on the matter, I believe that it has achieved its goal. The normative argument on international relations is only just possible. It would be wrong to expect it to provide us with conclusions at such an early stage.

But what if a different disappointment were in store? What if it were to come, not from actual applications of the natural law model to international relations (in any case, such experiments have never been attempted *positively* by natural law scholars), but from the realization that the natural law model as such simply cannot be applied to them? Does the fact that it was *the* model for the modern state guarantee that it is also the model for modern international relations as well? This doubt is voiced in *Normative Politics and the Community of Nations*, which rejects the entire contractarian framework, contesting the fact that it has been applied to the state with one logic and to international relations with another; as a theoretical construct in the first case and as an effective empiric condition in the second.[72] Fain observes that states must not be considered exclusively in their pure individuality, like juridical persons with an exclusive sovereignty of their own (they may be properly defined as such when viewed from their borders but not from within). He suggests that they should also be seen as co-partners in a different political system, formed not by citizens but by other states. In this way, each state would have a double constitution, one for domestic political relations and another for international relations.[73] These two 'corrections' prompt Fain to discard the applicability of the natural law model to the international realm, which, he claims, has a nature of its own and hence does not imitate others.

This originality has another important feature: it is the foundation which Fain sets at the base of the constitution of international society; a system, that is, in which different states share common ends, concerned with the defence of the interests of single member states and the protection of citizens on the outside, or of natural resources. All this of course also implies that decision-making powers combine and/or intersect (and hence clash). But it is not so much the possible malfunctions of this system that are at stake here as its founding logic. States are of course different from citizens in some ways. Citizens, for example, can elect a governor, something which states will never be able to do. Thus, relations between states must be organized on the basis of their specific common ends, not of the distribution of power. Although it may be unfeasible, this proposition is a fruitful one in so far as it reminds us, first and foremost, that states really do have common ends, for the achievement of which some form of organized solidarity seems inevitable. This is true, for example, of the protection of fish in the world's seas, not to mention the problems of territorial waters or the Amazon jungle, and so on. It thus becomes clear that, like the challenge of nuclear power (including the production of energy), the state of the planet is not only a problem of national public policies. By its very nature, it cannot be addressed by states as single entities. (In general, Italy, for instance, can do nothing about the deforestation of the Amazon or the nuclear arms race.) The planet may be considered the *sum* of all its states, unlike the international system, which is not a *sum* of foreign policies. But if, as Fain suggests,[74] the basis of relations between states is founded on their sharing a (artificially divided) territorial space,[75] and not on the pursuance of respective national interests,[76] the prospect of their *unification* on the basis of their duty to conserve the planet in acceptable conditions of life helps us create a new way of viewing international relations themselves. The matter before us tends to be transformed into a *super*-issue (the function of the prefix being neither superlative nor ornamental, but designed instead to convey a sense of excess or overlapping)[77] due to the immensity of the issues it has to dominate: from specialized study of international politics it is elevated to global analysis of international life, by which I mean the conditions in which states and citizens of different states live together in the same (planetary) space. Of course the horizontal organization of subjects already covers every aspect of relevance: from economics to law, from technology to communications theory, from political geography[78] to international politics itself and hence also – and why not? – to international ethics. By the term 'international ethics' I mean a reflection on the conduct of states, whose existential dimension is not just that of their artificial borders but also of the planet as a whole – the characteristics and problems of which (something resembling Teilhard de Chardin's 'Noosphère')[79] affect their unprejudiced possession of nature forcing them to act under the conditions which nature itself dictates.

Reflection upon *international life* will thus entail both research into the birth of the international social contract (if we endorse the contractarian approach) and, more generally, into the foundation of relations between states. It will be necessary to investigate the best arrangement for such relations and the nature of international politics,[80] to study political relations *strictu sensu* and, finally, to consider the *quality* of international life or international ecology. In this way, far from perverting the specific nature of international relations, we adjust them to the nature of the problem in hand. For too long we believed that (1) the foreign policy of every state had to be somehow reserved, (2) the decisions which affected the destinies of populations were not open to free debate, (3) all states had as their sole, unique duty the defence of their own national interest, (4) other states had to be left equally free to act, (5) events elsewhere in the world were irrelevant except in terms of growth and loss of power or influence. According to the ideological interpretation of international life, the survival or death by starvation of citizens of one country may be of interest to others solely and exclusively in terms of ideological assessments: is it an ally or an enemy, is it democratic or not? Such exclusiveness must now be replaced by consciousness of the fact that, if we supply aid, we do so to save human life, not that of white man or yellow, of democrat or communist; that health protection is a duty in itself and does not end at state boundaries;[81] and that, if the protection of human rights is confined within boundaries, it is no longer the protection of human rights. Even in this, an age in many respects free of the most dramatic aspects of thermonuclear survival, the argument in favour of an ethics for international relations may appear easily acceptable.

The normative problem is not new to international life:[82] this is not the first time in history that it has been posed. It is indeed inherent in the nature of international life in so far as it emerged at the very moment in which modern states were formed. The international community as a legal entity, the international system as a political entity, the human community as a cosmopolitan manifestation – these are the principal levels to which the nascent ethic of international relations must appeal. Research into ethics thus prompts a veritable *re*foundation of international relations, which, almost paradoxically, are now asked to address the most dramatic problems of the human condition. How is it possible to abandon all this to an anarchic, hence amoral conception of international life?[83] A variety of albeit fragmentary contributions have been made in recent years to fill the anarchic 'gap' which has opened up. First, there has been a growth in legally regulated international economic relations (according to an extraordinarily broad set of standards which ranges from jurisdiction over natural resources, raw materials and energy, to different forms of regional cooperation; from the regulation of trade and commerce to the consolidation of the international monetary system; from rulings on movements of capital and foreign investment to strategies of financial aid for development).[84] A second, highly original element is the 'support' offered to the international system by the political community and its network interrelations to allow crossover 'demands' to be met or, at least, reconciled.[85] Such demands thus 'regiment themselves' according to the hypothesis advanced for some years now by those who believe that most of the daily problems of international life (from the fixing of strategic raw material prices to the charting of territorial waters; from ecological legislation to the management of undivided collective goods such as the South Pole) may be, and very often are, solved by the (spontaneous or negotiated) forming of problematic, local 'regimes' determined by collective acceptance of 'some basic procedures and rules relating to the means through which controversy over demands was to be regulated and work out some ends that would at least broadly and generally guide the search for such settlements.'[86]

This institutional image of international reality still has a challenge to address, nonetheless. For is it not true that war and its material function (victory) have often been allotted the task of 'beating time' to the history of humanity? This at least is the impression one receives observing the way it periodically reappears to an almost existential tempo. It is, therefore, to this fascinating, mysterious chapter in the philosophy of history that we must now devote our attention.

5

Cycle of Wars and Philosophy of History

All historians agree that the external activity of states and peoples in their conflicts with one another is expressed in wars, and that as a direct result of greater or lesser success in war, the political strength of states and nations increases or decreases.... All the facts of history (as far as we know it) confirm the truth of the statement that the greater or lesser success of one army against another is the cause, or at least an essential indication of an increase or decrease in the strength of a nation.

L. Tolstoy, *War and Peace*

1 PREMISE

There is no more ingenuous activity than rummaging through the philosophy of history to grasp the main strands of international life: all the more so if one bears in mind that the grand designs of the philosophy of history have never centred round states collectively, but round the destiny of humanity and civilization, round the reasons for conflict – not so much of states as of individuals – according to their nature.[1] Albeit not from an internationalist angle, the experiment was repeated on numerous occasions in past centuries: when, for example, there was the notion that the history of humanity was bound to happen and repeat itself in continuous recurring cycles,[2] to wallow in continuous decadence,[3] or condemned to oscillate incessantly.

It may be observed that provinces amid the vicissitudes to which they are subject, pass from order into confusion and afterward recur to a state of order again; for the nature of mundane affairs not allowing them to continue in an even course, when they have arrived at their greatest perfection they soon begin to decline ... and thus from good they gradually decline to evil, and from evil again return to good.[4]

Or when A. Comte, somewhat more optimistically, discovered, in 'the great philosophical law of the succession of the three states – the primitive theological state, the transient metaphysical and the final positive state',[5] the fundamental law of human evolution.

The encounter between history[6] and international politics[7] takes place on the battlefield, as it were. How can one fail to wonder whether war is endowed with meaning or not by the trends of history? Whether, that is, the function which war supposedly exercises in history is not unveiled in this way? All philosophies of history have to endow wars with meaning, if they are to justify their function. Indeed, wars almost always have the effect of a kind of caesura, as if they marked the climax of a period of decadence, as if their job was to bring into being new empires and new historical eras. The principal models which the philosophy of history[8] offers are the *linear* model, that of continuous development (whether for better or for worse is a further distinction that remains to be made); the *cyclical* model, whereby everything repeats itself; and the *chaotic* (or *static*) model which precludes interpretation. All these models consider war as akin to a disease; evolutionary (or transient, but also painful and necessary) or terminal in the first case, a turning point or about-turn in the second, and a chance occurrence in the third. In each of the three formulations, none of which actually offers more than an initial attempt at *description* (since none of them amounts to an *explanation*), war appears by its very nature to be an insoluble problem. For the end of war as such is, nonetheless, victory,[9] not historical destiny. To understand the meaning of war – if it has one – or to allot it a role, it is necessary to transcend contingency. What is needed is an explanation capable of setting war in a broader design, of revealing its global significance. War is not self-explanatory: it has to be interpreted. Through this lens, the cyclical logic appears not only the most suggestive, but also the only one prepared to come to direct terms with the mystery of the never-ending alternation of peace and war.

It may strike the reader as odd that I should introduce such a seemingly irrelevant issue into a discussion of the ethics of international relations. The fact is that, as the twentieth century draws to a close, an extraordinary phenomenon – namely, the decline of two great empires which were formed at the end of World War II – seems set to dominate the 'turn of the millennium'. For several years now,[10] there has been talk of the decline of the US empire, but the demise of its Soviet counterpart – much more unpredictable but no less sudden for all that – is more conspicuous still. This may lead to a significant new historical turnaround, although we are as yet unable to appreciate its scope. Yet if it is wars which provoke the great turnarounds in history, are we to infer that the decline mentioned is irrelevant, or that a sort of 'Unfought World War III' has taken place, triggering due consequences? Are not the end of bipolarism and, along with it, the obliteration of the ideologies of capitalism, in its 'limited' imperialist version, and of socialism, with its dream of a world revolution, bound to leave their mark, in some totally unforeseeable way, on the end of our millennium?[11] Confronted by a cyclical situation such as this, one inevitably wonders whether some new framing of international relations might offer humanity original, as yet unenvisaged, models of organisation, or whether (as the Gulf war, provoked by the Iraqi occupation of Kuwait on 2 August 1990, and begun on 17 January 1991, would appear to suggest) the theory connecting international order and war has been proved once and for all. Now that the 'government' which, for a long time controlled the fortunes of the international system, has collapsed, hasn't anarchy resumed the upper hand, with (as its logic demands) aggressive conduct running in its wake, followed close behind by conflict; that is, by a sort of 'civil war' which only a new 'constitutive war' can stifle?

2   THE CYCLE AND THE PENDULUM

The twentieth century, like those before it, has witnessed the elaboration of grand designs. Spengler 'found' (as Thucydides might have said)[12] a 50 year rhythm in the 'political, spiritual and artistic progress of every civilisation',[13] while Jaspers has evoked the 'two long breaths' of history.[14] Q. Wright, in turn, in a chapter of his monumental *A Study of War*, observed that, 'There appears to have been a tendency in the last three centuries for concentrations of warfare to occur in approximately fifty-year oscillations, each alternate period of concentration being more severe.'[15] A few years later, in a work with a symmetrical title, *A Study of History*, A. Toynbee devoted a chapter to 'Laws of Nature in Civilisations', in which he discovered in the modern history of the western world an 'overture' from 1494 to 1568, followed by four 'regular cycles', each with an average duration of between 87 and 116 years.[16] Other somewhat more naïve theories also deserve to be cited. F. Klingberg, for example, claimed that every state passes through alternate phases of extroversion and introversion which wind round one another like a spiral.[17] L. Farrar, on the other hand, imagines a periodization determined by three successive models of war (of hegemony, adjustment and challenge) and, without actually specifying the duration of each cycle, concludes that the next great war of hegemony could take place in around the year 2060.[18]

This idea is by no means outmoded or neglected. In recent years, there has been a significant revival in research on the cyclic nature of international politics from the sixteenth century to the present day, following the scansion criterion of a series of great wars: the Spanish–Dutch War (1585–1609); the Thirty Years' War (1618–48); the Franco-Dutch or Third Dutch War (1672–78); the Nine Years' War (1688–97); the War of the Spanish Succession (1701–13); the Seven Years' War (1756–63); the Napoleonic Wars (1792–1815); World Wars I (1914–18) and II (1939–45).[19]

All versions of the historiographical problem of cycles (on the basis of the 'turnarounds adopted', four or five different cycles have been discovered) share one common characteristic: they all predict that, on the basis of the cyclical rhythm noted in the history of the past, the next turnaround (read *war*!) will come to pass within the next 20 or 30 years at the most![20] One should also mention, however, that the results of the most important empirical studies – using the term 'empirical' in its most technically sophisticated meaning – are much less drastic. Singer and Small, for example, rule out 'uniformity in the intervals between the beginning of successive wars over the last 165 years', if we except 'the modest periodicity which emerges through peaks of 15–20 years.[21]

The cultural climate in which these intuitions turned into an agenda for research certainly owes a great deal to the success of I. Wallerstein's fresco of world economic history, which was, in turn,[22] inspired by the precepts of Braudel, who identified in the period 1460–1560 a cyclical fluctuation scanned by wars.[23] It may thus be useful to learn more about this alternation. Systematic reconnaissance of the subject has been facilitated by the outstanding work of J. Goldstein, who in 1988 published an exhaustive study of historical cycles, which he sees as the product of the alternation of prosperity and war.[24] The distinctive feature of the most recent formulations has been the idea that the *rhythm* of history is anchored to an external element which is responsible for binding the cycle of power (of states) to that of wars: that element is economic performance (of industrial and consumer price trends, of all or strategic goods, of the national product, wages, inflation and so on) taken as an independent variable. (How can we fail to observe though that the *law* of the succession of prosperity and war is, in turn, not so much cyclical as circular, in so far as, if the one succeeds the other continuously, we are unable to establish whether one prevails over the other – whether, that is, one is the cause of the other?) Hence, partly on the basis of N. Kondratiev's classical studies on economic cycles,[25] Goldstein has ended up proposing the following synthesis: (1) the existence of tidal waves in price trends from 1495 to the present day is empirically demonstrable and the mounting level of the gravity of wars is closely correlated thereto; (2) the most serious wars take place during phases of economic expansion, not of stagnation; (3) development produces the economic surplus necessary for primary powers to fight their most important wars; (4) the cost of these wars exhausts the surplus and interrupts economic development.[26] This framework may help to plot the future course of the spiral (a motion which is both cyclical and linear)[27] from a situation (the late eighties) of slow economic development, a reduced level of war, and moderate inflation. We should find: (1) an increase in the development of production, followed by (2) an increase in warfare by the great powers and (3) a rise in prices.[28] The most plausible projection reads as follows:

> 1995–2020:   Phase of productive growth
> 2000–2022:   Phase of increased warfare
> 2010–2035:   Phase of price rises

At the end of which process, humanity should embark on its next great war.[29]

Does the material history of international life offer us any evidence of the development of cyclical trends? To attempt to answer this question, one might analyse the transformation – unquestionably original and exceptional – undergone by the international system following the disintegration of the Soviet empire, which has indeed signalled the end of a historical era. Is it possible to see the conditions for a turnaround here? And if so, a turnaround from what?

Few attempts have been made to put the international system into a historical context: the first problem is to identify proper criteria of interpretation, the second is to periodize in such a way as to single out the eras to which such criteria may be applied. One might nonetheless seek, for example's sake, to apply the method to the period from 1815 to the present day (with the additional specifications which I shall shortly be making). Using as scansion criteria some of the great international conflicts or general upheavals caused to the international order, we might single out the following five periods:

> 1815–1848
> 1849–1870
> 1871–1914
> 1919–1939
> 1945–1989

They have been split up according to two criteria designed to assess their effectiveness. Hence, distinguishing systems that are ideologically homogeneous and heterogeneous from others that are totalizing and limited (in terms of the differing intensity with which the rules established at the beginning of each period are imposed and shared), we observe that, while the first period is characterized by homogeneity and the totalizing intensity of its rules (ideological homogeneity; predominance of the legitimist principle; restoration without opposition; intensity of rules; states or future states questioning existing order incapable of asserting themselves), the second displays diametrically opposite features (in it, the nation principle grew uncontrollably, as the great crisis of 1848 was to highlight, so that the system tended to be heterogeneous, a trend reinforced by the incapability of the great powers to ensure anything more than limited obedience to the rules of the game). This initial alternation is followed by a second symmetrical one. The period 1871–1914 is homogeneous and totalizing (as evinced by the fact that the conflictuality of the system extended more to the competition of colonial conquest than to 'Eurocentric' tension, and that nationalist protest movements had by now achieved their ends with the unification of Italy and of Germany), while the period 1919–39 (defined by E. Carr as the 'twenty years' crisis')[30] only registers a slacker enforcement of the rules of the game (as the success of Mussolini and Hitler demonstrates) and immanent heterogeneity (the Soviet Union even had visions of a socialist world!).

Was the alternation of these two pairs of systems (homogeneous and totalizing on the one hand, heterogeneous and limited on the other)[31] perhaps the embryo of a cycle?

It certainly gains in significance if we compare it with the international system that came into being at the end of World War II; when that is, the global framework was self-evidently heterogeneous (the clash between the United States and the Soviet Union and their respective blocs of alliances even degenerated into the *Cold War*) although according to the law of alternation, a homogeneous system ought to have developed. What is more, whereas in previous heterogeneous systems the intensity of rules of the game had been limited, now it became unquestionably totalizing. In practice, only two great powers remained to control events virtually anywhere in the world. It is not difficult to explain this anomaly. It is simply the consequence of the step forward in quality caused by the advent of the atom bomb, which consequently modified the very framework of international politics, making war 'almost impossible'. (The most obvious example of the innovation was that the greatest armaments race in history developed without the armaments in question being used directly.) If we accept that the system formed in the aftermath of World War II has now faded, it is possible to compare its *duration* with that of previous periods:

1815–48	1849–70	1871–1914	1919–39	1945–89
homogeneous	heterogeneous	homogeneous	heterogeneous	homogeneous
totalizing	limited	totalizing	limited	totalizing
33 years	21 years	43 years	20 years	44 years

After cycles are interrupted, the first thing one notes is the duration element, which would appear to confirm the perspicuity of each pair.[32] Homogeneous/totalizing systems tend to last longer than heterogeneous/ limited ones: the reason is an intuitive one. When the system is dominated by the latter two elements, this means that it has a high dissent rate, whereas when the first two reign it is clear that, perhaps even without consensus, the various states are prepared to adapt to the rules. Yet the same element also begs the question of the duration of the international system, which has been founded since 1989 on elements that seem once more to match in an original way: the limitedness of the rules of the game (following the lapse of the grand government agreement between the United States and the Soviet Union), accompanied by growing ideo- logical homogeneity (which may be deduced from the rapid decline of the socialist model of society). Limited rules ought to produce instabil- ity, while homogeneity should lead to stability: limitedness generates systems with a brief duration, homogeneity fosters longer lasting systems.

3   A DEFEAT FOR POLITICAL THEORY?

Making predictions is a fascinating business, but also a risky one. How many conditions have to be respected if the spiral is to unwind as expected? What must we discover to establish that the nature of history is cyclical? How can we unveil the nature of history, how can we feel its pulse?[33] The debate on progress has been so intense over the last few years, it is impossible to review it here. How do we argue that in no case can what has been recur exactly as before? How can we claim that the great transformations experienced by humanity in the last few cen- turies have not shifted – not 'changed' – the trends that preceded them? Was it possible for the framework of economic life a hundred years ago to effectively obey the same natural laws as it does today? How, for example, can we rule out the possibility that the three great material *modifications* (demographic growth, growth in quantity of energy, growth in amount of information) – on the basis of which K. Pomian, in the conclusion to his entry on cycles in the *Enciclopedia Einaudi*, argues that human history has a linear, cumulative and irreversible character[34] – have really influenced global reality? And how, on the contrary, can we argue the central importance of the connection between industrial development and war, or claim that there are no possible alternative hypotheses, and hence that war (great war) periodically and inevitably blights humanity, regardless of the different ways the latter adopts to reorganize itself? In this way, the cyclical logic unconsciously turns into a formulation based on economism. If the war cycle depends on evidence of an economic type it should follow that economic causes explain wars. Yet this appears anything but automatic: the history of thinking on this possibility offers a multiplicity of contrasting solutions. For B. Constant, as for Saint-Simon or James Mill, there was no doubt that development, industrial and commercial, would ultimately demonstrate the non-convenience of war, and N. Angell reiterated the argument almost a century later when he suggested that the alleged advantages of any war were to be considered nothing other than a *grand illusion*. That war and industrial development were indissolubly linked was also the central idea of the Marxist-Leninist interpretation of international politics, on the basis of which the interplay of the two would, sooner or later, force the great imperial powers to clash and annihilate one another (and it is difficult to imagine a more teleological interpretation than that!).[35] In the first case, war is bound to become extinct. In the second, as soon as it reaches its acme, it is banned!

Whereas these formulations attribute some degree of dynamic intentionality to history, the one which has dominated interpretations of international relations for centuries, and which goes under the name of international equilibrium theory (although it may be described in an infinite variety of other ways),[36] chooses not to pursue this goal. It may suffice for the moment to stress its substantially anti-teleological outlook (as well as the fact that it is not a cyclical, but a dynamic *circular* logic of 'eternal returns'):[37] it tends not to an end, but to an unstable (and repetitive) oscillating motion between peace and war (each of which 'corrects' the excessive presence of the other) meant or destined to restore the state of the system to its origin. Equilibrium may be modified and reproduced, but it makes no progress and has no ends. The balance metaphor describes its mechanisms but not its reason nor its rationality. Why, in any situation in which one party has excessive power, should an equilibrating coalition develop, necessarily bound to generate conflict? In its apparent neutrality,[38] natural equilibrium must deprive the players in the game of any capacity to intervene, if it is true (as it must be) that diverging individual interests ultimately reach a spontaneous agreement. The destinies of international politics are incorporated in its very nature. Its ability to elude normative criteria[39] and as a consequence, any principle of assessment, serves us the ultimate disappointment. So is international politics *nature*? Moving from metaphor to straightforward simile, we might be tempted to ask whether international life is not simply regulated by motion akin to that produced by a pendulum, a body suspended on a thread and oscillating round a fixed point, swinging from one extreme (peace) to another (war) and back again. Obviously, the fundamental feature of a pendulum is the *fixed axis* which regulates its oscillation: for this *line* explains both its oscillating motion (its range) and its speed (rhythm of alternation); it is also at the centre of the thrust which sets the oscillation (change) from peace to war in motion. Albeit simpler than that of the cycle, the pendulum simile is just as mechanistic, but it does come closer to the little we know about the alternation of war and peace. It manages, that is, to suggest the irrepressible nature of the shift (once it reaches one extreme, the pendulum is irresistibly and inevitably drawn towards the other) as well as its natural unmodifiability. Isn't this a good representation of the history of the modern state? In the emphatic words of C. Tilly, 'War made the state and the state made war.'[40]

Is that as far as our understanding of international life extends? Here is how one of the leading international relations theorists describes what might be defined as the 'original position' of states.[41]

> States in an anarchic order must provide for their own safety by themselves, and threats to it, true or presumed, abound. The preoccupation of having to identify dangers and reacting to them becomes a way of life. . . .
> Each on its own account, states can do this exclusively to sustain their own security. Apart from their individual intentions, collectively their actions provoke armaments races and alliances. . . . In an anarchic milieu, the source of wellbeing of one is a source of preoccupation for another.[42]

Like teleological logics, cyclical logics provide a limited image of war as something which stems inevitably from given conditions. In the final analysis, they too make do with a solution which purports to *explain* processes by *describing* them.

War can (and must) be explained. Or, when it breaks out, is it just another mishap in the relational life of states? Is the alternation of war and peace a natural, spontaneous fact of life, like that of night and day? No, to fight a war is no action-packed adventure, while to lose one is more than just a regrettable accident: 'it means in very truth that *we* are lost: our character, our cause, our hope our history.'[43]

The anarchic imagery which describes war as a spontaneous event, determined solely by states exclusively bent upon power, supremacy and dominion, thus appears extremely abstract. Even if history had laws to obey, they would not always regard the same men and the same states. The latter do not experience a cycle but a reality: a war lost is the *end* of one story, not the continuation of another, invisible to its protagonists, reduced to blind, unconscious puppets. By dispensing with the justifications discussed here, are we dispensing with any attempt to understand war? There could, after all, be some rationality behind it: perhaps it is merely hidden to our view. If we accept the hypothesis of a mutation in international life[44] as a result of the advent of the atomic bomb in contemporary history,[45] it is realistic for us to admit that any philosophy of history has to recognize that a new epoch or historical age has begun. In turn, at whatever stage we consider history to be, we must acknowledge that it has been *interrupted*. Although this problem is theoretically the exclusive preserve of the philosophy of history, since it contains the element (war, but not just any war, as we shall see below) which normally acts as a caesura or break between one epoch and another, it fully deserves to be addressed by international theorists as an example of *change*. Compared to the linear, cyclic and chaotic formulations described above, the mutation hypothesis necessarily implies recognition of an 'upright nature' with respect to which it is possible to observe the alteration that has taken place.

The idea of the heterogenesis of ends[46] seems to adapt particularly well to the international problem for the simple reason that it provides it with a refuge from its own incomprehensibility, freeing it from the randomness and inscrutability that were among the principal causes of its lack of appeal (in the past). By appealing to a reason which produces results *other* than – as opposed to, or as well as, different from – the natural or expected or apparent ones, we would immediately make war an event which lends itself to rational analysis, however complex or difficult that analysis may be. Faced by a reality that is, instead, unverifiable and obscure, without revealable meaning (which is how many interpret international politics), our 'magic wand' – the heterogenesis of ends – might prompt the following consideration: even if none of the protagonists of historical actions can explain their motives, such motives do nonetheless exist, as the future will reveal. Even if evil sometimes generates good, even if, in general, a straightforward factual event may have unforeseen consequences, this does not mean that what happens after explains what happened before, but simply that it is possible to hypothesize that the modifications made to reality by that event detach themselves from it; they thus acquire a capacity of their own, if not to shed light on the past (that the atom bomb may at last have brought peace to humanity[47] does not explain why it exists nor why the first atom bombs were built), at least to illuminate its historical scope and allow possible explanations to be formulated.[48] The mechanism of the heterogenesis of ends prevents us from resigning ourselves to the inscrutability of history since it suggests that even what appears evil may be good and vice versa,[49] and hence that what seems incomprehensible at first sight may instead have aprioristic meaning. It may thus be possible to apply it to the anarchic image of international life (and what 'ends' could international life then have?). It might also be possible to apply it to the image's redundancy (that is, its surplus explanatory capacity which incorporates both description of and judgement on reality). If it were, the mechanism would thus help us to discover the meaning (admittedly hard to recognize) of international relations. Here, though, we are weighed down by an excess of explanation, on the basis of which everything that has happened is justifiable, hence rational. To steer a middle course between too little (war is inexplicable) and too much (that it is in all cases explicable), it might be useful to stipulate that, more than motives or causes (the most problematic concept possible in this context), there exist tentative propositions which, remaining necessarily outside reality, purport to be hypothetical explanations, not *de facto* proof. Since our survey of the various attempts to fit history to some form of heterogenesis of ends (isn't that what the cycle idea is?) cannot achieve definitive, satisfactory (scientific) solutions, we must deduce first that the problem of international life has a specific autonomy of its own, that it does not fit into excessively broad, general (and to some degree providential) solutions in which war is but one of the many elements; and resign ourselves secondly to the fact that no real *general theory* of international relations[50] (that is, a systematic, global attempt to understand[51] this particular dimension of reality) exists for the moment, nor will it ever exist unless we formulate a theory of international change as the driving force of international politics. A subject's theoretical agenda cannot confine itself to describing the events which fall within its range: it also has to explain their relevance and the reason why they happen. It must thus make an effort to recognize and distinguish the subjectiveness of real conduct and the objectiveness of the frameworks used to interpret that conduct. It must, in short, assess the comparability of the two categories of data on which scientific knowledge is based. A general theory should contain both descriptions and explanations, but must keep the two rigorously apart. It will be accepted, criticized or rejected in terms of its ability to explain or otherwise, not of its ability to describe or otherwise.

Is it possible to make a first step in this direction (which I am inclined to describe as *non-ideological* in that it does not concern itself with 'strong' value assumptions) by resorting to a rudimental chaos hypothesis? Although it does not return us to anarchy, which I have been at great pains to keep out of my argument, it does accept the 'original' primacy of chance and/or the unforeseen. Isn't a teleological model a prerequisite for avoiding the limits typical of the 'strong' formulations we have seen? The fact that chance determines that given events necessarily lead to others is that prerequisite. One possible misunderstanding needs, in any case, to be clarified: a casual formulation cannot be turned into some sort of lesson on the past. If it were, we would have a dissembled version of the general linear conception, which would, at the same time, seek to stand out from that conception. Its modest proposal would be that, while the linear hypothesis indicates a tendency towards – and hence sets a seal on – the future, it would merely be prolonging the past, which as such is incontrovertible and and in no way prejudices the future.[52] It is not 'historical laws' (discovered by looking to the past) which determine history, but vice versa. It is merely circumstance that the international system prior to the reorganization brought about by the Napoleonic and post-Revolutionary wars experienced mainly dyadic wars, and that since 1815 this model has been progressively replaced by a coalitional one; that is, the spontaneous action of the political movements which had to deal with those situations. The fact cannot be *explained* by a law, but exclusively *interpreted* as a sign of the time.[53]

All this leads to a consideration that might help us to reconstruct the problematic field of international relations. It is based on the premise that, since it is not guided by any external will, international life must have an internal history of its own, different from the sum-total of the histories of states. If we reconstruct this internal history, it may also be possible to understand its nature and specificity. We are thus able to adapt to international relations (but with totally different contents from Rawls's) the image of the 'original position' of individuals, by which we mean the 'appropriate initial status quo', but without its ability 'to ensure that the fundamental agreements reached in it are fair'[54] – international analysis being as yet a long way short of such a refined level of elaboration. The great difference which separates original conditions is demonstrated basically by the obviousness of the principles which, according to Rawls, typify the original position of states: equality, self-determination, self-defence, observance of treaties.[55] There is no 'veil of ignorance' that can convince states to judge these four as the basic principles of a *just* international life simply because states are not equal one to another, their national autonomy is a product of history and not an initial condition, they are not always strong enough to

protect themselves and they do not observe treaties. Yet the great difference between the two situations lies not in some imperfection in the
assessment of the original position of states with respect to that of
individuals, but in the diversity of their origin (partly because the one
described for states seems, if anything, to adapt to a 'final' or ideal
situation rather than to an original one). No state has the right to live
enjoyed by the individual. The birth of a state is the product of history,
or, better still, of the material development of a given conception of the
organization of human relations, first statist and then interstatist.[56] We
have always devoted so much attention to the origin of the modern
state[57] that we have lost sight of the origin of international relations: of
the modern state we have considered its centralizing capacity, its consolidation through the setting up of boundaries and their defence and
its claims to external sovereignty. In doing so, we have neglected the
'original' condition, the artificiality of each of the states which began to
take shape from the sixteenth century. For example, how can we justify
the fact that, in the space of almost four centuries, the number of
sovereign states had reached 23 in 1815, while in as few as four years
(1959–62) it increased by 20 (from 89 to 118)?

States are the product of historical evolution, or, better still, of a
series of transformations achieved almost invariably by the recourse to
war. Our ongoing preoccupation with the domestic function which they
perform in regulating interindividual relations prevents us from having
even the vaguest understanding of their true *nature*. In this way, we
observe exclusively their material matrix. Yet states also share an external reality with dozens of analogous institutions, all engaged in age-long
controversies over issues such as coexistence, the sharing of available
resources, the affirmation of ideological preferences and, last but not
least, the management of a common political space (which, due to the
artificial origin of each, has been distributed to date exclusively as a
result of inevitable conflicts between opposing wills). Are we right to
consider such matters residual?

4   THE FUTURE OF PEACE AND PEACE IN THE FUTURE

So is the history of relations between states to be invariably, solely
and exclusively one of war? The state is the organizational principle
which has dominated world history over the last five centuries. During
the same period, about 500 wars, large and small, have taken place,
so many that in our everyday language we acknowledge their great
importance metaphorically when we speak about war against poverty,

press wars, the war between the sexes, trade wars and so on.[58] Has war always been the same or is it possible to frame it in a historical context, considering, for example, that its scope has grown progressively with time? It may suffice to read that extraordinary piece of literature, *The Adventurous Simplicissimus*,[59] to appreciate just how unmodifiable the laws of war are: devastation, pain and death are always the same, never changing, under any sky, at any time. Thus, if war's material dimension has changed, the same cannot be said of its functions, which does not preclude that its models have diversified. Wars are fewer but intenser, a myriad of dyadic wars having been progressively replaced by a concentration of wars between large-scale coalitions and so on.

Yet if we were to calculate the incidence of war in the life of each single state, we might conclude that the problem is not one of quantity anyway. In the two centuries following their independence (excepting domestic wars of conquest against native Indians), the United States spent one year (1898) at full-scale war with Spain, two years during World War I, four years during World War II, three years during the Korean war and four or five years in the Vietnam war:[60] a total of 15 years in a period of more than 200. Analogous observations might be made about Italy or even 'warlike' Germany (while the cases of Great Britain and France are entirely different, mainly because their history has been much longer). This fact does not mean that war's incidence in the history of states has decreased, but rather that states devote most of their historical life to weaving peaceful daily relations with each another. What then is the content of these normal peaceful relations? Can we identify the links in the war–peace chain?

To address the war–peace cycle – which is logical, not historiographical or historical-philosophical – we must delve right to the roots of international life. Is the *original* position one of war or of peace? It is impossible to establish the effective 'date of birth' of international relations, but the story must have a beginning at some stage in time! We might, hypothetically,[61] imagine that the first meeting of states was a belligerent one; that the outcome of this first war was the establishing of an unequal relationship between the two states involved (and/or their other allies). In this way, the differentiation would originate from one crucial test: what, after all, is more final, more definitive than victory or defeat? But once peace was achieved, relations between states must have drawn their inspiration from the outcome of the war, hence any subsequent modification of the content of their unequal relations must necessarily have been revised by further conflict. If we were to extend this mechanism to international relations in general, applying it to great wars in particular, we would have an extraordinarily precise, clear tool for the conceptual reconstruction of international history. Using war as a caesura between different configurations of international relations, we would be able draw a map of successive international systems, dominated – or better still, constituted – according to the will of victorious states. Peace, the long period which goes from one 'constitutive war'[62] to the next would thus be hinged on the will of the state (or states) which has gained from its victory in war the power to determine the content of international order. It will evidently endure as long as conditions remain unchanged. The international realm is hence peaceful for most of the time, but owes its content to war.

This means that it is not as important to take stock of the belligerence of international life as to realize that change takes place exclusively through wars. More precisely, this historical law of the international system may be applied over an arc of time that spans from the beginning of the sixteenth century up to the last decade of the twentieth, in which – following a mutation perhaps?[63] – we have witnessed a series of modifications to the constituted order without precedent in the history of the modern state. It is irrelevant to our purpose to know whether what happened in eastern Europe in 1989 (another '89 that will go down in history!) will be enduring and whether it will have further consequences. What is in any case certain is that, unlike Hungary in 1956 or Czechoslovakia in 1968, some states, situated in a position determined by the 'stratification' imposed by the victorious states at the end of World War II, have radically modified their domestic arrangements (another element established by the victors in wars), as well as their alliance system, *peacefully*. By so doing, they have infringed a hitherto iron law. It is of course impossible to establish whether this is the beginning of the break-up of the international order. Nevertheless, surely the end of bipolarism (as we knew it) represents at least the overriding of a system of coercive order resembling that in force inside states. This mutation may lead to a series of positive consequences; such as the assertion of a series of (at least embryonic) principles of effective equality between states, or the preconditions for democracy, fostered perhaps by the success of techniques of regime formation[64] of major international problems, designed to limit if not to avoid the traditional recourse to violence. The 'life breath' of war in almost half a millennium of history appears to have grown progressively quicker. As we have seen, cycles of roughly 100 years gave way to 20-year cycles (between World Wars I and II). Then it began to gasp only to relax and grow longer in the contemporary period. Certain signs also induce pessimism: the excessively abrupt rebirth of the national idea, the lust for revenge against fallen despots, regression towards forms of quasi-anarchy which risk reigniting tension and aggression. Whatever future awaits international politics, whatever destiny awaits each one of us, there can be no doubt that, viewing contemporary events, one detail stands out above all others. It is that the necessary, albeit inevitably insufficient, condition for the nonviolent revolution in the countries of eastern Europe has been, and is, a curious but most welcome contradiction; the fact that local changes have failed to provoke extended conflict has depended on international peace at the highest level, but the speed and intensity of such change may, in turn, jeopardize peace. This is anything but an exceptional circumstance for international life: hasn't the 40-year success of nuclear deterrence always been bound to the precarious equilibrium of threat and reassurance, of arms race and arms reduction, of deceit and promise, of tension and detente – of war and peace? This situation can be described in one way only – as the *realm of uncertainty*? While, for the state, law represents *certainty*, international life is characterized by deep-rooted *uncertainty*, which, however, should be assessed not in terms of the traditional idea of insuperable anarchy, but as the founding, structural element of international relations. Such 'uncertainty' has the task of reconciling liberty (of action) and constriction (on the basis of each state's limit), innovation and conservation, responsibility and adventure. So on what criteria are statesmen, governors and peoples to base their choices? Such 'uncertainty' might, each day that passes, cause everything to be questioned all over again under the thrust of new, and not always immediately perceivable, collective challenges and threats. Last but by no means least, such 'uncertainty' also extends to decisions to be taken and directions to be followed, as well as to the moral consequences that may arise from them.

6

The Future of International Justice

Now it appears that the terms Justice and Injustice are used in several senses, but as their equivocal uses are closely connected, the equivocation is not detected; whereas in the case of widely different things called by a common name, the equivocation is comparatively obvious: for example (the difference being considerable when it is one of external form), the equivocal use of the word *kleis* (key) to denote both the bone at the base of the neck and the instrument with which we lock our doors.

Aristotle, *The Nicomachaean Ethics*

1 THE ARGUMENT

The very idea that principles of universal scope may be applied to a number of states together seems to clash head-on with the concept of sovereignty. Since when have states been prepared to accept external judgement? The picture would change completely if we imagined that no states existed, that no boundary separated huge masses of citizens. A minimal principle of equality could be applied everywhere, and the idea that some criterion of planetary justice had a chance of asserting itself would no longer seem absurd.[1] But since states do exist and it is impossible to tell if and when they will be overtaken by some superior form of organization (not that this would necessarily be a good thing in the short term), the relevance of an international theory of justice would soon become bankrupt.

Is it then merely an ingenuous coincidence of names that, aping analysis of domestic justice, underpins the arguments on international justice which, for some years now, have characterized the philosophical and political debate on the nature of international life? Inside the state and outside, is the same word – justice – really weighted with as many different meanings as Aristotle's *kleis*? It once appeared highly unlikely that relations between states could be observed in terms of their justice, chiefly because each state entered into contact with the others almost exclusively during wars (and nothing could be less suitable than war for assessments of this kind). Today, however, the worldwide diffusion and consolidation of very similar forms of state has rendered states comparable; while infinite opportunities for non-belligerent contact have developed among them thanks to the immense transformations which their material culture, as well as that of individuals, has undergone. Unconsciously, increasingly consistent, common models of conduct have been disseminated to such an extent that today, when a head of state defines the international conduct of the Libyan leader Qadhafi as 'criminal', international public opinion has an immediate, basic understanding of what he means.

Be that as it may, what we are faced with here is yet again nothing other than the extension of a practice habitual within states, as opposed to a specific conception of justice applied to states. So what are the preconditions for 'exporting' the problem of justice to international relations? The first is obviously the overriding of the so-called 'anarchic prejudice', while the second is acceptance of a sort of saving clause against premature failure, a waiver of the proposal for the mere transposition to states of the theory of justice among individuals.[2] It should be observed, besides, that any intention to formulate a theory of international justice cannot avoid being totalizing – comprehensive, that is, of both peacetime and wartime justice – not so much because 'inter arma silent leges'[3] as because war may at times be considered as nothing more than an attempt to take justice into one's own hands.[4]

Likewise, it is not enough to imagine that just states by their very nature give life to a just international system – as if the sum of just domestic policies necessarily generated just international policies. States which behave democratically in the domestic sphere may subsequently implement an aggressive foreign policy.[5] The same applies to justice too. The passage from one realm to the other necessarily entails an improvement in quality. This is determined by the difference that exists between a reality in which citizens delegate the right to govern them to a legal authority (thus giving shape to a vertical relationship) and another in which little more than a hundred subjects (although the number is actually immaterial), on a joint basis, seem to have exclusively horizontal – that is, equal – relations.[6] Nonetheless, although we are dealing here with materially incomparable entities,[7] and the hypothesis whereby the same principles of justice that are valid for individuals ought to be applied directly to states appears untenable, why rule out the possibility that, in so far as they are composed of individuals, states too may be subject to value judgements?

2   CAN INTERNATIONAL MORALITY EXIST?

As external representatives of a collectivity of citizens who identify with them, do states (and their governments) have obligations to each other of the type that we all believe the individuals who live together in a state have? This problem, which once appeared irrelevant, has today become an object of circumspect, but nonetheless careful, consideration. The only stumbling-block is the difficulty involved in fully grasping the fact that those citizens to whom criteria of justice are applied form states, without which not only international justice but also justice in general would never have been administered at all. The question is an exceedingly subtle one, but it may, nonetheless, be referred to the two extreme positions imagined thus far. A first, generically realist position confines problems of morality within the state, beyond whose boundaries anything goes. A second, cosmopolitan formulation turns the situation on its head. By supplanting the state it suggests that we consider *all* individuals (all equally moral subjects). The position which I have defended here (according to which the same ethical theory must embrace states and individuals) argues instead that, if it is possible to speak of morality in politics at all, then this morality can be one and one alone, be it domestic or international: the moral duty of *states* is to be just towards *individuals*. Individuals, joined together into states, are united round values – those introduced into their respective bills of rights, for instance.[8] States, joined together into an international community, must promote these values, defend them or ensure their affirmation.

If all the moral rules of states dealt exclusively with one state's way of conducting itself in its relations with another, we would have no need to override a sort of diplomatic code logic. More generally speaking, it would suffice to equalize international and moral law, cementing them with the principle of 'pacta sunt servanda', which would, on its own, define as morally praiseworthy the conduct of the state which observes the agreements it has undersigned, and as unjust that of the state which violates them. There would be nothing at all scandalous about this onus on positive law: unlike citizens, states, in so far as they do not exist in nature, can claim no *natural right*. In so far as they are artificial creations, why should they adapt to anything other than legal artifice? The problem is much more complex than that, however, for not even positive international law can be assessed by analogy with domestic law (international law is not for states what state law is for citizens). The reason for this is to be found not in the traditional view that there is no judge capable of having an international sentence enforced, but in the historical (but not irrelevant) fact that not all states are bound to the same agreements, whereas that of equal application is a basic principle of contemporary domestic law. A state may be a friend or an enemy of other states, conducting itself accordingly with all of them. It may help its allies and harm its enemies. It may even recognize the right to exist of some and not of others. This is a vital, discriminating point since on no grounds might anything of the sort be granted by domestic law (only under extremely restricted, extenuating circumstances is domestic homicide excusable). It was thus, for example, that for a number of centuries a small group of European states used their colonial domination to prevent other states from being formed (indeed, the vast majority of the world's former colonies eventually achieved sovereignty and independence through 'wars of liberation'). Likewise, after a war, a state may decide to contribute to the reconstruction of beaten allies without feeling similar obligations to other countries in the same predicament. Wasn't this the case of the Marshall Plan, named after the US Secretary of State who launched it on 5 June 1947? Did anyone have the right to criticize US wishes? In short, the crime of failure to assist does not apply in international relations as it does in relations between individuals.[9]

It is this latter aspect which began to attract the attention of moral philosophers about 20 years ago. The question they asked themselves was whether rich states are morally obliged to supply aid to poor ones. It is obviously a very short step from this notion to that of international justice, bearing in mind that the two fundamental applications of justice that have always been considered feasible internationally are distribution of weights and benefits, and compensation for any damage suffered.[10] One thus feels compelled to question whether it is right to consider just the rich state that squanders assets which might considerably alleviate the predicament of a poor neighbouring state. I shall use three positions to explore the problem, two of them extreme and one intermediate.

The first may be summarized in P. Singer's forceful argument in favour of the obligation of rich nations to prevent, wherever possible, crippling poverty in underprivileged nations. His main points are: we are duty-bound to prevent evil whenever we can; absolute poverty is evil; the rich can given up some of their wealth without thereby suffering moral damage; hence, we are duty-bound to intervene to avoid the death by starvation of millions of people scattered throughout the world.[11]

The second, diametrically opposed, position is J. Fishkin's, when he argues that there is no limit (or restraint) on the demand for the rich in rich countries to reduce their income in so far as an additional extra fraction of it might always be allocated to the poor in the poor countries.

The easily imaginable consequence of this would be the impoverishment of the rich and hence the cyclical reversal of the problem. Basically, in Fishkin's view, if we move from the domestic to the international realm, we upset a system of rigid, impartial consequentiality in so far as, 'We are left to balance morally incommensurable considerations' (or considerations referring to realities considered as such).[12] In conclusion, no one can be forced to act the hero. At most, as long as we find ourselves in a 'zone of indifference', each one of us can decide as he deems fit.[13]

The intermediate position is that held by B. Barry, who starts from the consideration that there is nothing to prevent us from thinking that a common international morality might be based on shared acceptance of a conception of 'The insistence on cooperation as a condition of morality [which] stems from a conception of morality as a scheme of mutual advantage from mutual restraint.'[14] Since this principle implicitly suggests that there can be nothing wrong with helping one's neighbour, with the proviso that it be shared by all the subjects of the argument, Barry addresses what might prove to be the greatest obstacle of all; namely, that it might be impossible to reach the required consensus, since anyone could withdraw from co-operation if there were no reciprocity.[15] Then, acknowledging that western liberal-democratic states have always appeared particularly favourable to unforced agreements, Barry concludes that, even without the consensus of the whole international community, liberal-democratic countries might, in any case, supply aid to poor countries; first, because states are less dependent on the co-operation of others to achieve their 'moral ends';[16] secondly, because the motive for acting morally resides simply in the 'desire to be able to justify our conduct'.[17]

Only in one of the three positions explored – that of Singer – does the conclusion envisage the obligation to supply aid, while Barry alone refers his considerations to states as opposed to individuals. Fishkin, finally, joins individuals and states in the zone of ethical indifference. What the three examples have in common is that their arguments regard the problem of economic aid as if it were the only sphere in which questions of international morality can arise. It is evident, nonetheless, that by defining the problem in this way, one runs the risk of countering the morality of theoretical intervention with the problem of its practical feasibility, hence leaving oneself vulnerable to the liberalist critique. This argues hard-nosedly that any economic-type entails co-ordination between the donor state and the recipient state, a fact which cannot but influence their political relations and may even give rise – through modifications to the respective positions of the states in the international stratification – to 'a less ordered system',[18] a system that is more egalitarian, hence more anarchic, on the basis of the notion that greater equality equals less order. This argument does not *de facto* damage the moral one:[19] but how can one deny that, 'there is a world of difference between the competition for power and status within most domestic societies affording scope for equal opportunities',[20] and that another value – international order or the conservation of peace – might, paradoxically, be threatened if successful redistribution were to upset the balance of power? Are we to resign ourselves to the consideration that international politics is 'the worst of all possible liberal worlds'?[21] Are we to strive 'to ensure that the intractable difficulties of international relations do not infect the integrity of liberal politics at a national level',[22] by barricading borders against external danger? We might even develop the point further and argue that what happens inside another state does not concern us, or even that respect for the sovereignty of others is an insurmountable principle.[23]

The sense of dissatisfaction with which these formulations leave us suggests that an element is still missing from the general framework. How can we accept that an individual lives or is left to die simply because he was born in one place rather than another? It is true that international politics has addressed even more elementary, dramatic problems such as war (in the context of which, it is enough to belong to another state to be killed by the enemy). It is true also that each single state is duty-bound to provide, first and foremost, for the well-being of its nationals: but does it do so because these nationals are its own, or because they are human beings, and hence possess equal birth-rights?[24] The same point might be reformulated as follows: assuming that it is the state's end (more than that of others) to guarantee minimum conditions of survival for its citizens, it must necessarily do the same for any foreign citizens on its territory. Why should it not do the same too for foreign citizens who have not taken the fortuitous step of crossing a border? History is full of cases in which states have carried on relations with citizens of other countries without the mediation of their respective governments. The history of subversion offers a welter of evidence of non-institutional external interference or intervention, of cases in which whole armies of spies or special corps have been sent into enemy countries to engineer the downfall of their governments.[25] It is hard to argue that the government responsible for such intervention is acting in self-defence or for its own survival. When the USA perpetrated episodes such as those in Latin America, or when the Soviet Union followed suit in countries in Africa, no great domestic interests were at stake.

We thus edge closer to the central question: is it possible to separate morality *in the* state from the morality *of the* state without submitting its action to global (domestic *plus* international) assessment? For why should a state mislay its principles whenever its view wanders outwards? The pursuit of a foundation for international morality can be neither continued nor discussed as long as morality is thought to be confined within boundaries – national boundaries. Unjustifiable though they may be,[26] national boundaries are a tangible, established fact. They are the result of the historical progress of the idea of the state which has now developed in substantially the same way all over the world. No formulation of international moral problems can be discussed without taking them into consideration. Whether the rich state's duty to aid the poor state is discussed with passion (Singer) or disenchantment (Ackerman), the common denominator of the two formulations is their difficulty in proposing lines of action capable of crossing national boundaries. The problem therefore, is to define the state's sphere of jurisdiction, or even to establish its duties. If we acknowledge that the state is at least duty-bound to ensure its citizens' survival,[27] this does not depend on their being its own citizens, but on the fact that all sentient human beings are entitled to equal birthrights. Why should a state's duty cease at its boundaries? Why not acknowledge that 'government coercion that extends across international borders is governmental coercion nonetheless'?[28] The scope of the state's judgement (in its effort to get acquainted with the world, or to understand it) cannot be restricted to the state itself, as if there were nothing outside but a world full of individuals abandoned in the state of nature. The problem, therefore, is not so much the justification or feasibility[29] of aid[30] as the *boundlessness* of the moral scope of principles – or better still of their universal value. That the state may recognize other states as different from itself is one thing: the protection of the wellbeing of a human being who, regardless of his flag, is entitled to the same guarantees that the state offers its nationals is another. (The only exception to this idea of the state in the contemporary world is the Islamic one, in which the foreigner is an enemy in so far as he is an infidel, not because he was born under a different sky!)

The problem of rich countries supplying aid to poor countries (which is no longer a short cut round the broader problem of the state's morality) should not be addressed submissively, as has been the case with most philosophical analyses, which are content to leave the intractable aspects of the practical application of principles to politicians and economists.[31] As I have stressed all the way along, at the core of the issue is the state or, better still in the context in question, the state's foreign policy. A single state can, if it wishes, refuse to recognize others

(I say this in the abstract, purely for argument's sake, since this does not happen in reality). It may, nonetheless, act in the same way towards non-citizens simply because they, unlike their state of origin, exist in nature, so to speak, and, as possessors of birthrights, ought to receive the same treatment from every state. This formulation is preferable to its alternative: that is, that ideals are one thing and practice another and, therefore, that 'what is just in theory' is unfeasible in practice or, more realistically, that it is a complex business for the state to guarantee the minimum rights of its own nationals, let alone those of the citizens of other nations. Is it possible or even acceptable for the state to have no conception of the world, for it not to seek to contribute to the realization of the model of world order it most prefers? (Remember that virtually the whole of the twentieth century has been dominated by the clash between two ideologies – international economic liberalism, or capitalism, and proletarian internationalism – each with its own clearcut vision of international order.) The realist theory upon which this formulation rests is well known: it maintains that the state's sole task is to pursue the national interest, and that its attitude towards the outside world is functional to that interest. Each and every external intervention – from aid to aggression – may be justified solely by the superior end of the strengthening of the state.

The difficulties that arguments in support of the state's external duty[32] inevitably lead to are no proof that aid is useless or unjustifiable. They simply reveal the short-sightedness (or lack of what Jonas calls the '*far-sightedness*' of the wealthy nations' selfishness)[33] of the predominant conception of foreign policy, according to which the only problems that really count for a state are domestic ones.[34] It would be wrong to forget also that foreign policy is part and parcel of government policy as a whole: it cannot be swept under the carpet whenever convenience demands. Granted that each state must concern itself, first and foremost, with the protection of its own nationals (albeit exclusively for material reasons of proximity), it often determines the destiny of foreigners too. We are thus forced to rule out the possibility that the same state adopts different criteria in the two cases, and that the second requires special justification. If we accept that in Vietnam the United States were not in the least way defending vital interests or the wellbeing of their population, what reason could they have for resorting to forms of chemical warfare which they denied ever using, and which they helped to have banned by attending international conferences on the issue? This argument does not of course refer to military actions against enemy troops (regular and irregular alike, war being an extenuating circumstance), but to actions against the local population. What difference is there between Vietnamese peasants and the farmers of the American Midwest or Deep South?

We naturally condemn brutal methods of warfare, but the question we must answer here is this: is it acceptable to treat human beings in different ways? Plainly, the US government would never use the methods it implemented in Vietnam to quell a riot at home. The crux of the matter is, therefore: is such schizophrenia justifiable? Unless we argue that human nature changes in value according to geographic position, colour of skin, race and so on, it evidently is not! If the state is a moral entity,[35] in the sense that its relationship with its citizens is not one of indifference, and has as its end their wellbeing (without necessarily achieving or wishing to achieve it), its action outside its boundaries cannot appeal to principles that are in total conflict with those followed at home. The fact is that, unlike domestic policy, which is regarded as *continuous*, foreign policy is normally (and erroneously) conceptualized as something *inconsistent*, intermittent and hence, so to speak, logically *subsequent* to its domestic counterpart. A state is formed within two contexts, its constitution has two souls: one domestic, the other external, one aimed at its citizens, the other at all other states.[36] (If a state were not to be recognized by only one other, then it would not exist at all!) Neither of the two policies can be unique since they incorporate links with the other. Which is the state whose citizens never cross its borders and which has no external pretensions? If we recognize the continuity between domestic and foreign policy,[37] we must verify whether the two realms are coherent or consistent with one another. This will tell us, for instance, whether a state acts democratically at home and in an authoritarian, imperialistic way abroad. The nature of things no doubt has its importance, but it is, nonetheless, impossible for the principles of humanity and civilization that are pursued internally to be totally and immediately ignored externally.[38] This implies that the state, in so far as it is a member of the international community, is not merely a possessor of rights – as realistic thinking has always maintained[39] – but also, and to the same extent, of external duties in as much as the society of all other states is composed of citizens, all equal and all entitled to the same fundamental birthrights.

Continuity and coherence connect 'internal' and 'external' in structural terms, first of all (only subsequently do political terms, the contextual differences and specific natures of the two realms,[40] come into play): it is they which guide our assessment of the conduct of states. How is it possible to differentiate between Tzarist Russia's defence of its national interest in World War I and Lenin's decision to sign the Treaty of Brest-Litovsk? How is it possible to admire a government which rides roughshod over its citizens' rights (as Brezhnev's Soviet Union did, for instance) at the very moment in which it champions the liberation of other citizens from the oppression of others. How can we compare Eisenhower's foreign policy with Kennedy's, or Stalin's with Khrushchev's? The international political conditions from which each drew the inspiration for his political decisions were not all that different, at least not so different as to allow leeway for the traditional argument of the so-called 'challenge to national security'.[41] It follows that, before we judge its morality, we must base our assessment of a state's standard of conduct on the fundamental nexus between domestic and international conduct, which is not merely or only intermittent (either one or the other), but global and unitary. Hence programmes of aid to underprivileged countries (this is just one example, but the whole of the politics of collaboration or hostility might be analysed according to the same criteria) cannot be justified if they are carried on solely inside boundaries, or if they are solely in favour of allied or friendly countries or influenced by changes of an ideological nature towards others still. Finally, if we view the state as a whole, we will be able to extend to it the categories of analysis elaborated by political theory, adding the moral criterion to the others used for assessment of international politics in peacetime.

This is possible not only because, as we have seen, it offers us vital pointers to the quality of international politics, but, more importantly, because the nature of a state influences its external stance as well. A state is a state is a state. Its domestic actions alone have no relevance: the state must respond for them to its own population, but must be judged also by other states and, subsequently, by world opinion. Likewise, in its external actions it must not only be responsible for itself, but also for the contribution it makes in terms of the conservation of peace, the establishing of a shared order and the development of *just* international life.

This reunification leads to an extremely important consequence. It undermines one of the traditional prejudices of international relations analysis: namely, that the elaboration of foreign policy completely – or almost completely – eludes the control of the ruled.[42] Empirical analysis appears to suggest that this prejudice has now been largely overcome for reasons that are easy to understand even in general terms. It may suffice to note the number of times public opinion has intervened in foreign policy decisions taken by states over the last few years,[43] while it is also worth remembering that the justification for prejudice does not derive from intrinsic reasons, but from the cunning of rulers (who are blatantly less democratic than they would like to appear) and also from the poor coverage which the media used to (and continue to?)

reserve for international problems, an object more of condemnation and execration than of news, debate and comment. The 'ruler–ruled' relationship ought instead to feel the weight of the ruled's responsibility to formulate judgements on the ruler's external conduct – which must not infringe the principle of non-interference in other states' affairs.[44] The latter, in turn, must not have priority over the violation of general principles of equal value for all citizens, hence for all states. A regime's level of democracy does not depend exclusively on the domestic components of political life, but embodies external components too, transforming or, better still, widening the horizons of democracy itself.

3 JUSTICE: INTERNATIONAL, INTERSTATE AND COSMOPOLITAN

With this reconstitution of the logical unity of citizens, their state and other states,[45] international morality may be founded on the conception that judgement of a state depends on its treatment of human beings, and that judgement of the human being[46] depends on his relationship with the state as an institution – his own but all others as well. This formulation is strictly linked to a principle of reciprocity: just as the state must be fair towards other states, so its citizens must be fair towards the citizens of other states. In other words, both the state and its citizens must foster equity in both domestic and international political life. This is not to suggest that justice is possible in relations between states only with reference to individuals, although this position is the one most commonly adopted in philosophical analysis (which sometimes ignores the existence of *states* altogether) and is largely to demonstrate the untenability of any theory of justice applied to the international realm. In abstract terms, it is possible to speak of justice at various levels: with regard to individuals in their reciprocal relations; with regard to states in their reciprocal relations; and, finally, with regard to a state's relations with citizens, nationals and foreigners alike.[47] Moreover, any theory of international justice must needs be *global* in view of the multiplicity of levels it has to embrace.[48] Before exploring this particular aspect, however, let us attempt to outline the different positions that have been taken on the problem.

Broadly speaking, it is possible to link international justice to the notion of international law. In as much as 'justice as a moral concept is not concerned to prescribe ends but only to govern their pursuit',[49] international justice must fit into the consolidated legal practice produced by the fact that no state may live in isolation, nor can it make the many opportunities it has for external contacts materialize without following legal rules.[50] Since (and rightly so) the most important material problem highlighted by cosmopolitan formulations (which consider individuals as opposed to, or instead of states, even in the international realm) regards the observance by states of a series of minimal conditions in their treatment of individuals (the question of democracy emerges powerfully yet again), the most realistic approach is to found the respect for human rights 'in the common rules of conduct governing the society of states, that is, in international law'.[51] The argument focuses on the ability of the community or society produced by the historical development of international law to promote the reforms necessary to adjust existing standards to the demands for greater equity advanced by states disadvantaged by centuries of legal (as well as material) inequality. It would not be difficult, in principle, to accept this type of proposition, provided that states actually demonstrated their willingness to share the globalist, unitary sensitiveness and goodwill required to rebalance relations which, historically speaking, have always been extremely asymmetrical.[52] Without this goodwill, can states still concern themselves progressively with their neighbours? If the answer is yes, this means that they do adopt one empirical principle: that of intervention at least in situations with which they cannot help but be acquainted.[53]

Although from the point of view argued in this book – namely that states and individuals share a series of moral obligations with regard to the natural rights of individuals (of all individuals, compatriots and foreigners alike) – the 'proximity' argument on its own is unacceptable, the force of the opposite argument, normally used to refute the doctrine of universal duties, appears (at least from the empirical point of view) anything but slight. It may be summarized in the 'lifeboat' image used by G. Hardin and O. O'Neill (Bruce Ackerman also resorts to it in one of his dialogues between passengers in a spaceship),[54] a dramatic simile in which the rich (survivors in the lifeboat) are surrounded by other survivors who will die if they are not brought on board. Yet if they were saved, the boat would capsize and rich and poor would all die together! Referring the image to population policy, it appears anything but abstract. As Hardin observes, the disproportion between the number of people born poor and people born rich is growing constantly:[55] in other words, the simile increasingly bears a striking resemblance to reality. Yet the plausibility of these conclusions prompts a number of observations.[56] First of all, as O'Neill points out, it is precisely the persuasive force of this simile which ought to lead the rich to promote population and food policies different from those currently being implemented (for the problem is not one of a lack of food in the world, but of how to distribute it), at least in observance of the right of human beings not to be killed.[57] Singer develops the point by arguing that, even if we accept Hardin's consequentialist viewpoint, the politics of 'refusal' entails a very great evil – namely, population control by famine and disease – and that millions of people would thus die a slow death.[58] By defusing the 'demographic bomb', commitment to aid for the world's needy would ultimately benefit not only the poor but also the rich.

From the point of view of the fundamental equality of birthrights, it is possible to make two more observations; the first from the point of view of the rich, the second from that of the poor (that is, in terms of how they might counter the rich). In the first case, one asks the following questions. (1) How is it that only one part of humanity has managed to climb into the lifeboat? Only the rich have been able to book their passage, and they have done so with the money they have acquired by exploiting the poor. Even if we leave aside the question of compensation (for the reasons already explained), the fact remains that the success of their exploitation in the past does not automatically give them the 'right of way'. Applying primitive equitable logic, this if anything would oblige them to offer their seats to the poor. (2) Is it really true that we are not all in the the same boat together? One might argue against this that the progressive interpenetration of the different regions of the world makes the image of the separation between classes (some passengers on board, others rejected) unrealistic. Even more conspicuous is that to date it has been the rich themselves who have pushed the poor on board – in return for their services! And so, on closer examination, wasn't the appeal to uniqueness and interdependence one of the background arguments on which the theory of reciprocal deterrence rested, when the balance of terror was preached as the only alternative to total destruction of the planet?

Let us now move over to the other side, the one which asks the rich for help. It argues that (1) the poor may, in the first place, claim the right to reappropriate natural resources, as well as to exploit and market them freely.[59] If they so wished, the rich could help to redistribute benefits among the poor; and even if they were to do this, they would not be pushed out of the boat, for the poor are aware that they cannot survive by themselves. (2) The poor actually possess great blackmailing power since they could, if they wished, sabotage the lifeboat, causing it to sink and dragging the rich down with them to a common (and, at last, unitary!) destiny. This risk, which is anything but unfounded,[60] plainly has a much more devastating potential than the rebalancing of wealth, which would of course ultimately reduce the privileges of the rich. Despite its limitations, the lifeboat argument provides a rather effective picture of the problem. Only if the latter can be framed in the context of *just* international politics will it be possible if not to solve it, at least to address it and assess its full significance – which is much greater than the example alone might suggest. Simile or no simile, the lifeboat represents our planet and, whether we like it or not, we are all on board,[61] as the development of the international economy (with all its asymmetries) and the problem of peace by threat have demonstrated, and which the ecological problem has highlighted even more frankly and unequivocally. The handling of the problems of the Amazon rain forests is no longer (if it ever was)[62] the *reserved dominion* – the most sacred of sovereignty's traditional prerogatives – of Brazil, simply because the consequences of deforestation have in practice spread all over the planet. Likewise, the trawling of the shoals of fish which migrate southwards from Greenland is not a private affair between Denmark and Iceland (the sea-going nations closest to the area of sea in question) but also affects at least Great Britain, which risks seeing no fish at all reach its coastal waters.[63] It is possible to fit similar considerations to the different forms of pollution which industrial development or technological decisions have procured (Chernobyl *docet*), which is why the conservation of healthy living conditions is rapidly turning into the gravest problem humanity has ever had to collectively address on a world scale.[64]

The ecological question exemplifies more than just the conclusion of the process of world unification and the common destiny of every individual on this earth. What emerges most is the specificity of the issue. Unless we acknowledge the state's central role as a pivot or keystone in the reality of the planet, the problem would appear to be absolutely intractable. In short, the state is the only single tool (today, at least) technically equipped to address the collective problems of humanity. The problem is no longer to seek separate solutions for local problems, but solutions that regard all states and all citizens. The only comparable precedent is that of wars, but even world wars, like great epidemics or plagues, invariably fail to transcend the local dimension. Proof of the *difference*? It may seem self-evident but its scope is enormous: in fact, for the first time since states have existed, reciprocal interest seeks no longer to favour one side against the other, but addresses globality. (Remember that for centuries when one state intervened in the affairs of another its sole aim was to destabilize it – through secret or underground support to one faction against another or against the government, to one party rather than another and so on.)[65] Now for the first time in history,[66] we have proof of the existence of universal conditions: the ecological issue highlights the even chances of living of every member of humanity. In other words, the passengers in the lifeboat can no longer be divided into different classes, so that the 'quality of life' issue can no longer be reduced to the local, specific problems of given categories or groups. What better proof than this of the fact that a framework of equality – albeit as yet badly distributed – has now been imposed on the world?[67]

Boundaries, borders, frontiers and differences are changing, and as they change they lose their traditional meaning. It is now possible at last to create *natural* contacts and bonds between bodies that were once distinct. We are even witnessing the formation of 'a contemporary society which is global twice over: since it occupies the whole earth, as solid as a block thanks to the crossover of its interrelations, it no longer has loose change to spend. . . . It knows on the other hand how to build and utilize technical means of spatial, temporal, energetic dimensions of the world's phenomena. Our collective power thus reaches the limits of the global habitat. We are beginning to resemble the Earth.'[68] The totalizing, all-encompassing nature of the ecological question consequently makes any utilitarian argument founded solely on the duty of proximity obsolete,[69] since what is at stake now is a principle and not a psychological sentiment, a judgement of unity and sharing and not of personal and social preference.[70]

The most complete antithesis to the restriction of international problems of justice to local situations is the cosmopolitan formulation, which, as we shall see below, may be right to criticize the narrowness of the localist view, but ultimately goes too far in the opposite direction and loses its capacity to refer to the real world (as opposed to a dream world). On a largely contractarian basis, much indebted to Rawls's abstract contractualism in section 58 of *A Theory of Justice*,[71] C. Beitz (who actually regards Rawls's discussion as incomplete in important respects) founds his justification of the relevance of a theory of (distributive) international justice on 'the observation . . . that international relations is coming more and more to resemble domestic society in several respects relevant to the justification of principles of (domestic) social justice'[72] (a position very close to the one I have maintained in this book). It is from this observation that he draws his conclusion: 'International distributive principles establish the terms on which persons in distinct societies can fairly expect each other's cooperation in common institutions and practices.'[73] If we eliminate the state and replace it with more than one society, we still fail to avoid the difficulty involved in an individualistic–cosmopolitan image of international life: for if citizens do not effectively recognize themselves in this image, it is hard to understand how, with no directive bodies, they can try to build it and accept intrinsically just redistributive principles. If contractarian theory provides an extremely persuasive reconstruction of the birth of the state, how can we transpose this model by analogy to an international life peopled by individuals, each of whom struggles – as natural contractualism highlighted so clearly – to apply criteria of justice? It is true that

> although today this federation of states appears only a rough idea, a presentiment is emerging in all members interested in conserving the whole, and this raises hopes that, after some revolutionary crisis of transformation, the supreme end of nature will finally surge up, that is a general *cosmopolitan order*, the matrix in which all the original dispositions of the human species develop.[74]

But it is clearly difficult for the time being to demonstrate that the transformation hypothesized by Kant has already taken place. In reality, the cosmopolitan formulation merely abolishes (without replacing it) the distinction between states and individuals, which, if it were feasible, would leave the way wide open for a definition of principles of justice. In this way, however, justice would no longer apply to states and would still not apply to individuals, so it would have to apply to the international system as it stands.

The extremism of this formulation pushes us back to the opposite solution (only apparently a 'compromise') defended by S. Hoffmann who, after equitably acknowledging that international justice is a question of both states and individuals,[75] suggests we make do with an eclectic conception which strives to do what it can with moderation, observing the rules of prudence as opposed to those of morality.[76] Whereby, alas, we would plummet back to the realistic formulation, which governed the formation of the world as we know it today – unjust and unsympathetic towards international justice!

4 INTERNATIONAL JUSTICE MIDWAY BETWEEN ETHICS AND POLITICS

In any case, the cosmopolitan formulation highlights the minimal prerequisites for any theory of justice seeking to comprise the society of states, which 'have duties toward individuals as well as toward other states'. Hence:

> The essential element of cosmopolitan justice in the circumstances produced by the state system is the idea of an international minimum *standard*

to be observed by states in their treatment of individuals, regardless of whether these are their own nationals or those of another country.[77]

We shall thus assume, first of all, that the application of criteria of justice is aimed (materially and effectively) at individuals but also that, *without* the mediation of the state, no justice can be really achieved. In other words, justice is an interindividual fact but is regulated by states. To the point that, to date, precious little international justice has been witnessed in the world, one might counter with the psychological, impressionistic argument that it no longer appears as irrelevant as it used to be to talk about it. Perhaps this is due to the reduced frequency with which states resort to warfare, perhaps to a certain growth in democracy within many states and in relations between them, or perhaps, finally, to the mutation[78] which has taken place in international life as a consequence of the advent of 'the weapons of the end of the world' and the process of globalization and interconnection typical of contemporary living. All of which tells us nothing about the content of justice, but justifies our attempt to delineate its minimal principles, now that we are aware that, in any case, it can no longer be the object only of 'national', but also of totally impartial global reflection; not because justice theories in the past did not seek to have universal scope, but because now it is the very life of states which has been made 'boundless'. Hence, if for centuries the only form of justice known was war, the outcome of which produced the only redistribution possible,[79] today the impartial unification of the destiny of the citizens and states of the planet gives us the full measure of the gap that has opened up between the hypothetical initial condition (the original state of nature of international life) and the present one. And it enables us to recognize systematically the principles which might inspire a just international life (albeit imperfectly), in which there are no longer barriers between domestic and international, local and global justice, and hence between domestic and international politics.

What situations must a possible theory of justice fit into? Let us imagine that we have to take a position on one of the most serious and important problems facing contemporary society: drugs and their system of world distribution. The facts are that, on the one hand, (1) many young people take drugs, thereby fuelling drug production and the drug market; (2) drugs originate chiefly from southern Asia and Latin America. On the other hand, concerned by the harm provoked by drugs, (3) the governments of many countries want to stop the drug trade; (4) the governments of many drug-producing countries (often extremely poor and governed by absolutist oligarchies) want to maintain their drug production, since it has become their only source of local wealth. Faced with this situation, our first consideration is that drug consumption is evil because it causes irreversible physical damage and (like arms!) provokes premature death. Elementary humanitarian principles ought, therefore, to make states put a stop to the drug market. But in this situation a number of dual relationships are at work: between the governments of drug-producing countries and those of drug-consuming countries;[80] between the populations of drug-producing countries and sectors of the population in the many drug-consuming countries; between governments in abolitionist countries and foreign citizens who produce or trade in drugs; between each government and those of its citizens who take drugs; between the governments of the drug-producing nations and drug consumers throughout the world. The issue's multiplicity of facets make it an excellent example of the complexity of the problems which a theory of justice would have to address. Domestic and international aspects, which in their political and social diversity are inextricably intertwined, implicate heterogeneous actors and subjects at various different levels of power and responsibility. Is it just, therefore, for one or more states to intervene outside their own boundaries (as the United States have done in Colombia) to stop the production, hence the distribution, of drugs? If outside commandos destroy crops, this will progressively impoverish the populations for whom they were once a staple source of income: it will also violate one of the most sacrosanct principles of international law – the inviolability of frontiers. And it is extremely unlikely that intervention in only one drug-producing country would suffice to dismantle the international market anyway! Other similar cases raise similar questions, albeit less dramatically. For example, why not intervene, militarily if need be, to stop the devastation of the Amazon rain forests, or to ban CFC gases, pollutant industrial waste and so on? Or why not intervene to destroy the toxic gas factories that are being built in countries in Africa or nuclear weapons plants everywhere?

Is it possible to get out of this fix and still conserve some principle internationally recognizable as *just*? The pre-condition for success is of course the conceptualization of international life as a consolidated entity with a *constitution* of its own, something resembling the constitutions of single states. This may in turn give rise to a set of general rules and standards for coexistence (whether they are consensual and democratic or not is an altogether different and, at this point in the argument, irrelevant matter). The constitution would be based on a fundamental, preliminary condition; that the subjective differences of its various recipients be considered relatively immaterial, just as a debate on a state's domestic constitution does not specify – unless there are conspicuous disproportions – the varying status of individuals. That a wealthy capitalist is relatively incomparable with a tramp does not upset the arrangement of the bourgeois–democratic state; the type of state, that is, which, comparatively speaking, has always offered most guarantees for the individual as such. It is also important to remember that my argument does not purport to locate the forms of international justice that exist in practice, but simply to enunciate them in the abstract. As any normative system demonstrates, practice is a different matter again.

Excluding the possibility that there can be effective domestic justice unconnected with international justice, we see the development of a series of hierarchically linked concentric circles: the first generating the second and so on. Once the series is complete, *it might* transform both political life among states and the political life of states.

1 *Overriding anarchy*: the idea that the international system is made up of states that are peremptorily and perfectly sovereign, among which the only relations are relations of alliance and hostility, of peace and of war, is unacceptable (not to say outdated).

2 *Tendential repudiation of the use of interstate violence*: war is a state's last, not its first or only, resort if it wishes to take the law into its own hands.

3 *Interstate pluralism*: states have neither a civilizing nor an emancipating mission in their intercourse with others (mutual respect is thus not merely functional to alliance but also acknowledges the alterity and liberty of the most diverse forms of organization).

4 *Democratization of the international system*: states are prepared to coexist, if they mutually recognize the equal prerogatives, rights and duties both of their own nationals and of foreign citizens.

5 *Collective acceptance of elementary principles of equity*: respect of the fundamental rights of individuals, wherever they are and regardless of their citizenship, with consequent slackening of boundaries – the international circulation of individuals, the promotion of a sort of 'racial confusion' (of which today's migration problems are a spontaneous, if disorderly, harbinger).

Were these five hypotheses to be endorsed and practised *de facto* by the states coexisting on planet earth at any given instant (and since none of them entails the abolition of the normal prerogatives of state sovereignty), we would have to verify whether they offered any pointers for assessment of the example presented earlier. Is it *just* to stop the drug traffic (with all its various ramifications)? *Must* forests be protected internationally? *Must* poison gas factories be destroyed? Let us see how the five principles described above act in relation to the different configurations of state–individual relations implied in these three cases. The relations at stake concern: (1) states in their reciprocal relations; (2) each state both in relation to its own nationals and with the citizens of one or more other countries (an original, innovative aspect this precisely because, as I explained above, it is one of humanity's collective duties to guarantee fundamental individual rights, wherever necessary); (3) relations between the citizens of different countries.

Except in the first case, the relations we are dealing with here are vertical (state with citizens) or crossed (citizens of one state with another state or vice versa). They embrace the examples both of the drug trade and deforestation, and in them the fifth principle of justice (which in so far as it is the most specific follows from the first four and hence presupposes them) suggests we approve the conduct of all states and citizens that take action to prevent or interrupt harmful conduct (producing and selling drugs, speculative deforestation and so on). In the case of the poison gas or nuclear weapon factory, the relationship is a prevalently horizontal, state-to-state one. It is unlikely, however, that only one state would be opposed – many might be. Hence, albeit horizontal, the relationship would also be top-heavy (and the fact that international public opinion would most likely be opposed would also carry weight). Here, however, we would not be applying a complete version of justice, but only the one that envisages acceptance of the principle of pluralism (which of course precludes the production of harmful gases) and which confides in the weight of world public opinion to delegitimize the action of the producer state. Didn't news about the famous gas factory in Libya or the discovery of an international network of cannon manufacturers trigger something similar to this? It is possible to summarize the reasoning in a general formula: since global (or, better still, unlimited) justice concerns both states and citizens, the fundamental principle of the protection and promotion of the wellbeing of citizens (which is the aim of the state, anywhere and on any grounds) is the value that it is *just* to assert, along with the right to survive of any existing state (although not necessarily any type of government).[81] A more muted version of justice will apply instead whenever the violation of the same principles is attributable only to states, in which case sovereignty continues to exert its influence, even though it is no longer either absolute or indiscriminate.

Wouldn't it have been possible to reach the same conclusions by appealing simply to the general principles of public international law, not to mention the content of the different international conventions now recognized by the overwhelming majority of states? In reality, the elements of justice listed here imply a series of duties for states and citizens in which positive international law cannot – as yet – intervene. We must not forget that the practical consequence of the acceptance of some principles of justice is the moral duty to intervene to stop the production and marketing of drugs (in Columbia, Turkey, Burma and elsewhere), to block deforestation in the Amazon jungle, to have factories observe rigorous anti-pollution standards and so on. The question of power is not at stake here. I am not disputing the fact that the United States have the power to cut off sources of drugs in Columbia, or that Columbia is in no position to argue with foreign interference in its domestic affairs. What I am questioning is whether it is possible to excuse the state which violates the sovereignty of another to save human lives and not the state which, observing positive law standards, fails to protect personal rights. Hasn't the Columbian government the duty to fight without quarter against drug producers? In turn, the right/duty to intervene exceeds the limits of traditional international aid simply because – again using the example of Columbian drug production – it is not enough to destroy crops to produce justice: it is also necessary to offer more acceptable, non-harmful sources of income to those who have avoided death by starvation by producing drugs. Another problem (which follows on from the last, but which I shall not discuss here) regards the possible realization of these principles by authoritarian imposition. Can this take place through slow but relentless progress? One thing is certain: the very nature of international problems rules out the possibility of unilateral solutions. If questions of pollution and redistribution of resources are extremely clear-cut examples of the fact, so is international life. It is precisely for this reason that states are not barred from morality. They have the possibility of addressing common problems jointly. On the rules (few to date) which they have used to regulate their mutual relations, states might at last build a morally acceptable international policy.

Are the principles we are speaking of here only suitable for situations of peace, contexts far removed from the predominant reality of international life? If we attempt to compare this model with the 'legalist paradigm' proposed by M. Walzer in *Just and Unjust Wars* – which consists basically of the idea that only when a state is a victim of aggression is it and/or the international community justified in reacting violently and punishing the aggressor[82] – it is possible to observe just how distant the two are. Walzer's is a *minimal* proposition in as much as it rules out the possibility of justifying principles except in the case (fundamental but not unique) of war, whereas mine seeks to embrace the political and social scope which results from the multidimensional interaction of the contemporary international realm. More precisely, the international system encompasses a set of interactions – among individuals, groups, states, international and supranational bodies and so on – so complex that the reduction of international life to the alternation of peace and war would now appear to be *a thing of the past*. This way of reasoning fitted a problematic world that no longer exists.

Recognition of the boundlessness of the world today is crucial if we are to formulate judgements on international relations; that is, on an immense system of billions of individuals and almost 200 states, no longer schematically confined to the interplay of alliances or military politics, but now in wholehearted pursuit of the fundamental laws of coexistence. States must no longer be viewed in splendid isolation or independence, but as elements in a larger system, the internal conditions of which are not the sum-total of single contributions. The collective problems of humanity transcend single states, which would encounter insurmountable difficulties if they were to act on their own. Recognition of the fact that destinies (from peace to war) are shared is the *sine qua non* for acceptance of collective compromises and agreements, simply because only the concerted and coherent action of all states (here we see the great importance of states in their present arrangement) as a sort of moral community may permit appreciable improvements in the conditions of international life and, of course, in ecology, the defence of human rights, weapon reduction and the redistribution of resources among rich and poor countries. Only if they are civilized can international relations be moralized.

If we accept these conclusions, we upset the customary image of international relations founded on three possible levels of analysis: in the words of the title of one of the most famous studies on the subject, the man, the state and the war (or anarchy, or the international system according to theoretical tendency).[83] The 'true international' is supposedly the supporter of the third level since he believes that any event that crosses the borders of a state and consequently crosses at least one other border can be explained neither from the point of view of the single agent nor from that of the state, but only in terms of international political reality (hence the domestic reality of states as well), seen as an overall, unitary system (whether its organization is anarchic or systematic is a question that comes later). The results which exploration of international ethics have achieved now question this cornerstone of international theory.[84] As we have seen, the system of international justice rests on the inseparability of our judgements on the individual and on the state (the only two material realities of international life, for the system is a concept, an organizational instrument, but not a fact). Their conduct cannot therefore be split, as if they belonged to two different realms. Individuals join together in states, states join together in international societies.[85] If there were no communication between them, it would be absolutely impossible to judge their respective actions, and there would be no contact between domestic and international politics, between domestic and international justice, between ethical theory for the state and ethical theory for states. At which point, the results would appear to be totally false! Yet the uniqueness of the various problems will not disappear. What will fall will be the artificial barriers which prevented us from addressing a reality that has proved more complex but also more fascinating than we believed.

7

Conclusion

Of the gods we believe, and of men we know, that by a necessary law of their nature they rule wherever they can. And it is not as if we were the first to make this law, or to act upon it when made: we found it existing before us, and shall leave it to exist for ever after us; all we do is to make use of it, knowing that you and everybody else, having the same power as we have, would do the same as we do.

Thucydides, *The History of the Peloponnesian War*

1 THE ARGUMENT

It is possible to trace the roots of more than two millennia of international politics to the celebrated words used by the Athenians to explain the irresistible allure of power politics to the Melians. Well nigh a thousand wars have been fought between then and now as a dramatic testament to the truth of what they had to say.[1] Their message, however, is diametrically opposed to this book's pursuit of the conditions under which it might become possible to speak of ethics in international relations (albeit justifying the possibility rather than explaining the content). In my programme, I have dispensed with the classic intellectual baggage of international relations theory, grounded as it is in the heritage left by Thucydides. At the same time, however, I have been unable to appeal to the findings of autonomous philosophical studies, since the latter concern themselves prevalently, though not only, with the domestic, state-centric sphere of ethics. We have thus travelled through a sort of no man's land, reconnoitring unexplored territory – that of the duties of states. International studies have always explored the rights of states, while philosophical studies have often overlooked the possibility that subjects other than citizens might be recipients of rights and duties. However, the relevance of this theme is no mere legacy of humanity's progress as it organized itself into states, or the fortunate, fortuitous consequence of an age of unforeseen (although intermittent and uncertain) international peace. It is justified by the very nature of the relations of states; that is, by the fact that their coexistence will inevitably produce rules of conduct derived not from the strength of their respective claims but from reciprocal recognition, hence from a shared destiny, as well as from the fundamental duty of states towards individuals, irrespective of their citizenship. Nonetheless, now that, on the one hand, wars have acquired the potential capacity to destroy the whole world and, on the other, original conditions of peace reign in much of the world, international ethics might generate fresh, autonomous progress in the life of states. In a certain, almost paradoxical, sense, unexpectedly and regardless of the forecasts of federalism, world peace has thus been achieved on the basis of the general, universal sharing of the *same* conditions of survival and organization of social life. Acceptance of this argument is not devoid of prescriptive implications; for it signifies that peace must nevertheless be preferred to war, and that extraordinary modifications must then be made to the morality of states. An unforeseeably high contribution is being made today by the assertion of new rules of international coexistence that would have been unimaginable only ten years ago. The increased sense of *responsibility* which states feel in their relations with each another and with their citizens also fosters the democratization of international and domestic political life. We do not know, nor can we assess today, what consequences the progressive concurrence of economic–political regimes – until yesterday so different as to be, in many cases, incompatible – will have on international order. For the moment at least, the process seems likely to help the *civilization*[2] of international life, pushing it closer to the standard reached by most of the world's states. Who can forget the way in which this optimistic picture was suddenly and drastically marred by the Gulf conflict, which cast the world back into the war spiral once more? Has the progress described above been interrupted already? Since we have no proof either one way or another, let us try in this conclusion to reconnect politics and war, facts and moral judgement. My argument thus turns full circle: can we subject states to ethical judgement?

2   ON THE APPLICABILITY OF PRINCIPLES OF INTERNATIONAL JUSTICE

It would be hard to deny that in the course of the last few years the quality of international life has changed in a basically positive way. The role of violence, domestic and international, has declined (although it would be wrong to forget or erase the misdeeds of the not so recent past). Wars, *coups d'état*, abuses of power and violations of international law have not disappeared altogether, but they have grown rarer and rarer. That the analysis of international democracy has increased in importance over the last few years is not a product of chance, but of the widespread sensation that the standards of international life are changing. As a result, scholars are devoting more and more attention to the issue, and an attempt is being made to override the conception of international life simply as a repetition of its domestic counterpart. The state not only expresses the will of individuals and of its nationals, but also represents them externally.[3] However a ruler achieves power inside a state, he assumes a dual representative role: he represents citizens before state authority and the state itself in its intercourse with all other states. The relationship between ruler and ruled does not stop at state boundaries: it crosses them.[4] Whether a government is capable or not of reconciling the requests and interests of the diverse groups which interact in the domestic political arena, it must, nonetheless, offer a unitary image of itself when it performs on the international stage. Does this lead to the idea that, on the international stage, each state finds itself in a situation to some degree analogous to that of the citizen within it (although whereas the representation of citizens takes the form of a legal authority, that of states does not give rise to anything that is formally comparable)?

Albeit devoid of legal legitimation, there has always been an 'international government'; from the supremacy of Charles V to the long period of British hegemony, from the Concert of Europe in the first half of the last century to the quasi-legal government of the United States and the former Soviet Union over the last 40 years and more. In no case has this form of 'spontaneous government' assumed the form that regime formation ought to inspire: namely, equality among all parties to collective government. Self-government has always been basically a *hetero*-government founded on subordination, on daily relations of inequality produced by its own superiority. It has derived its strength either from more highly developed forms of social organization (colonial exploitation) or from the outcomes of direct military confrontation between equally developed states (great wars). Hence the argument that the fracture between domestic and international politics cannot be healed. Although both realities originate from the recourse to force and violence, in the case of the first, historical evolution seems to have led to the progressive annulment of the right to use force, or the replacement of violence with nonviolent procedures, whereas this has not (nor could have) happened in the case of the second.

Can we continue to accept the idea that there is no contact between the two worlds? The fact is that in international as in domestic life, no event can be regarded as ethically irrelevant, even though domestic life is richer and more composite, and hence tends to allow citizens (and also their authorities) a sphere of autonomy and indifference that is not to be found in international life, which is in turn *basic*, and in a certain sense, *intermittent* (given that events of great scope are not produced there at every moment). Yet this is no reason to consider international life primitive. It is instead original and unique (besides being, at least at the present day, unitary). Everything to do with the relations of states has to do with the fortunes and misfortunes of citizens. Since everything is basic, nothing can be irrelevant: hence the need for an ethic of international relations. Since we all judge, let us express our justifications and defend them if necessary, but let us never consider them either unquestionable or, worse still, superfluous. This leads to a consequence of considerable methodological relevance: namely, that domestic and international politics can no longer be studied distinctly, each in its own autonomous sphere. The age of the prevalence, of the alleged explicative authority, of the one over the other, has now come to an end. The two political spheres are indissolubly intertwined and must be restored to substantial unity. Which does not of course mean that the student of political parties has to search out international objects to apply his knowledge to directly, nor that the international coalitions theorist can address government coalitions directly. Levels of analysis, objects of knowledge and specialization are not in question here. What is being challenged is prejudice against the qualitative difference between the two spheres. If this prejudice ceases to exist, new and original programmes of research and theoretical hypothesis may be proposed in this, a territory until recently unexplored, which is now generating extraordinary explicative potential.

The reasons why, for some years, a number of countries supported a punitive trade policy against South Africa, guilty of implementing an odious racial policy at home, are admirable (if they are sincere) and evidently acceptable. But it is vital to stress also that states which refused to sell arms to South Africa for humanitarian reasons should have been (morally) coherent enough to apply the same criteria not only in their domestic sphere but also in their relations with other countries. This, of course, is something which rarely happens. And, more generally, is the arms trade, very often accompanied and backed by thriving contraband, always permissible, as if arms were a commodity like any other? Market freedom must have some limit somewhere: to produce and push drugs, to make and sell arms are not actions conducive to improving the conditions of life of the purchaser! If a person sells arms in good faith, can he be sure that he is not being deceived? Can he have any influence on the way the purchaser uses the arms?[5] It is even harder to justify other types of conduct by states (when fundamental rights are not at stake), which stem from the judgement they formulate on other countries, and in particular on their regimes. This has traditionally been a reserved domain for each sovereign state (provided it did not violate fundamental human rights). It is precisely conduct of this type which one notes in Italian decree law number 65 of 26 March 1990, on the basis of which Italy allocated 127 billion lire 'to *support the process or liberalization* of the Polish economy' (article 1: my italics).[6] Italy thus declared itself prepared to come to the rescue of a foreign country in distress. This is all well and good, but the problems of Poland were born yesterday, not today. Why was humanitarian aid, denied to citizens in a communist state, granted as soon as they embarked on a 'process of liberalization'? If we change our regime, are we entitled to be judged differently? Support for *a certain* Poland has ideological justifications, but this is not a moral argument. Can I influence the survival of a foreign citizen only if he agrees with me, only if he shares the same political values? My intention here is not to condemn Italian aid to Poland in 1990,[7] but to endeavour to understand why Italy (or any other western country, for that matter) did not feel the duty to help Poland before. More generally speaking, I wish to raise the problem of international solidarity, which cannot be subordinated to the closeness of relations between regimes, but should be geared to the effective and dramatic needs of far-off populations – such as those of the Sahel, for example. The scope of the humanitarian or charitable conduct of the more fortunate states towards the less privileged is an initial, fundamental testing ground for so-called *international morality*. If this exists, it will have to be supplemented in the near future by collective commitment towards what the newspapers describe as the ecological or environment problem. Yes, for the first time in history, all the world's governments and populations have joined together in this common struggle: for, in the present conditions of industrial and technological growth, it would be unthinkable to safeguard the collective goods of humanity through individual or partial initiatives alone.[8]

There is of course a conspicuous difference between my two examples. Italian aid to Poland is aid from one state to another, whereas the aid Italy sends to the peoples of the Sahel is aid not to a state, but to citizens – humanitarian aid. The first aims to consolidate a respected regime, the second to help unknown people survive. The first derives from ideological reasons, the second from reasons of principle (the

whole immense question of North–South relations is obviously bound
up in the example). Regardless of the result of aid (if, that is, it is
sufficient to improve the conditions of the people who receive it), the
two types of conduct are motivated by very different justifications. It is
necessary to acknowledge that motivations of an ideological nature
seem stronger (though not juster) than humanitarian ones, simply because humanitarianism (if that is what it is) cannot be intermittent. It
must be continuous and systematic; it must leave its mark on a situation.
Since, as we know, this has never happened to date, we are forced to
conclude that international humanitarian aid has never been more than
charity.[9] When, instead, the justification is ideological, its motivation
appears much clearer and easier to accept. It is every state's wish to be
surrounded by friendly neighbours, governed by analogous, ideologically
consonant institutions. If we help them to survive, we help and reassure
ourselves. The most fortunate states act in a utilitarian fashion, but in
doing so they do not improve the world (although it is true that they
might be able to help the poorest even without losing their own
wellbeing). But the true lesson to be learnt here regards the fact that
states can no longer reason as states:[10] they simply cannot allow egoistic
motivations to prevail over humanitarian ones. They can no longer
justify their particularistic reasons with talk of 'sacred egoism' or the
need to survive, for such reasons are patently the fruit of ideological
assessments, of value choices which, as such, are criticizable. Not only
does the institution of the state exist, it also continues to appear very
solid. A radical new alternative to it is as yet nowhere to be seen. Which
is why it is with the conduct of states that international ethics must
concern itself, avoiding simplistic criticism of their cosmopolitan in-
sensitiveness and the consequent impossibility of a foundation for international morality.

3   TESTING THE FACTS WITH NORMATIVE ANALYSIS

It is unthinkable for all the minimum principles of international justice
discussed in the previous chapter to be effective in situations other than
one of substantial or prevalent peace: for that matter it would be unthinkable even within a single state. I have assumed the existence of
such a situation as the tacit precondition for my argument. Without this
assumption, it would have been impossible even to present the problem,
although (as I have made clear from the outset) my intention has been
simply to defend the plausibility of the international ethical argument,
not to claim that international life *per se* should be inspired by moral

criteria. Sweeping, largely nonviolent transformations in eastern Europe, which led, in turn, to an equally peaceful, unforeseen mutation of the framework of the international system, seemed to lend weight to my proposal. Then, out of the blue, a dramatic new large-scale conflict – the Gulf war – set the the world on fire again. Its prelude, which began on 2 August 1990, was a disturbing repeat of the *drôle de guerre* model, while the war proper broke out on 17 January 1991 and lasted for roughly 40 days. The 'dizziness of war' – the object, in the past, of R. Caillois's disquieting reflections[11] – seems to have swept away all hope or prospect of the international harmony which ought to have ensued from the overriding of the hierarchical foundation of the international order.

War demands certainties: it is the struggle of good against evil. It cleaves the world in two, dividing friends and turning them into foes. Only the victory of one over the other can reunite them. War causes death, pain, hatred, destruction, the lust for revenge. Has all – peace, order, the promise of justice – been lost for good now? From a multiplicity of different points of view, the Gulf war seemed to herald significant innovations.[12] Never before had such shared, joint, direct and collective commitment been harnessed to avoiding war and, once war broke out, to framing it within a legal context. Although good intentions were eventually drowned in a spiral of violence, this was undoubtedly the most concerted effort ever made by the international community to emerge from anarchy (to return to the formula I used to draw the first of the concentric circles of international justice).[13] The United Nations' Organization's function as a superior parliament within which any controversy must be presented and discussed was recognized (alas, too late), and the most intense diplomatic exchanges ever witnessed were entered into. *Iraq's conduct* – against the defenders of the established order[14] – *was reminiscent of that of the anarchist who acknowledges no authority, not that of someone acting in the anarchic state of nature.* Following the material violation of one state's sovereignty, many vain efforts were made to foster forms of non-military pressure – such as the trade blockade and the embargo – on the aggressor (the trend to dispense with violence was contained in my second circle). Arguably, they failed not only because Iraq possessed the capacity to resist, but also because they were violated on numerous occasions. They constituted, nonetheless, a model of nonviolent international pressure. Inspired by the third circle of international justice, the assertion that the anti-Iraq coalition's aim was not to affirm one culture's superiority over another,[15] but to safeguard a now *effectively* recognized principle (the right of self-order)[16] – which is, in turn, the prerequisite for any form of democratization of international life (my fourth circle) – does not appear to be unfounded.

Am I being too ingenuous here? War does appear to be a clear-cut feature of the history of humanity,[17] yet it would be wrong to overlook the unprecedented fact that, during the Gulf war, international public opinion (both of states and of citizens) interpreted an attack on one state by a larger, more powerful neighbour as an unjustifiable challenge to international order. The formation of states which, for months on end, opposed Iraq's invasion of Kuwait, really did appear determined to assert elementary principles of equity (my fifth circle).

Nevertheless, principles prevented neither war nor the ensuing massacre and devastation. Yet it is not their job to do so: principles serve to assess war and all it entails. As I suggested at the beginning of the book, I could not have developed my analysis without resorting to normative principles, and the ones I have identified allow us to make an assessment of the conduct effectively held by the sides at war. As a result, our considerations on the universal duties of states towards citizens the world over inevitably cloud our analysis of the United States' decision to protect the lives of its combatants through contempt for those of enemy citizens (not only soldiers but also civilians). The principle applies to all parties in the conflict, hence to Iraq as well, but is no less fundamental for all that. It was at the heart, 30 years ago, of the first ever large-scale philosophical controversy on nuclear war. Jasper's claim that the mere protection of life cannot be worth more than the defence of liberty from totalitarianism was countered by G. Anders and B. Russell, precisely on the grounds that value of life holds priority over quality of life.[18] As long as the material – not ideal – criterion of the organization of the planet into state-form is as widely adopted and shared as it is today, all governments will have the unconditional obligation to *reduce* the artificiality of the boundary concept by treating all individuals equally, wherever they come from, wherever they live. Of course this is also the circumstance which might justify the recourse to war. Even without making full use of the conceptual framework of the 'just war' doctrine, the classical distinction between the decision to make war and the way in which it is conducted ('jus ad bellum' and 'jus in bello') may apply. From the point of view argued thus far, the entry into war of a coalition of states (representative of a large part of the community of states) in defence of Kuwait would be justifiable.[19] The way in which military operations were conducted[20] must be analysed differently, in terms of their disproportion and indiscrimination[21]; for it is hard to deny that what we might term a *supererogatory* attitude was adopted on the battlefield, a way of using military necessities to justify the indiscriminate use of force against civilian populations. Are we to content ourselves with the success of military action? The United States' powerful war machine satisfactorily achieved the rational end of winning the war. Yet analysis cannot stop here. The wave of feeling which swept the world, when oil wells in the Persian Gulf were set on fire, demonstrates as much. Can any means be excused in the pursuit of the proposed end – victory? It is possible to answer the question on a series of counts. First, one might argue that it is impossible to justify war in the nuclear era. Secondly, one might refuse violence unconditionally. Thirdly, one might look for the answers by observing the facts and the circumstances. Let us examine the three possibilities, one by one.[22]

For over 30 years, the dominant strategic theory founded its exploration of the nature of reciprocal deterrence on *escalation*, which, by linking traditional war and nuclear war, generated the fear that any local conflict might conceal the epidemiological germ that would increase its scope and intensity beyond the conventional threshold. How did politicians react to such considerations? They responded that if there was effective continuity between the two types of conflict, the only solution was to avoid *both*. This was the official repressive-deterrent message conveyed to people all over the world. It was precisely its repressive function which, in the period of dominance of the nuclear duopoly, we criticized and condemned. Who could have imagined that the hypothesis of *escalation* would become more realistic in the Gulf war? In other words, it is necessary to reject the specialism of strategic justifications rather than seeking to counter them from the inside. This is probably the reason why a great many people motivated their opposition to the Gulf war in terms of an unconditional rejection of violence. The sole limit of this otherwise strong argument is that it is implausible. Are we really to believe that the justifications of 'peace at all costs' have been interiorized by such a large section of public opinion? There had been no sign of this before, after all. To condemn war and violence, when we are at their mercy, is understandable but insufficient. It is against this type of intermittent moral judgement that the whole of this book has been directed. While it is true that we pronounce judgements only as circumstances require, it is also true that, by necessity, such judgements are an expression of our most deep-rooted beliefs, or at least of the ones we will hold in the future. Can't the discovery of such widespread pacifism be regarded as an omen for the future?

Thus, all we have left is the third hypothesis, according to which – albeit amidst countless difficulties – we ought to seek to consider single cases, setting them in a general reference framework embracing both the nature of international politics, the differing political styles of states and the intrinsic quality of the facts. We should, in other terms, grow accustomed to scrutinizing international political affairs on a daily basis, without letting ourselves be deceived by their seemingly episodic nature. Much greater democratic control must be exercised over the interventions of single governments and over their liberty of action. (For example, shouldn't stricter checks be made on arms production and trading?) It would also be wrong not to consider the levels of democracy of domestic regimes. Although democratic regimes are not automatically peaceful (and the cohesion of US opinion on the Gulf war proves the point), there can be no doubt that the procedural obligation of public debate and discussion offer important tools for controlling and pressurizing public opinion. What distinguishes my application of the traditional justification of war is its relevance for *both* parties in the conflict. Normally, one party is justified and the other held totally responsible. I believe, instead, that in some cases war may be *unjust* on both sides.[23] Just as purely strategic arguments cannot be exploited to refute ethical assessments, so the observance of principles is compulsory at every stage in a conflict. The application of values cannot be deferred, neither in wars fought in the traditional age, nor in nuclear war, nor in wars fought traditionally in the nuclear age.[24] Is my application too legalistic or traditional?

Inspection of specific cases confines analysis to the facts. Not even the purest application of the nonviolent doctrine precludes some ultimate form of defence. This does not derive from the inevitability of war as such, but from the fact that it is but the last link in a chain. Just as nonviolence is an ongoing, daily discipline, not an occasional, impromptu stratagem, so the ethics of violence is a routine that is hard to break. If it is difficult to unravel the web of conditions, excuses and mitigating or aggravating circumstances which justify war, this neither derives from the nature of things nor can it spell failure for every programme of assessment. The simplistic conclusion that all wars are justified or, on the contrary, all unjustified or unjustifiable, does not follow from the exercising of free judgement but from undue narrowing of our field of vision. Paradoxical as it may seem, to apply 'just war' case history *only* to war is useless and sometimes misleading. In one of his less famous pages, Clausewitz helps us clarify the misunderstanding: 'War never breaks out wholly unexpectedly, nor can it be spread instantaneously. Each side can therefore gauge the other to a large extent by what he is and does, instead of judging him by what he, strictly speaking, ought to be or do.'[25] If war is not an isolated, self-contained act, but the continuation of policy by other means, shouldn't we apply our criteria to politics and not to war? Only if it is intertwined with politics can war be explained. It is impossible to judge war without also judging the policy that has produced it. War is more than just a fact or an event, it is the violent materialization, the conclusion of a procedure. Thus, if we confine ourselves to considering the detail and not the whole, we will ultimately miss the target. Where does war come from and where will it lead us? Why should we limit our judgement to the state of war, neglecting what has generated it?[26] The final conclusion of research into the ethics of political life is that judgement criteria should be extended to politics as well as – and more than – to war. And it is thus that our journey comes to an abrupt end.

It is only interlinked with politics that war – such a fundamental event in international life – may be understood and judged. At which point, I now wish to summarize the progress we have made. I have sought, first of all, to reverse the traditional conception of the rights of states,[27] arguing that it is necessary to view them in terms of their duties as opposed to their rights, the latter being attributable to all individuals equally. An assumption as strong as this necessarily seeks its foundation in redefinition of the international ethical-political space produced by overriding the deception of state sovereignty (not so much in practice as in theory, since we can hardly expect to understand international politics simply through the absoluteness and unconditional nature which typify sovereignty in the abstract). I then sought to demonstrate that the attempt to unhinge the state's ethical–political centrality is neither possible nor a wholly new idea. I did so by exploring the 'morality' of deterrence and the consequent mutation that it has produced. By demonstrating that the policy of deterrence and its effects were not, in actual fact, neutral, I was able to address the strongest, most deep-rooted prejudice in philosophical analysis of international life: namely, the image of international anarchy. I attempted to demonstrate that the international state of nature is a thing of the past (if it ever existed at all), and hence that the content of principles of coexistence is no longer founded on the terror of destruction but on the moral obligation to contribute to the survival of the planet and of the type of structures (states) which have developed on it. Yet the greatest menace that international politics can bring to bear is of course war (especially large-scale wars), which would appear to be simply an offshoot of politics itself. Without pretending to fathom the unfathomable, I have proposed a way of emerging from the fatalistic impasse in which we are liable to stray, by constructing a minimal model of international justice. Thanks to the system of principles expounded, its task is to move the emphasis from the prerogatives of states to the rights of citizens. It also aims to achieve forms of fair rebalancing of economic and financial resources, which are currently distributed in an alarmingly unbalanced way.

My conclusions concern the transformation of our very image of war. If we trace its nature to its political matrix, war ceases to appear mysterious and hence unjudgeable, and emerges as the material expression of a political dispute prompted by a conflict of values, or, better still, of preferred world images. (I have attempted to demonstrate this by constructing a model for judging a real war – the Gulf war.) Blinded by the glare of nuclear explosion, for decades we entrusted the fate of humanity to the specialism of strategic theory, which is by nature incapable of making pronouncements on the great problems of humanity. In view of the extraordinary transformation which international reality has experienced over the centuries, of sociocultural unification on a whole series of different levels, is it reasonable to expect citizens, joined together in states, to continue to be ruled solely by strategists? International relations are still living in a pre-revolutionary age. Rights of citizenship are still not distributed equally – neither among states nor among individuals. This is not caused by nature but by the will of states which, 'by birth', have had the fortune and the privilege to dominate and not to be dominated. The 'third state'[28] has never had the chance to enforce the elementary principles of equality and mutual respect that provided the basis of the 1789 Déclaration. But wasn't it the development of a moral judgement that made the Déclaration possible in the first place?

4   UTOPIA OR DISILLUSIONMENT?

Specific ethical principles (subjectively interpreted by rulers and potentates) have always existed. One is inclined to admit, however, that their ability to manifest themselves or, at least, to be recognized by states is, in turn, a product of history. It derives from the material and specific conditions which first determined the prevalence of certain values, then reconciled them, allowing them to coexist, and eventually discarded their unconditional nature, causing the emergence of a set of common values, including the need to accept restraints and to limit the absoluteness of 'brute' sovereignty. The same process is visible in numerous other objects of 'scandal': in the condition of women, of children, of homosexuals, the emancipation of the working classes, of oppressed peoples and of slaves. Who knows if the conditions of international life will ever progress in the same way? An American scholar uses the example of slavery in an essay (more seductive than convincing) to suggest that war will follow the same course:

If it is no longer ethically acceptable for one human being to use brute force to extract economic benefits from another, then a decreasing tolerance for states that 'enslave' their counterparts by means of military conquest can be expected to follow.[29]

Under what conditions can this materialize? Moral progress is the answer. As in the case of slavery, warlike conduct, once considered just and legitimate, has been progressively and increasingly condemned thanks to ' "moral progress" [which] has brought about a change in attitudes about international war.'[30] It is thus possible or at least desirable that, after abolishing slavery (not to mention other evils), humanity's moral progress will also lead to the abolition of war.[31] H. G. Wells, author of *War of the Worlds*, recounts that in 1914, driven by the horror of war, he published a pamphlet, which no publisher was prepared to print, whose title was to become proverbial: *The War To End Wars?*[32] His prediction was wrong. War will never end war: only peace can do that – provided, of course, that men are prepared to let it.

The subject is more fascinating than it is reassuring. To accept its being expounded at all demands a good deal of optimism. But how can we rule out the possibility that it is feasible? Individuals are different from states – that much is certain. For many centuries, they succeeded in modifying, correcting and improving the conditions of life of more and more of their number. But each existential dimension has its own spontaneous speed of development. Now that it is on the verge of self-destruction, isn't it possible for war to kill itself instead of killing the soldiers who fight it? And, likewise, now that its most elementary possessions – life, the air we breathe – have been ridden roughshod over, isn't humanity ready to embark on a new stage in its progress?

Notes

Introduction

1 For example, 'in international relations, by contrast with domestic politics, the scope of moral conflict is infinite, whereas in domestic order the scope is normally much more restricted.' S. Hoffman, *Duties Beyond Borders. On the Limits and Possibilities of Ethical International Politics* (Syracuse: Syracuse University Press, 1981), p. 18.

2 Isn't it highly significant, not to say revealing, that we resort to this idea of citizens *belonging*?

3 During the Vietnam war, the United States were certainly very democratic at home (up to the standards we currently ascribe to this quality), but their foreign policy was aggressive and imperialistic. Is this difference irrelevant – due, that is, to the difference in context – or not? The opinion I favour is the second one, essentially on the basis of a principle of justice whereby states must not treat human beings differently, no matter where they may be. How could one remain indifferent to the Italian government's shabby treatment of the Albanian citizens who suddenly and illegally docked in Italy in early August 1991? Detailed analysis of the government's actions would highlight the immorality of the lies it told and the decisions it took, inspired, all of them, by the most cynical opportunism. There is a tragic precedent for this type of conduct: one is, in fact, reminded of the way in which the Nazis sent unknowing Jewish prisoners to their death in extermination camps, but lied to them about their true destination! This episode is a compendium of the principal circumstances of a problem central to my argument: the need to clearly distinguish between the rights and duties of states (i.e., of their governments) and the rights and duties of citizens, irrespective of their place of birth.

4 R. L. Holmes, *On War and Morality* (Princeton: Princeton University Press, 1989), p. 21.

5 This, basically, is the subject of my book. I discuss the analogy between domestic and international politics in ch. 4, section 4 in particular.

6 Yes, the task of developing a social order comprising all humanity is a fact men objectively have to face, whether they are aware of it or not. See N. Elias, *Humana conditio. Beobachtungen zur Entwicklungder Menscheit am 40* (Frankfurt: Suhrkamp, 1985), section 11.

7 An extraordinary example of which is the 'tractatus technologicus-ethicus' proposed by H. Jonas, *The Imperative of Responsibility* (Chicago: University of Chicago Press, 1984).

8 Perhaps Kant's affirmation that 'a violation of rights in one *part* of the world is felt *everywhere*' – the third definitive article in 'Perpetual Peace', in *Kant's Political Writings*, ed. H. Reiss (Cambridge: Cambridge University Press, 1970), p. 255 – was somewhat ahead of its time!

Chapter 1   States and Morality

1 Cf. W. K. Frankena, *Ethics* (Englewood Cliffs, New Jersey: Prentice-Hall, 1973), pp. 113–14. Even the briefest review of the issue ought to range from Machiavelli to Max Weber, at least. On the implications of the value reference in political theory, cf. A. Dal Lago, 'Il ruolo dei valori nella teoria sociale e politica', in A. Panebianco (ed.), *L'analisi della politica* (Bologna: Il Mulino, 1989), pp. 341–63.

2 To cite just one example of this type of apodictic liquidation, B. Moore Jr, *Reflections on the Causes of Human Misery* (Boston: Beacon, 1972), ch. 2, sees international politics as pure or straightforward, largely unfettered by law and morality.

3 Cf., for a general framing of the problem, N. Bobbio, 'Etica e politica', in W. Tega (ed.), *Etica e politica* (Parma: Pratiche Editrice, 1984), pp. 7–17; N. Bobbio, 'Etica e politica', *Micromega*, I:4 (1986), pp. 97–118. R. Polin, *Ethique et politique* (Paris: Editions Sirey, 1968), ch. 3, provides a rare overview of the question. For analysis of the principal theoretical aspects of the debate, cf. F. E. Oppenheim, *Moral Principles in Political Philosophy* (New York: Random House, 1968). A critical update is to be found in E. Lecaldano, 'Etica e significato: un bilancio' in C. A. Viano (ed.), *Teorie etiche contemporanee* (Turin: Bollati Boringhieri, 1990), pp. 59–86. F. Oppenheim returns to the theme in 'Non cognitivismo, razionalità e relativismo', *Rivista di filosofia*, LXXVIII:1 (1987), pp. 17–28.

4 On the meaning of the word, cf. U. Scarpelli, 'La "grande divisione" e la filosofia della politica', the introduction to *Etica e filosofia politica* (Bologna: Il Mulino, 1971), the Italian translation of Oppenheim, *Moral Principles*, now in U. Scarpelli, *Etica senza verità* (Bologna: Il Mulino, 1982). For the development of the debate, cf. G. Carcaterra, 'La "grande divisione", sì e no', and E. Caldano, ' "Grande divisione", legge di Hume e ragionamento morale', *Rivista di filosofia*, LXVII:1 (1976), pp. 26–73 and pp. 74–100 respectively. For von Wright, directives may also be defined as 'technical norms', almost akin to user instructions: cf. G. H. von Wright, *Norm and Action: a Logical Enquiry* (London: Routledge and Kegan Paul, 1963), ch. 1, section 7, and the discussion which follows.

5 Cf. M. Bovero, 'Gramsci e il realismo politico', in F. Sbarberi (ed.), *Teoria politica e società industriale* (Turin: Bollati Boringhieri, 1988), p. 62.

6 Cf. the famous first chapter ('A Realist Theory of International Politics') of H. J. Morgenthau, *Politics among Nations* (New York: Knopf, 1949). For a recent revival of realistic thinking, cf. M. Donelan, *Elements of International Political Theory* (Oxford: Clarendon, 1990), who, with a touch of coquetry, omits virtually all reference to Morgenthau.

7 Taken as 'discovery' and 'description'. Cf. G. H. von Wright, *Explanation and Understanding* (London: Routledge and Kegan Paul, 1971), ch. 1, section 1.

8 According to realistic thinking, an 'imperfect world' results from 'forces inherent to human nature' which act in a situation of 'opposed interests and conflict': cf. Morgenthau, *Politics among Nations*, p. 3.

9 H. J. Morgenthau, *In Defense of the National Interest* (New York: Knopf, 1951), p. 38. (The italics in the citation are mine.)

10 To ask 'a nation to embark on altruistic policies, forgetting national interest' would certainly be immoral! Cf. Morgenthau, *In Defense*, p. 36.

11 Oppenheim suggests that it may be disappointing to realize that there can be no objective basis for our fundamental moral and political convictions. Nevertheless, he argues, it is a sign of a person's – and a civilisation's – maturity if he is able to stand on his own two feet without the support of a philosophy. Cf. Oppenheim, *Moral Principles*, ch. 5.

12 Cf. N. Bobbio, 'Sul fondamento dei diritti dell'uomo' (1964), now in *L'età dei diritti* (Turin: Einaudi, 1990), pp. 5–16.

13 These enunciations are of course in tune with axiological values: equal rights to live and to enjoy the various liberties, wellbeing and social security, education etc.

14 Cassese, *I diritti umani nel mondo contemporaneo* (Bari: Laterza, 1988), p. 62. According to Cassese, the agreement rests on the hierarchy of fundamental rights, on the particular gravity of violations of human rights and on the importance of Declarations or Bills of Rights and the principal pacts (cf. pp. 62–3).

15 Apart, obviously, from those deducible from specific pacts.

16 Cf. the last two sections (VIII and IX) of N. Bobbio's entry 'Politica', in *Dizionario di politica* (Turin: Utet, 1983).

17 Albeit generally favourable to the principle of non-intervention (chiefly in the case of states with a high degree of social development), J. S. Mill seemed willing to excuse cases like the one hypothesised here. Cf. J. S. Mill, 'A Few Words on Non-Intervention' (1859), now in 'Essays on Equality, Law and Education', *Complete Works*, vol. XXI (Toronto and London: University of Toronto Press, Routledge and Kegan Paul, 1984). The Millian view is reiterated by M. Walzer, *Just and Unjust Wars* (London: Allen Lane, 1978), pp. 87–96.

18 Precisely in the strong sense reaffirmed by von Wright, *Explanation and Understanding*, ch. 1, section 3.

19 Not 'necessarily'. Anything that cannot be subordinated to a rule easily leads to abuses of power. It is thus obvious that, historically (and not in

the abstract), international anarchy has permitted cases of bullying, considered unfair by at least some of the actors in international politics.

20 The editions of Hobbes's works used here are *De cive*, ed. H. Warrender (Oxford: Oxford University Press, 1983), and *Leviathan*, ed. R. Tuck (Cambridge: Cambridge University Press, 1992). An extremely lucid analysis of the Hobbesian formulation of these problems is to be found in M. Geuna and P. Giacotto, 'Le relazioni tra gli stati e il problema della pace', *Comunità*, XL:187 (1986), pp. 77–126.

21 Leaving aside the considerations one might make on the legal, economic and cultural civilization which has come into being in international life, and within which there are extraordinarily intense peaceful and efficient interactions.

22 What is important, at this stage in the reasoning, is that they obtain obedience: how and why is an altogether different matter.

23 Isn't 'Pax est quaerenda' the 'first, and Fundamentalle law of Nature'? Cf. T. Hobbes, *Leviathan*, XIV, p. 92.

24 Peace might be likened to an international equivalent of a situation of pluralism or tolerance within the state.

25 To demonstrate the unfoundedness of naturalist subjectivism, Oppenheim refers precisely to the principles of Nazism and the impossibility of rejecting the latter as abnormal: they are, he argues, *moral* principles of politics in so far as they can be judged immoral by those who undertake to achieve the wellbeing of all. He concludes that similar ethical systems may be and have been adopted in good faith by 'normal' people and assumed as a basis for rational behaviour. Cf. Oppenheim, *Moral Principles*, ch. 4. Frankena, on the other hand, is much more peremptory: 'we do not and cannot simply excuse the Nazis for their crimes against humanity even if we think they sincerely believed that what they were doing was right, partly because the wrong is too heinous and partly because a man may be responsible for his moral errors.' Frankena, *Ethics*, p. 60. T. Nagel also addresses the point but concludes that here one is still morally in the hands of destiny, and that however irrational it may appear upon reflection, our ordinary moral attitudes would be unrecognizable without it. T. Nagel, *Mortal Questions* (London: Cambridge University Press, 1979), ch. 1.

26 'My claim is that morality has its sources in conflict, in the divided soul and between contrary claims, and that there is no rational path that leads from conflicts to harmony.' S. Hampshire, *Morality and Conflict* (Oxford: Blackwell, 1983), p. 152. Of course this does not mean that conflicts can never be resolved: 'there is also unmixed evil. The Nazis tried to establish a way of life which entirely discarded justice and gentleness', ibid., p. 156. Frankena too dwells upon the problem of the conflict of the principles, but his conclusion is, all things considered, unsatisfactory in so far as he merely acknowledges that it is insoluble in practice, and suggests that it be dealt with on a case-by-case basis: cf. Frankena, *Ethics*, pp. 52–3. Albeit applied to moral conflicts of an entirely different kind, G. Calabresi and P. Bobbit,

Tragic Choices (New York: Norton, 1978), is one of the most brilliant expositions of this problem.

27 For a discussion of international justice, cf. ch. 6 below.

28 With the exception of course of those principles which derive from *jus gentium*. 'For centuries, individuals were protected by international law only in as much as they were foreigners; only, that is, if they went abroad (and provided of course that their national state was prepared to protect them and had the capacity to do so).' Cassese, *I diritti umani*, p. 210.

29 This is, more or less, the type of relationship which L. Brilmayer, *Justifying International Acts* (Ithaca: Cornell University Press, 1989), pp. 84ff., calls 'diagonal'.

30 For example, towards one's own, that of paying taxes; towards others, that of not stirring up disorder or insurrection.

31 Citizens will obviously continue to be bound to the different rights imposed upon them by the civil law of their own countries, which cannot prescribe them anything that is incompatible with the international commitments contracted.

32 For a traditional legal formulation of the problem, cf. the paragraph devoted to 'Rights and Duties' by H. Kantorowicz, *The Definition of Law* (London: Cambridge University Press, 1958), ch. 3, section 6. The circumstance whereby the right of one subject always corresponds to the duty of another is restored to the moral sphere and discussed by F. Fagiani, 'Etica e teoria dei diritti', in C. A. Viano (ed.), *Teorie etiche contemporanee* (Turin: Bollati Boringhieri, 1990), p. 89.

33 'Moral language must not necessarily make use of the two deontic principles of right and obligation typical of legal language, but at the very moment in which it has recourse to them, the assertion of a right implies the assertion of a duty and vice versa.' N. Bobbio, *L'età dei diritti* (Turin: Einaudi, 1990), p. XIX.

34 'Truth is dependent upon a degree of longitude', remarks Pascal before going on to exclaim, 'A strange sort of justice that is bounded by a river! What is true on this side of the Pyrenees is false on the other side.' B. Pascal, *Pensées*, tr. J. Warrington (London: Dent, 1973), frag. 108, p. 35. The other celebrated fragment, dedicated to the dialogue between two people separated by a river, a fact which justifies their shooting and killing one another (frag. 233) was introduced by Goldmann as follows: 'Pascal knows that no legal or moral rule achieves true justice or true good.' L. Goldmann, *Le dieu caché. Étude sur la vision tragique dans les 'Pensées' de Pascal et dans le théâtre de Racine* (Paris: Gallimard, 1955), ch. 14.

35 Bobbio, *L'età dei diritti*, p. VII. Bobbio has dealt on several occasions with the possible democratization of the international system: cf. 'Democrazia e sistema internazionale', in L. Cortesi (ed.), *Democrazia, rischio nucleare, movimenti per la pace* (Naples: Liguori, 1988), pp. 37–52 and 'Della democrazia tra le nazioni', *Lettera internazionale*, V:22 (1989), pp. 61–4. I myself argued the relevance of the issue in 'Democrazia internazionale:

utopia, mito o tragedia?' and 'Pace o democrazia?', both in *Teoria politica*, respectively II:2 (1986), pp. 33–62, and III:3 (1987), pp. 43–61.

36 We also speak about a 'thaw' or 'a cooling off' in diplomatic relations and so on. There are so many metaphors of war, it is almost superfluous to list them here: we talk of 'the sex war', 'the generation war', 'the wine war', 'the trade war', 'the war against poverty', 'the telematic war' etc.. Sometimes, however, it is the language of international theory which supplies everyday life with metaphors. This was the case of the 'cold war', the term coined by W. Lippmann to describe the state of US–USSR relations after World War II, and now common parlance. Another sphere often referred to by analogy is that of economic science, in which the international system is compared to the free competitive market: cf., for example, Barrington Moore Jr, *Reflections on the Causes*, ch. 2; or K. N. Waltz, *Theory of International Politics* (Reading, Mass.: Addison-Wesley, 1979), ch. 6.

37 For an interesting, albeit inconclusive, dissertation on the causes of World War I, cf. von Wright, *Explanation and Understanding*, ch. 4. section 3.

Chapter 2   The International Ethical and Political Space

1 A. C. Bradley, 'International Morality: the United States of Europe', in E. M. Sidgwick, G. Murray, A. C. Bradley, L. P. Jacks, G. F. Stout and B. Bosanquet, *The International Crisis in its Ethical and Psychological Aspects* (London: Oxford University Press, 1915), p. 54 (my italics). On the philosophical climate which characterized the outstanding debate on international affairs which raged in Britain at the start of the century, cf. P. P. Nicholson, *The Political Philosophy of the British Idealists* (Cambridge: Cambridge University Press, 1990).

2 It would suffice to follow the themes which recur in the periodical *International Organization* to evaluate the dimensions of the phenomenon. In any case, the pages which follow contain references, some bibliographical, to all of them.

3 Cf. R. Gilpin, *The Political Economy of International Relations* (Princeton: Princeton University Press, 1987).

4 The master in this area of study is without doubt G. Modelski, to whose writings I refer frequently in the pages of this book.

5 K. N. Waltz, *Theory of International Politics* (Reading, Mass.: Addison-Wesley, 1979). An example of the debate which Waltz's study triggered is R. O. Keohane (ed.), *Neorealism and Its Critics* (New York: Columbia University Press, 1986).

6 J. Der Derian and M. L. Shapiro (eds), *International/Intertextual Relations* (Lexington: Lexington Books, 1989).

7 Another recent example of which was the debate (with papers by K. J. Holsti, T. J. Biersteker and J. George), introduced by Y. Lapid, 'The Third

Debate: On the Prospects of International Theory in a Post-Positivist Era', *International Studies Quarterly*, XXXIII:3 (1989).

8 'We must found a true international order and thereby put an end to the system of absolute national sovereignty.' E. McClennen, 'The Tragedy of National Sovereignty', in A. Cohen and S. Lee (eds), *Nuclear Weapons and the Future of Humanity* (Totowa: Rowman and Alanheld, 1986), p. 405. This is but one of the many possible examples of the dissemination of this form of intolerance.

9 D. Hume, *A Treatise of Human Nature*, ed. T. Hill Greene and T. H. Grose (Aalen: Scientia Verlag, 1964) vol. II, p. 330. The reference to Hume is not coincidental. He was one of the first philosophers (if not the very first) to deal extensively with international relations. Cf. for example, 'Of the Balance of Power', in Charles W. Hendel (ed.), *David Hume's Political Essays* (Indianapolis: Bobbs-Merrill, 1953). For an anthology of writings on the relationship between the doctrine of natural law and international politics, see L. Bonanate (ed.), *Diritto naturale e relazioni tra gli stati* (Turin: Loescher, 1976).

10 T. Hobbes, *Leviathan*, ed. R. Tuck (Cambridge: Cambridge University Press, 1991). The anti-Hobbesian polemic is a recurrent one as the following recent example reveals: 'Hobbes, for example, argues that in the absence of a state there is no morality. Since nations exist in a virtual state of nature with no authority over them to compel obedience and punish disobedience, the notions of right and wrong have no applicability to their conduct. But this is a *non sequitur*. Assuming the international system is a state of nature, the most this shows is that *a morality* does not exist among nations, not that their conduct cannot be judged by moral criteria.' R. L. Holmes, *On War and Morality* (Princeton: Princeton University Press, 1989), p. 98. As I argue in ch. 4, section 3 below, the problem is, more generally, to avoid imitative applications of Hobbesian thinking to international relations and to adopt a formulation by analogy, which seems to me much more fruitful. M. Cohen, 'Moral Scepticism and International Relations', *Philosophy and Public Affairs*, XIII:4 (1984), pp. 299–346, discusses the positions of both Hume and Hobbes (coming out in favour of the former).

11 G. F. Kennan, 'Morality and Foreign Policy', *Foreign Affairs*, LXIV:2 (winter 1985–6), p. 206. Kennan was the author of the famous report, marked with an 'X', which the US embassy attaché in Moscow forwarded to the State Department in July 1947, and which shaped the United States's attitude towards the Soviet Union at the height of the Cold War.

12 R. Niebuhr, *Moral Man and Immoral Society: a study in ethics and politics* (London: SCM Press, 1963), p. xi and p. 88.

13 Stephen Decatur (1779–1820), an American naval officer who fought in the War of 1812.

14 This, basically, is a more ingenuous, indifferent way of saying what Nazi war criminals replied to the Nuremberg war crimes tribunal: *all they did was to obey superior orders.* Cf. A. Cassese, *Diritto e violenza nell'età nucleare* (Bari: Laterza, 1986) esp. ch. 6 and bibliography.

15 This problem is well presented by R. M. Hare who, with regard to citizens' obligations to the state, rejects neutralistic or 'local' solutions, pointing out that, on the basis of the 'logical universalism of moral judgements', citizens cannot recognize more rights to their own state than to others. Cf. R. M. Hare, 'Have I a Duty to My Country as Such?', *The Listener*, 20 October 1955, p. 652. On the previous page, Hare deals fleetingly with 'my country, right or wrong'.

16 I refer of course to the terms in which the distinction is presented in ch. 1 above.

17 In our linguistic tradition, when we say that something *breaks out*, we refer to something that cannot be avoided, almost as if to suggest a sort of natural *inevitability*.

18 This kind of injustice is simply the consequence of the insoluble clash between two 'justices', which, as such cannot be applied on a universal basis.

19 For updated reappraisals of realistic thought, cf. F. E. Oppenheim, 'Interesse nazionale, razionalità e moralità', *Teoria politica*, III:2 (1987); M. Cesa, 'La teoria politica di H. Morgenthau', ibid.; P. P. Portinaro, 'La concezione della guerra nel realismo politico moderno', in C. Jean (ed.), *La guerra nel pensiero politico* (Milan: Angeli, 1987); R. B. J. Walker, 'Realism, Change and International Political Theory', *International Studies Quarterly*, XXXI:1 (1987); J. T. Johnson, 'Giudizio morale e questioni internazionali: i limiti del realismo', *Teoria politica*, V:1 (1989); D. P. Lackey, 'Su un errore sistematico della critica realistica all'etica politica', ibid.; J. Rosenberg, 'What's the Matter with Realism?', *Review of International Studies*, XVI:4 (1990), pp. 285–303.

20 But I do not mean that it is rare: on the contrary, this is, albeit unconsciously, the prevalent attitude to the problem. Holmes, quite rightly, exemplifies the more radically alternative position: 'in elevating the preservation of an abstraction – the state – above individuals, it [political realism] places no limits upon what may be done to achieve that objective.' R. L. Holmes, *On War*, p. 112. Nevertheless, albeit recognizing the right to apply ethics to international relations, by reducing the state to a sumtotal of individuals, this position also leaves several problems unsolved.

21 B. Croce, *Etica e politica* (Bari: Laterza, 1956). These two extracts from the ch. 'L'antieroicità degli stati' may be found at p. 182 and p. 179 respectively.

22 Cf. the anthology, S. Pistone (ed.), *Politica di potenza e imperialismo* (Milan: Angeli, 1973).

23 B. Croce, 'L'Italia in guerra', ch. 6 'Ancora dello stato come potenza, *Pagine sulla guerra* (Bari: Laterza, 1928), p. 90.

24 Ibid., p. 91.

25 'The theme of war is traditionally connected with the theme of the state in its relations with other states. . . . The theory of the modern state proceeds apace with the theory of war.' N. Bobbio, 'Rapporti internazionali e marxismo', in *Filosofia e politica. Scritti dedicati a Cesare Luporini* (Florence: La Nuova Italia, 1981), p. 303.

26   If we put the various catalogues together, it transpires that exactly 503 wars have been fought in the five continents from the early sixteenth century to the present day! Cf. G. C. Kohn, *Dictionary of Wars* (New York: Facts on File, 1986); M. Small and J. D. Singer, *Resort to Arms* (Beverly Hills: Sage, 1982). It may be worth mentioning in passing that there is still no definitive, accepted source for the calculation of the number of all historically recorded international wars.

27   R. Aron, in 'Battre la guerre', ch. 5 of *La violence*, coll. Récherches et Débats, no. 59 (Brussels: Desclée de Brower, 1967).

28   Bobbio, *Rapporti internazionali*, in particular pp. 314–16.

29   F. Nietzsche, *Thus Spake Zarathustra: a Book for All and None*, tr. Thomas Common, 6th edn (London: Allen and Unwin, 1967).

30   C. von Clausewitz, *On War*, ed. and tr. Michael Howard and Peter Paret (Princeton, New Jersey: Princeton University Press, 1984), vol. VIII, ch. 2 (italics in the original).

31   R. Aron, *Penser la guerre, Clausewitz* (Paris: Gallimard, 1976), pp. 92–3, and note XVI, pp. 405–6.

32   von Clausewitz, *On War*, p. 605.

33   The whole passage reads: 'Is war not just another expression of their thoughts, another form of speech or writing? Its grammar, indeed, may be its own, but not its logic.' Ibid., p. 605 (the whole passage is italicized by Clausewitz).

34   Ibid., p. 607 (these words too are italicized in the original).

35   Not that I intend to somehow justify war *as a source of law*. I simply wish to argue that *post-war* is more interesting than *pre-war*, and hence that the framework of order imposed by the victors over the vanquished will occupy the foreground. On the relationship between law and war, cf. N. Bobbio, 'Diritto e guerra' (1965), now in *Il problema della guerra e le vie della pace* (Bologna: Il Mulino, 1984).

36   That the distinction has a sociological foundation was already clear to M. Weber, who represented it explicitly in his distinction between acting rationally 'with respect to the aim' and 'with respect to the value'. Cf. Weber, *Economy and Society: an Outline of Interpretative Sociology*, ed. G. Roth and C. Wittich (Berkeley: University of California Press, 1979), where the first form corresponds to *Ziel* and the second to *Zweck*.

37   C. M. Santoro, *La perla e l'ostrica. Alle fonti della politica globale degli Stati Uniti* (Milan: Angeli, 1987), analyses this distinction in practice by reconstructing the American government's 'war aims' (Clausewitz's *Ziel*) and 'post-war planning' (*Zweck*) during World War II.

38   Cf. ch. 3, section 3 below.

39   Cf. ch. 3, section 1 below.

40   How can a state guarantee the health of its nationals by dumping toxic waste downstream of rivers which cross through the country, and which hence harm the health of inhabitants of another country? How can it be argued that the value of an individual's health varies according to the territory in which he or she is born?

41 H. Kelsen, 'Der Wande der Souveranitatsbegriffes' in *Studi Filosofico-Giuridici dedicati a Giorgio del Vecchio*, vol. 2 (Modena: Società Tipografica Modenese, 1931). Albeit with less emphasis, Kelsen makes analogous considerations in *General Theory of Law and State* (Cambridge, Mass.: Harvard University Press, 1945), ch. 6, section C, h.

42 'For the theory of the primacy of the state legal system, its own sovereign state, that is to say its own state system taken as a supreme system of rules, cannot be derived any further. Other "states" are comprehensible for it only in so far as they are recognized, delegated by their own state system, that is to say conceived only as partial systems.' H. Kelsen, *Das Problem der Souveranitat und die Theorie des Völkerrechts. Beitrag zu einer Reinen Rechtslehre* (Tubingen: Mohr, 1920), ch. 11, section 63.

43 Ibid., ch. 11, section 63.

44 Ibid., ch. 11, section 64, note 2. Kelsen takes the argument to its extreme consequences: 'Is there any other way that surely leads to the negation of every ethical element other than subjectivism, since any ethicality is connected to objective rules, to a duty whose validity must be independent from the subject, if we are to speak in general of validity?'

45 Ibid., ch. 11, section 64. The passage continues: 'Its legal unity, the *civitas maxima* as world organization: this is the political core of the legal hypothesis of the primacy of international law, which is, however, at once the fundamental idea of the pacifism which, in the realm of international politics, constitutes the reverse image of imperialism.' In *General Theory*, Kelsen recognizes that in choosing one or other of the two formulations, 'we are evidently guided by ethical and political preferences', but whatever the content of the latter, 'the choice is important since it is linked to the idea of sovereignty', ch. 6, section C, i, 3. It is to this equidistance that F. Riccobono, *Interpretazioni kelseniane* (Milan: Giuffré, 1989), ch. 6, traces his reappraisal of the link in Kelsen's thinking between the pre-eminence of international law and pacifism.

46 Albeit with results that are often by no means satisfactory, this is what is happening increasingly intensely in the USA. Of all the many classical readings one might suggest, cf. at least ch. 9 of H. Arendt, *The Origins of Totalitarianism*, 2nd enlarged edn (London: Allen and Unwin, 1961).

47 An altogether different matter, frequently discussed in the international relations field, is that of the state's centrality as a unit of analysis. Cf. the classical studies of J. H. Herz, 'Rise and Demise of the Territorial State', *World Politics*, IX:4 (1957); and 'The Territorial State Revisited: Reflections on the Future of the Nation-State', *Polity*, I:1 (1968). There is nothing obsolete or outmoded about this debate: for an update, see R. Haass, 'The Primacy of the State . . . or Revisiting the Revisionists', *Daedalus*, no. 4 (1979).

48 S. Hoffman, *Duties Beyond Borders* (Syracuse: Syracuse University Press, 1981), p. 108.

49 Somewhat tentatively, I use this term here to suggest the idea that states as a whole should be seen as a specific reality, the sum-total of a set of

units whose very existence is, nonetheless, determined by the *necessary* existence of other similar units. I later replace it with the more technical 'international system'.

50   I shall develop this point in ch. 6, section 4.

51   The spectre of the national idea rears its ugly head once more!

52   That the nation is not always and exclusively a negative idea may be evinced, in any case, from works such as F. Chabod, *L'idea di nazione* (Bari: Laterza, 1961). For other more recent studies, cf. A. H. Birch, *Nationalism and National Integration* (London: Unwin Hyman, 1989); J.-Y. Guiomar, *La Nation entre l'histoire et la raison* (Paris: La découverte, 1989).

53   For an extremely detailed account of different outlines of the frontier concept, cf. M. Foucher, *Fronts et frontières* (Paris: Fayard, 1988). For a philosophical approach to the problem, cf. A. H. Goldman, 'The Moral Significance of National Boundaries', *Midwest Studies in Philosophy*, VII (1982). Cf. also P. G. Brown and H. Shue (eds), *Boundaries: National Autonomy and Its Limits* (Totowa: Rowman and Littlefield, 1981). An entire chapter is dedicated to international analysis of frontiers by E. Luard, *Conflict and Peace in the Modern International System* (New York: State University of New York, 1988). I return to the problem, especially in terms of its effects on moral theory, in ch. 6, sections 2, 3 below.

54   J. Herbst, 'The Creation and Maintenance of National Boundaries in Africa', *International Organization*, XLI:4 (1989), p. 681.

55   R. H. Jackson and C. G. Rosberg, 'Why Africa's Weak States Persist', *World Politics*, XXXV:1 (1982), p. 24.

56   For instance, the fact that Saudi Arabia is extremely rich in oil and Italy has none at all inevitably produces natural inequality.

57   To be victors or vanquished in a war is another example.

58   One can hypothesize that this takes place according to the model with which Rousseau described the origin of private property: 'The first man who, having enclosed a piece of ground bethought himself of saying, "This is mine," and found people simple enough to believe him, was the real founder of civil society.' J. J. Rousseau, 'Discours sur l'origine et les fondements de l'inegalité parmi les hommes'; English translation, *A Dissertation on the Origin and Foundation of the Inequality of Mankind: The Second Part*, in R. Maynard Hutchins (ed.), 'Great Books of the Western World', no. 38, *Montesquieu/Rousseau* (Chicago: University of Chicago, 1952), p. 348.

59   In Clausewitz's words: 'The decision by arms is for all major and minor operations in war what cash payment is in commerce. Regardless how complex the relationship between the two parties, regardless how rarely settlements occur, they can never be entirely absent.': *On War*, vol. I, ch. 3, p. 97.

60   It is the title of section b of ch. 3, vol. VIII of *On War*, p. 585, in which Clausewitz discusses the elements which 'introduce uncertainties that make it difficult to gauge the amount of resistance to be faced and, in consequence, the means required and the objectives to be set', pp. 585–94.

61 Not to mention suffered! Cf. the extremely interesting observations of E. Scarry, *The Body in Pain: the Making and Unmaking of the World* (New York: Oxford University Press, 1985), ch. 2 of which is entitled 'The structure of war: the contiguity of the suffering body and the abstract objectives of war'.

62 Also in individual and subjective terms: physical death, the destruction of property, the perception of pain, engrained hatred, impotence and thirst for revenge are there to prove as much.

63 That is, not equally appreciable by all.

64 Cf. on this expression, C. M. Santoro, 'Il sistema di guerra', *Il Mulino*, XXXIII:294 (1984).

65 The very composition of forces at war offers some pointers in this direction: only very rarely have dyadic wars given rise to great transformations, whereas multilateral wars or wars between coalitions often have. The point obviously requires deep empirical analysis. Cf. my 'La Rivoluzione francese e le relazioni internazionali. Questioni di metodo', *Teoria politica*, V:2–3 (1989), esp. pp. 130–3.

66 I use the expression in the sense assigned to it by D. Easton, *A System Analysis of Political Life* (New York: Wiley, 1965), ch. 12. For a general presentation of the problem, cf. A. Caffarena, 'Introduzione all'analisi dei regimi internazionali', in L. Bonanate (ed.), *Dopo l'anarchia* (Milan: Angeli, 1989), pp. 39–131. I return to the problem, combining it with the historicization of the regimes themselves, in ch. 5 below.

67 Cf., on this extraordinarily stimulating question, H. Suganami, *The Domestic Analogy and World Order Proposals* (Cambridge: Cambridge University Press, 1989).

68 Many years ago, one of the last great exponents of international political realism asked himself the question: cf. M. Wight, 'Why Is There No International Theory?', in H. Butterfield and M. Wight (eds), *Diplomatic Investigations* (London: Allen and Unwin, 1966). His conclusions were that international politics is to some degree 'reluctant' to let itself be theorized on (p. 33), that, all things considered, between absolute immorality and absolute morality, an intermediate stage exists after all (i.e., careful consideration of the real conditions of the action) and that, basically, it is not the end of the world if morality cannot be observed. Cf. M. Wight, 'Western Values in International Relations', in Butterfield and Wight (eds), *Diplomatic Investigations*, p. 130. Cf. my considerations in ch. 6, section 3, below.

69 I discussed the content of the answer to this question in ch. 1, section 3, above.

70 One might also feel that the state *per se* cannot have a moral value given that entities exist which may be 'good, bad, desirable, undesirable, and so on, but we do not mean that they are morally good or morally bad, since they are generally not the kinds of things that can be morally good or morally bad'. W. K. Frankena, *Ethics. An Introduction to Political Philosophy* (Englewood Cliffs: Prentice Hall, 1973), pp. 9–10. The distinction

between non-moral judgements may be traced principally to the fact that moral judgements are only made on aspects of character, motive and intention (ibid., p. 62): 'but since it will turn out that a consideration of what is good (non-morally) is involved in determining what is morally right or wrong, we must include a discussion of such value judgements anyway.' Ibid., p. 10.

71   Hoffman, *Duties Beyond Borders*, p. 23. The same author subsequently returned to the question in 'The Rules of the Game', *Ethics and International Affairs* (in a section of the yearbook dedicated to *Superpower Ethics*), I (1987); and *The Political Ethics of International Relations*, Seventh Morgenthau Memorial Lecture on Ethics and Foreign Policy (New York: Carnegie Council on Ethics and International Affairs, 1988).

Chapter 3   The Ambiguous Nature of Peace

1   For a historiographical overview of the problem, cf. J. T. Johnson, *Just War, Tradition and the Restraints of War*, (Princeton: Princeton University Press, 1981). Attempts to present the problem in contemporary terms have been made by M. Walzer, *Just and Unjust Wars* (London: Allen Lane, 1978), and by Johnson, *Can Modern War Be Just?* (New Haven: Yale University Press, 1984). For an exemplary argument of the incomparability of traditional war and nuclear war, cf. N. Bobbio, 'Il conflitto termonucleare e le tradizionali giustificazioni della guerra' (1962), now in *Il terzo assente* (Turin: Edizioni Sonda, 1989), pp. 23–30. This later volume, a collection of Bobbio's most recent essays and speeches, also includes 'Non aprì una nuova era' (pp. 218–20), which, at least in part, contradicts the thesis of the 1962 essay. G. Anders's classic argument according to which there is no longer any motive for war which would not lead to international ruin, and there can be no motive for war which might be justified as a *cause* of war – G. Anders, *Die Toten. Rede über die drei Weltkriege* (Munich: Oscar Beck, 1982), ch. 1 – has also been presented to the Italian reading public recently.

2   I have no idea whether it is easy or not to argue or demonstrate that the value of life changes as nationality changes. Cf. my broader considerations in ch. 2, section 3, above.

3   Robert J. Oppenheimer's speech on 2 November 1945 to mark the disbanding of the team of scientists, which not only devised but also built the first three atom bombs in history, is a most valuable document for reflections on the ethics of science, on the responsibilities of scientists and on the changes generated by the new weapon. Cf. R. J. Oppenheimer, *Letters and Recollections* (Cambridge, Mass.: Harvard University Press, 1980). The quotation used as an epigraph to this chapter is an excerpt from the speech. The story of this brilliant, contradictory character has yet to be fully told: for a general insight, the critical but touching H. Chevalier,

Oppenheimer: the Story of a Friendship (New York: George Braziller, 1965) is essential reading.

4 This historical 'paralysis' is evidently at once unnatural and inevitable. Cf. ch. 2, section 4 above for the impact it exerts on the 'constitutive function' of war, and ch. 5 below for the outlines of the philosophy of history which it implies.

5 Precisely to avoid erasing the possibility of conflict – and relinquishing politics in the light of the intractable alternative between 'all' and 'nothing' – strategic theory strived first to justify minor wars, explaining that they could not break out into great wars. Later, it tried another tack, adding that the escalation notion stressed how the principle was not an absolute one, but had to be handled with the utmost care. Yet, since the first rule of the game of deterrence is uncertainty, strategic theory was unable to settle on this position either. The very same dialectic was thus reproposed to the letter in the course of the seventies, when overconfidence in the stability of the balance of terror was countered by the danger of 'the window of vulnerability' which it opened. It was the Euromissile crisis which eventually, and suddenly, put things back into place. More than mere history of strategic doctrines, what we have here is a precedent currently worthy of due consideration, now that the oppressive image of nuclear war is, fortunately, fading.

6 The most important reference work on the relationship between armaments, technology and nuclear war remains W. H. McNeil, *The Pursuit of Power: Technology, Armed Forces and Society since 1000 AD* (Chicago: University of Chicago Press, 1984), esp. ch. 10.

7 K. Jaspers, *The Future of Mankind* (Chicago: University of Chicago Press, 1961).

8 Walzer, *Just and Unjust Wars.*

9 The novelty here is not deterrence, but the fact that a social relations technique has given life to a code of international behaviour so perfectly interiorized by all states that, in the course of half a century, it has never hit a single false note. Albeit now very dated, my *La politica della dissuasione* (Turin: Giappichelli, 1971) contains a detailed analysis of deterrence theory.

10 For a brief but exhaustive overview of the debate and the literature, cf. S. Frega, 'Strategia della deterrenza nucleare e paradossi della "ragion pratica" ', *Teoria politica*, V:1 (1989), pp. 47–65; *Etica pubblica e strategia della deterrenza nucleare* and *Deterrenza nucleare. Un'analisis normativa* (Milan: Ispi, 1989). Cf. also R. Hardin, J. Mearsheimer and R. E. Goodin (eds), *Nuclear Deterrence. Ethics and Strategy* (Chicago: University of Chicago Press, 1985).

11 Frega, 'Deterrenza nucleare', p. 44.

12 A. Rapoport, *Strategy and Conscience* (New York: Harper and Row, 1964), pp. 139–40. For a fiercely critical summary of the strategic thinking of Kahn, Kissinger and Schelling, cf. my *La politica*, ch. 7.

13 Discussed in philosophic terms by T. Nardin, 'Nuclear War and the Arguments from Extremity', in A. Ohen and S. Lee (eds), *Nuclear Weapons and the Future of Humanity* (Totowa: Rowman and Allanheld, 1986).

14 In my argument, I in no way imply that the problem of the incomparability of the atom bomb to any other weapon was a false one but that, if anything, its rationalization shifted the terms of the problem, as I argue more specifically in section 3 of this chapter below.

15 This is why arguments as sophisticated as those of G. Dworkin, 'Morality and Deterrence', in Hardin, Mearsheimer, Dworkin and Goodin, *Nuclear Deterrence*, pp. 37–52, are ultimately so abstract and dull.

16 It may appear ungenerous to name names, but only a handful of people avoided falling into the trap of the deterrent state of necessity: among them are Bertrand Russell, Günter Anders and Norberto Bobbio.

17 I use this word without valuational connotations: I am thinking here of past empires such as those of Charles V and Luigi XIV.

18 We must remember that, at that time, it would have been downright ridiculous to imagine that the Soviet Union had the strength to attack the West. Having said that, however, it is neither my wish nor my objective to attach all the blame to the United States.

19 Comparable to the building of pyramids and other useless objects, which Keynes suggested as a solution to the problem of unemployment, although, of course, the two examples are morally different!

20 The fact that now, in the early nineties, all this appears either dated or on the way out is an entirely different matter.

21 For the most diverse reasons: they are ex-colonies, they traditionally belong to a sphere of influence, they are historically and economically backward etc.. Having said that, however, such areas have become the object of much freer competition than the *centre* of the system.

22 In *Né guerra né pace* (Milan: Angeli, 1987), I tried to convey the paradox of the balance of terror, the strategic formula which synthesized deterrence strategy, through the metaphor of communicating vessels, cf. pp. 52–4.

23 Not because it is thus impossible to construct political peace *as well*, but because what is most urgent is peace *in* the present political reality.

24 In 'Il conflitto termonucleare e le tradizionali giustificazioni della guerra', (1962), now in N. Bobbio, *Il terzo assente* (Turin: Edizioni Sonda, 1989), pp. 23–30.

25 T. Hill Green, 'Political Obligation', in *Works* (London: Longman, 1888), vol. II, section 163.

26 L. Woolf, *International Government* (London: Allen and Unwin, 1916) p. 86. It is a great pity that this author has been completely forgotten by contemporary culture. All he is now remembered for is the fact that he was married to the much more famous Virginia.

27 For an introduction to the issues involved, cf. H. Afheldt, 'Una difesa difensiva?', *Problems of Socialism*, I:1 (1984), pp. 230–5; for a broader

introduction to 'nonviolent popular defence', of which defensive defence is an application, cf. the works of T. Ebert.

28 The refusal of 'despicable peace' referred to by C. Viano, 'I filosofi e la pace', in F. Baroncelli and M. Pasini, *I filosofi e la pace* (Genoa: Ecig, 1987), pp. 42ff.

29 In order to counter the perverse but by no means abstract logic of the so-called 'security dilemma', through which strategic theory has strived to exemplify the model of the spiritualization of international tension, cf. R. Jervis, 'Cooperation under the Security Dilemma', *World Politics*, no. 3 (1978), pp. 167–214; G. H. Snyder, 'The Security Dilemma in Alliance Policies', *World Politics*, XXXVI:4 (1984).

30 The classics of this formulation, which is liable to be more successful today than it was in the Seventies, are C. E. Osgood, *An Alternative to War or Surrender* (Urbana: University of Illinois Press, 1962); and E. Fromm, *May Man Prevail?* (Garden City: Doubleday, 1961).

31 This, in synthesis, is the central thesis of N. Angell's extremely famous but little read *The Great Illusion*, 4th rev. and enlarged edn (New York: Putnam's, 1913). On this master, almost completely forgotten by modern pacifists, cf. C. Navari, 'The Great Illusion Revisited: the International Theory of Norman Angell', *Review of International Studies*, XV:4 (1989), pp. 341–58.

32 The reason I have not included this type of alternative to war among the necessary evils is to stress that war is anything but impossible. Hence its alternative is not inescapable but, in turn, the product of a choice.

33 Cf. M. Riordan (ed.), *The Day After Midnight: The Effects of Nuclear War* (Palo Alto: Cheshire Books, 1982); P. R. Ehrlich, C. Sagan, D. Kennedy and W. Orr Roberts, *The Cold and the Dark* (New York: Open Institute, 1984). A more technical discussion is contained in C. Sagan, 'Nuclear War and Climatic Catastrophe', *Foreign Affairs*, Winter 1983–4, pp. 257–92.

34 The number of times wars themselves have been justified precisely by the desire to establish a *just* peace!

35 Which – as stressed by N. Bobbio, 'Il problema della guerra e le vie della pace' (1966), now in *Il problema della guerra e le vie della pace* (Bologna: Il Mulino, 1984), p. 71 – are the three subspecies of war's dimension as a necessary evil.

36 Since it is the weak link in the peace-war partnership: cf. N. Bobbio, 'L'idea della pace e il pacifismo' (1975), now in *Il problema*, p. 121.

37 The leading pioneer in this field is without doubt J. Galtung, founder of the first scientific peace research centre in Oslo, and of the *Journal of Peace Research*.

38 I use the word in its weak, descriptive meaning as a symbol of the conditions of cultural, economic, political and strategic integration which mark the contemporary world, and not in the strong, valuational sense used by K. N. Waltz, *Theory of International Politics* (Reading, Mass.: Addison-

Wesley, 1979), ch. 7, who considers it a form of weakness or reciprocal vulnerability of states.

39 Cf. R. Aron, *Peace and War: a Theory of International Relations*, tr. R. Howard and A. Baker Fox (Garden City: Doubleday, 1966).

40 Aron thus indicates *what* should change, but leaves us under no great illusion as to *how*. Ibid..

41 Cf. Bobbio, *Il problema*, p. 90. Bobbio also analyses the justifications of war in 'Il conflitto termonucleare', especially p. 24.

42 Except for the case of terror-based peace which, to all intents and purposes, was witnessed only after World War II.

43 A. Momigliano, 'Alcune osservazioni sulle cause di guerra nella storiografia antica', *Storia e storiografia antica* (Bologna: Il Mulino, 1987), p. 47.

44 Aristotle, *Politica*, VII, 1333a.

45 Plato, *Laws*, I, 626a.

46 One inevitably thinks back to Aron's celebrated formula, 'impossible peace-improbable war'. Cf. R. Aron, *Le grand schisme* (Paris: Gallimard, 1948), pp. 20ff.; R. Aron, *Mémoires* (Paris: Juillard, 1983), p. 285.

47 The principal, best known and most reliable source of quantitative information on war is M. Small and J. D. Singer, *Resort to Arms* (Beverly Hills: Sage, 1982). *Copdab* (Conflict and Peace Data Bank) is an archive set up by A. Azard to catalogue war and peace since 1945, whereas the Singer-Small collection covers the period 1815–1980.

48 Erasmus of Rotterdam, 'Letter to John Botzheim', in P. S. Akllen (ed.), *Opus epistolarum Des. Erasmi Roterodami* (Oxford: Clarendon, 1906), pp. 18–19. The complete passage reads: 'Opposed to this plan were those who judge quiet things to be useless, who . . . much prefer peace that is not peace, war that is not war.' Despite his cultural and chronological distance from Erasmus, one inevitably recalls similar words used by C. Schmitt in *Der Begriff des Politischen. Text von 1932 mit einem und drei Corollarien* (Berlin: Duncker und Humblot, 1966), corollary 2, section 4.

49 This particular theme is discussed in ch. 5, section 3 below.

50 This mutation is discussed fully in the section below.

51 R. Hardin and J. J. Mearsheimer, 'Introduction', in Hardin, Mearsheimer, Dworkin and Goodin, *Nuclear Deterrence*, p. 7.

52 Walzer, *Just and Unjust Wars*, p. 274.

53 The final draft of the pastoral letter may be found in E. Balducci and L. Grassi (eds), *La pace. realismo di un'utopia* (Milan: Principato, 1985), pp. 362–86. See S. M. Okin, 'Taking Bishops Seriously', *World Politics*, XXXVI:4 (1984), pp. 527–54; B. M. Russett, 'Ethical Dilemmas of Nuclear Deterrence', *International Security*, VIII:4 (1984).

54 T. Nagel, *Mortal Questions* (London: Cambridge University Press, 1979), ch. 5.

55 To whom I referred in the section above.

56 I think it worth remembering that, while Dworkin excludes good intentions being distinguished from bad whenever evil is threatened or committed, Nardin argues that extremity cannot be defined neutrally. Of the recent

analyses of the issue, cf. also A. Kenny, 'The Logic and Ethics of Nuclear Deterrence', and H. Shue, 'Conflicting Conceptions of Deterrence', both in A. Ellis (ed.), *Ethics and International Relations* (Manchester: Manchester University, 1986).

57 R. Tucker, *Morality and Deterrence*, in Hardin, Mearsheimer, Dworkin and Goodin (eds), *Nuclear Deterrence*, p. 70.

58 I discussed this issue fully in 'Per una teoria (pura) della politica (internazionale)' in S. Veca (ed.), *Filosofia, Politica, Società* (Milan: Bibliopolis, 1987).

59 S. Krasner, 'Structural Causes and Regime Consequences: Regimes as Intervening Variables', *International Organization*, XXXVI:2 (1982).

60 The 'international system regime' formula may be advanced by analogy with the use made of the word 'regime' in constitutional and political analysis of the state. The best introduction is still that of D. Easton, *A System Analysis of Political Life* (New York: Wiley, 1965).

61 For a critical presentation complete with every necessary reference, cf. D. Snidal, 'The Limits of Hegemonic Stability Theory', *International Organization*, XXXIX:4 (1985); and R. K. Smith, 'The Non-Proliferation Regime and International Relations', *International Organization*, XLI:2 (1987).

62 The book which more than any other has revived the polemic on the possible decline of US power is P. Kennedy, *The Rise and Fall of the Great Powers* (London: Unwin Hyman, 1988).

63 Cf. for example O. Hintze, *Staat und Verfassung* (Gottingen: Vandenhoeck and Ruprecht, 1962); M. Bloch, 'Feudal Society', in *Friends, Followers and Factions* (Berkeley: University of California Press, 1977), pp. 192–206.

64 The question of the overriding of the international anarchy model is discussed in ch. 3, section 2, below.

65 As a consequence of the INF treaty signed by Reagan and Gorbachev in Washington on 8 December 1987.

66 A *change* without *movement*: cf. N. Bobbio, 'La rivoluzione tra movimento e mutamento', *Teoria politica*, V:2–3 (1989), pp. 3–21.

67 Cf., for example, S. Hoffman, *Gulliver's Troubles, or the Setting of American Foreign Policy* (New York: McGraw Hill, 1968), chs 1–2.

68 Continuing to speak in economic language, we might say that war has become the 'flywheel' of the entire political *enterprise* of the modern state. As Hintze does in *Staat und Verfassung*, ch. 7.

69 I personally believe that, even for this second type of war, the problem is no longer to liquidate the past, but to adapt progressively to the new, unforeseen situation created by the advent of the atomic bomb.

70 From this point of view, Enrico Berlinguer's 'Eurocommunist' proposal was anything but senseless. On the contrary, it was arguably a step in the right direction.

71 Driving a scholar of the calibre of D. J. Singer to protest that the expression *global system* was becoming increasingly more appropriate than *international system*, cf. D. J. Singer, 'Accounting for International War:

the State of the Discipline', *Journal of Peace Research* XVIII:1 (1981), p. 4.

72 Here *hyperspace* corresponds to the international hyperpolitics I spoke of above. The quotation is taken from F. Jameson, *Postmodernism: the Cultural Logic of Late Capitalism* (London: New Left, 1984). Jameson observes first that postmodern culture is the domestic and superstructural expression of the whole new course of America's military and economic world dominance, then concludes that postmodernism is not only an ideology or a cultural fantasy, but has a genuinely historical (and socioeconomic) function as the third original stage in capitalism's expansion in the world. He ends by asking whether the increasingly global and totalizing new world system might not require the invention and elaboration of a radically new type of internationalism.

73 The prospects which open up by assuming this point of view are discussed in ch. 4, section 3, below.

74 I advise anyone who finds my recourse to the image of mutation somewhat excessive to read the description of the way victims died in the course of the first and last atomic bombardment in history: cf. *Hiroshima – Nagasaki. I superstiti* (Brescia: Queriniana, 1987). No one who follows my advice will ever argue again that atomic death is comparable to other forms.

75 Albeit ambiguously, the same sentiment is expressed by M. Fini, *Elogio della guerra* (Milan: Mondadori, 1989), who claims that, 'nuclear war departs from the human milieu and old-fashioned, honest war', p. 139. By way of a review of this thesis, that war has a physiological function, cf. at least the essay which M. Mead dedicated to the subject half a century ago: cf. M. Mead, 'Warfare Is Only an Invention – Not a Biological Necessity', *Asia*, XL, pp. 402ff.

76 Speaking of the 'means–ends' relationship, it is well worth recalling an extraordinary page in H. Arendt, *The Human Condition* (Chicago: University of Chicago Press, 1958), which, after first emphasizing the paradoxes implicit in the dichotomy, concludes that, 'As long as we believe that we deal with ends and means in the political realm, we shall not be able to prevent anybody's using all means to pursue recognized ends' (p. 243).

77 'As long as a situation of interindividual relations is characterized by reciprocal fear, the situation is one of the state of nature, that is of the state in which security is unstable and from which individuals seek all means to depart, among which the principal one is the institution of a common power,' N. Bobbio, 'Democrazia e sistema internazionale', in L. Cortesi (ed.), *Democrazia, rischio nucleare, movimenti per la pace* (Naples: Liguori, 1989), p. 46.

78 Cf. N. Bobbio, *Il terzo assente* (Turin: Edizioni Sonda, 1989).

79 Actually, the point is not whether we should feel nostalgia for war or *praise* it (cf. Fini, *Elogio*), but whether we should *judge* it.

80 In this sense, we are faced by a totalitarianism specular (i.e., contrary) to

that denounced over 30 years ago by Jaspers, according to whom the totalitarianism of the communist threat was even more evil than that of the bomb. Cf. Jaspers, *The Future*.

Chapter 4   Duties of States and Ends of Politics

1 J. Herbst, 'The Creation and Management of National Boundaries in Africa', *International Organization*, XLIII:4 (1989), p. 692.
2 On the relationship between the formation of the modern state and the foundation of international law, cf. the anthology, L. Bonanate (ed.), *Diritto naturale e relazione internazionale* (Turin: Loescher, 1976), which comprises essential passages on the subject from the works of seventeenth- and eighteenth-century natural law scholars.
3 Cf. the classic M. Giuliano, *La comunità internazionale e il diritto* (Padua: Cedam, 1950).
4 R. K. Ashley, 'Untying the Sovereign State: A Double Reading of the Anarchy Problematique', *Millennium: Journal of International Studies*, XVII:2 (1988), p. 229.
5 It is no coincidence that all international political realists begin, reluctantly or with conviction, from the *natural* connotation of anarchy.
6 For argument's sake – I do not intend here to address the moral problem which the example implies.
7 The first of which prescribes that 'every man, ought to endeavour Peace', and the second that 'a man be willing, when others are so too . . . to lay down this right to all things' (Hobbes, *Leviathan*, XIV, p. 125). They are thus comparable to instructions or directives.
8 Cf. C. Schmitt, *Der Leviathan in der Staatslehre des Thomas Hobbes* (Hamburg: Hanseatische Verlagsanstalt, 1938). Here Schmitt affirms that among states there is no state, nor is there legal war and legal peace; there is only the pre- and extra-legal state of nature of the reciprocally tense relations between Leviathans, uncertainly overridden by frail treaties.
9 That the conception of the fundamental nature of international life is the logical culmination of Schmitt's 'friend-enemy' theory also stresses the link that must therefore exist between domestic and international politics.
10 Cf. H. Bull, 'International Theory: a Case for a Classical Approach', *World Politics* XVIII:3 (1966).
11 Cf. K. Knorr, J. N. Rosenau (eds), *Contending Approaches to International Politics* (Princeton: Princeton University Press, 1969).
12 Cf. M. Wight, 'Why Is There No International Theory?', in H. Butterfield, M. Wight (eds), *Diplomatic Investigations* (London: Allen and Unwin, 1966).
13 Ibid., p. 18.
14 The best example is H. Bull, *The Anarchical Society: A Study of Order in World Society* (London: Macmillan, 1977).
15 As Pufendorf objected in his argument against Hobbes, it sometimes happens

that states are united by treaties and alliances: it would be contrary to general opinion to consider them as sides in a reciprocal state of war for the mere fact that they are not subordinated to a common lord. S. Pufendorf, *De jure naturae et gentium* (1672), tr. C. H. and W. A. Oldfather (Oxford: Clarendon, 1934), vol. II, ch. II: par. 8. Wight also cites Pufendorf.

16 Cf. K. N. Waltz, *Theory of International Politics* (Reading, Mass.: Addison-Wesley, 1979), p. 113.

17 M. Kaplan, *System and Process in International Politics* (New York: Wiley, 1957).

18 Cf., for example, E. H. Gombrich, *The Story of Art* (London: Phaidon, 1966).

19 C. Perelman, 'Analogia e metafora', in *Enciclopedia Einaudi*, vol. I (Turin: Einaudi, 1977), p. 524.

20 It is uncanny how Hobbes's formula seems to repeat Plato's. See *Laws*, I, II–IV for what is, arguably, the first major analysis of the significance of war in western culture. The resemblance is pointed out by D. W. Hanson, 'Thomas Hobbes's Highway to Peace', *International Organization*, XXXVIII:2 (1984), pp. 336–7.

21 Aristotle, *Politics*, tr. H. Rackham (Cambridge, Mass.: Harvard University Press, 1959), p. 553.

22 D. Hume, *An Enquiry Concerning the Principle of Morals*, 2nd edn, ed. L. A. Selby-Bigge (Oxford: Clarendon, 1902), section IV.

23 D. Hume, *A Treatise of Human Nature*, ed. T. H. Green and T. H. Grose (Aalen: Scientia Verlag, 1964), vol. III, part II, section XI, p. 330.

24 I. Kant, 'Perpetual Peace', in *Kant's Political Writings*, ed. H. Reiss (Cambridge: Cambridge University Press, 1970). Cf. also N. Bobbio's introduction to the Italian translation, *Per la pace perpetua* (Roma: Editori Riuniti, 1985), pp. X–XI, in which he explicitly refers to the procedure by analogy.

25 This formulation has always been one of the cornerstones of federalist thinking. Cf., for example, Lord Lothian, *Pacifism Is Not Enough*, ed. J. Pinder and A. Bosco (London: Lothian Foundation, 1990), p. 246: 'The inescapable result of anarchy is that morality is dethroned in international affairs.'

26 The distinction is discussed by C. Beitz, *Political Theory and International Relations* (Princeton: Princeton University Press, 1979).

27 Hobbes, *Leviathan*, XXX, p. 244.

28 This is easy to verify thanks to A. Garcia, *Thomas Hobbes. Bibliographie internationale de 1620 à 1986* (Caen: Centre de philosophie juridique de Caen, 1986).

29 Cf. 'Hobbes on International Relations', the appendix to D. P. Gauthier, *The Logic of Leviathan* (Oxford: Clarendon, 1969). Incisive as it is, I don't think that H. Warrender in *The Political Philosophy of Hobbes: His Theory of Obligation* (Oxford: Clarendon, 1957) can lay first claim to the discovery. Cf. also H. Bull, 'Society and Anarchy in International Rela-

tions', in H. Butterfield and M. Wight (eds), *Diplomatic Investigations* (London: Allen and Unwin, 1966); and the recent, but not particularly innovative collection, T. Airaksinen and M. A. Bertman (eds), *Hobbes: War Among Nations* (Aldershot: Avebury, 1989).

30 The 'international system' in Hobbes's time comprised no more than twenty or so sovereign states, among no more than half of which there were intense, ongoing relations!

31 According to Portinaro, with his extension of the state of nature hypothesis to international relations, Hobbes 'does not seem to get very far', hence if 'the concept of nature does not allow a realistic vision of the many facets of politics, that of the social contract does not seem capable of indicating a solution to the state of international anarchy.' P. P. Portinaro, *Il terzo. Una figura del politico* (Milan: Angeli, 1986), p. 43.

32 It is necessary to bear in mind the specification whereby 'the state of nature whose subjects are individuals is prevalently a state of actual, fought war: while the state of nature whose subjects are states is prevalently a state of potential, feared war': indeed 'the state of nature whose subjects are states is a condition which allows the development of industriousness and the growth of wealth.' Cf. M. Geuna and P. Giacotto, 'Le relazioni tra gli stati e il problema della pace', *Comunità*, XL:187 (1985), pp. 86–7.

33 M. Walzer, *Just and Unjust Wars* (New York: Basic Books, 1977), p. 59.

34 T. Hobbes, 'De Corpore Politico' [1650], *The English Works of Thomas Hobbes*, ed. W. Molesworth (London: John Bohn, 1845), p. 185. The fact that Hobbes referred specifically to civil war must not be construed as limiting the scope of my assessment, first of all because the stress is mainly on the relationship between ignorance and war (which is valid in domestic and international realms), secondly because Hobbes himself, in the lines preceding, refers more generally to 'war and peace', and finally because domestic and international war are associated in Hobbesian thought by the reference to human nature. This is why the assertion cited is so disconcerting. It is much more optimistic than we have come to expect from Hobbesian anthropology. Its faith in the capacity of moral philosophy to dispel our ignorance might almost be that of the Enlightenment. This passage from *De corpore*, which is not commonly cited as an example of Hobbesian thought on the case in point, is also referred to by D. W. Hanson, 'Thomas Hobbes' Highway to Peace', *International Organization*, XXXVIII:2 (1984), pp. 343–4.

35 This is the reasoning at least of those who accept the logic of the security dilemma which forces reciprocally suspicious states to reinforce themselves beyond measure, thus provoking a continuous armaments race. Cf. ch. 3, note 29 above, for bibliographical references.

36 Here I summarize pp. 207–12 of D. P. Gauthier, *The Logic of Leviathan* (Oxford: Clarendon, 1969).

37 In reality, the first discussion by analogy that I know is by I. L. Claude Jr,

who entitles a paragraph of a chapter in *Power and International Relations* (New York: Random House, 1962) 'The Analogy of Nation-State and World State' (pp. 255–71), although the context of his analysis is a totally different one. The most recent – anything but repetitive – is E. F. McClennen, 'The Tragedy of National Sovereignty', in A. Cohen and S. Lee (eds), *Nuclear Weapons and the Future of Humanity* (Totowa: Rowman and Allanheld, 1986), pp. 400–1.

38 Cf. H. Bull, 'Hobbes and International Anarchy', *Social Research*, XLVIII:4 (1981). This second essay (the first is cited in note 29) does not significantly modify the sense of the previous arguments. For an analysis of the analogy model of Bull and others, cf. H. Suganami, 'Reflections on the Domestic Analogy: the Case of Bull, Beitz, Linklater', *Review of International Studies*, XII:2 (1986).

39 I presented it for the first time in 'La costituzione del sistema internazionale', *Comunità*, XXVII:169 (1973).

40 Cf. N. Bobbio, 'Il modello giusnaturalistico', *Rivista internazionale di filosofia del diritto*, L:4 (1973).

41 Beitz, *Political Theory*, p. 54.

42 Cf. M. Forsyth, 'Thomas Hobbes and the External Relations of States', *British Journal of International Studies*, V:2 (1979), pp. 208–9. An interesting specification in the same direction is made by Geuna and Giacotto, 'Le relazioni tra gli stati', p. 85, with regard to the 'pure natural state'.

43 Cf. for a similar line to Beitz's, M. Cohen, 'Moral Scepticism and International Relations', *Philosophy and Public Affairs*, XIII:4 (1984), p. 31, according to whom whereas 'Individuals in the Hobbesian state of nature are anonymous and ahistorical . . . nations have names and reputations, geographies and histories, principles and purposes,' and this brings about the downfall of the analogy procedure.

44 Beitz, *Political Theory*, p. 53.

45 Cf. M. A. Heller, 'The Use and Abuse of Hobbes: the State of Nature in International Relations', *Polity*, XIII:1 (1980), p. 22.

46 Ibid., p. 31.

47 Another two essays, of the many dedicated by international relations specialists to the reappraisal of Hobbes, add nothing to the debate: Bull, 'Hobbes and International Anarchy', reiterates the arguments already advanced in his 1966 essay, while R. J. Vincent, 'The Hobbesian Tradition in Twentieth Century International Thought', *Millennium*, X:2 (1981), claims that elements of anarchy and order – i.e., state of nature and civil society – continue to exist on the international stage (which does not, of course, resolve the question at stake).

48 I find the following statement by Beitz biased but acceptable: 'To say that international scepticism is incorrect, then, is like saying that international political theory is possible.' *Political Theory*, p. 65.

49 Cf. J. D. Singer, M. Small, *Resort to Arms* (Beverly Hills: Sage, 1982).

50 J. L. Windenberger, *Essai sur le système de politique étrangère de J. J.*

Rousseau (Paris: Picard, 1899), p. 49. Cf. also the comments of the editor of the Pléiade edition of *Contrat social* (Paris: Gallimard, 1964), vol. III, p. 1431, pp. 1507–8.

51 I use the jargon term 'international system' to remind readers that the international political struggle does not actually take place among all states, but only among those reciprocally linked by relations of a certain intensity and continuity. For this problematique and a discussion of the relevant literature, I refer to the essays contained in L. Bonanate, *Il sistema internazionale* (Genoa: Ecig, 1986).

52 Whose forerunner is E. H. Carr, *The Twenty Years' Crisis* (London: Macmillan, 1939), and whose master was M. Wight, *Power Politics* (Harmondsworth: Penguin, 1986).

53 Cf. Bull, *The Anarchical Society*, p. 13. Cf., for a friendly and touching critical comment (Bull died in 1985), A. Watson, 'Hedley Bull, States Systems amd International Societies', *Review of International Studies*, XIII:1 (1987).

54 H. Bull, 'The Emergence of a Universal International Society', in H. Bull and A. Watson (eds), *The Expansion of International Society* (Oxford: Clarendon, 1984), p. 120.

55 Cf. T. Nardin, *Law, Morality and the Relations of States* (Princeton: Princeton University Press, 1983). Of the first discussions of the study, see T. W. Pogge, 'Liberalism and Global Justice: Hoffmann and Nardin on Morality in International Affairs', *Philosophy and Public Affairs*, XV:1 (1986); and M. Wright, 'Reflexions on Injustice and International Politics', *Review of International Studies*, XII:1 (1986).

56 Pogge in 'Liberalism and Global Justice', p. 77, rightly stresses the contradiction into which Nardin stumbles when he proposes the idea that procedural rules may exist, without justifying why they should be adopted.

57 Nardin, *Law, Morality*, p. 310.

58 In my 1973 essay 'La costituzione', I even conjured up the image of a 'two-headed Leviathan' to describe the ongoing international government relationship between the United States and the Soviet Union.

59 Besides the works already cited, Beitz, *Political Theory*, Nardin, *Law, Morality*, Walzer, *Just and Unjust Wars*, cf. also S. Hoffmann, *Duties Beyond Borders: On the Limits and Possibilities of Ethical International Politics* (New York: Syracuse University Press, 1981); N. A. Sims (ed.), *Explorations in Ethics and International Relations* (London: Croom Helm, 1971); A. Linklater, *Men and Citizens in the Theory of International Relations* (London: Macmillan, 1982); K. N. Thompson (ed.), *Ethics and International Relations* (New Brunswick: Transaction, 1985); M. Frost, *Towards a Normative Theory of International Relations* (London: Macmillan, 1986).

60 R. Niebuhr, *Moral Man and Immoral Society* (London: SCM 1963), p. 83.

61 I discussed the point in ch. 1 above.

62 Beitz, *Political Theory*, p. 55; cf. also pp. 181–2. By the same author see also 'Cosmopolitan Ideals and National Sentiment', *The Journal of Philosophy*, LXXX:10 (1983).

63 Cf. G. L. Scott and C. L. Carr, 'Are States Moral Agents?', *Social Theory and Practice*, XII:1 (1986), esp. p. 95.

64 M. Mori, *Le regioni delle armi* (Milan: Il Saggiatore, 1984), p. 87.

65 G. W. F. Hegel, *The Philosophy of Right*, ed. R. M. Hutchins (Chicago: University of Chicago Press, 1952), p. 110.

66 G. W. F. Hegel, 'Encyclopaedia of the Philosophical Sciences', tr. W. Wallace, in *Hegel's Philosophy of the Mind* (Oxford: Clarendon, 1894), p. 147.

67 D. A. Routh, 'The Philosophy of International Relations: T. H. Green versus Hobbes', *Politica*, III, p. 223.

68 J. Rawls, *A Theory of Justice* (Oxford: Clarendon, 1972). It would be impossible here to summarize the general, never mind the international-oriented, debate on this study. For the moment I shall mention only two analyses with an especially international slant: they are R. Amdur, 'Rawls's Theory of Justice: Domestic and International Perspectives', *World Politics*, XXIX:3 (1977); and G. Pontara, 'Giustizia locale e giustizia globale', *Biblioteca della libertà*, XIV:64–5 (also in *Filosofia pratica* (Milan: Il Saggiatore, 1988); cf. also the bibliography). Pontara judges Rawls's considerations in section 58 as 'the tritest in the work', and, in general, rejects the normative dualism which stems from Rawls's position. For two examples of application to international relations theory, cf. M. I. Midlarski, 'The Balance of Power as a "Just" Historical System', *Polity*, XVI:2 (1983); M. W. Jackson, 'Justice and Heroism', ibid. Further references are to be found in ch. 5, sections 1 and 2 below.

69 Cf. Rawls *A Theory of Justice*, p. 378.

70 Here I summarize from pp. 90–2 of Walzer, *Just and Unjust Wars*. A vast debate developed round this study as well. Cf., at least, the series of notes published in *Philosophy and Public Affairs*: G. Doppelt, 'Walzer's Theory of Morality in International Relations', VIII:1 (1978); D. Luban, 'Just War and Human Rights', IX:2 (1979); M. Walzer, 'The Moral Standing of States', X:3 (1980); G. Doppelt, 'Statism Without Foundations', X:4 (1980); J. Dubik, 'Human Rights, Command Responsibility and Walzer's Just War Theory', XI:4 (1982).

71 At least as far as Rawls is concerned, the same type of judgement is made by B. Barry, *The Liberal Theory of Justice* (Oxford: Clarendon, 1973), pp. 132–3. A more detailed assessment from the specific standpoint of international justice is contained in B. Barry, *Theories of Justice* (London: Harvester Wheatsheaf, 1989), pp. 183–9.

72 Cf. H. Fain, *Normative Politics and the Community of Nations* (Philadelphia: Temple University Press, 1987) p. 91. Another author who rejects the contractarian analogy for the foundation of international relations is M. Frost, *Towards a Normative Theory of International Relations* (Cambridge: Cambridge University Press, 1986): cf. esp. pp. 162ff..

73 Ibid., p. 42.

74 Admirable as it may be, his overall argument seems unacceptable in its ingenuousness.

75 As I suggested in ch. 1, section 3 above.

76 The following seems to me a noteworthy assertion: nations 'are all members of an egalitarian world political community, constituted upon essentially global tasks', Fain, *Normative Politics*, p. 112.

77 As when we speak of the superconductivity of a metal, in which case we do not make a quality judgement, but a judgement which heightens a phenomenon (in this case, a considerable, brusque reduction in a metal's resistivity).

78 Extremely significant examples of the role which an update in political geography can play in this context are R. J. Johnston, *Geography and the State* (London: Macmillan, 1982); J. P. Taylor, *Political Geography: World Economy, Nation-State and Locality* (London: Longman, 1985). Cf. also R. J. Johnston, J. P. Taylor (eds), *A World in Crisis? Geographical Perspectives* (Oxford: Blackwell, 1986).

79 Defined by the French theologian as 'the terrestrial sphere of thinking substance': cf. Pierre Teilhard de Chardin, *L'avenir et l'homme* (Paris: Editions du Seuil, 1959), p. 203, note 2 (see also the whole chapter entitled 'La formation de la Noosphère'). Jonas observes something very similar:

> It is at least not senseless anymore to ask whether the condition of extrahuman nature, the biosphere as a whole and in its parts, now subject to our power, has become a human trust and has something of a moral claim on us, not only for our ulterior sake but for its own and in its own right. *If this were the case, it would require quite some rethinking in basic principles of ethics.*

H. Jonas, *The Imperative of Responsibility* (Chicago: University of Chicago Press, 1984), p. 8 (my italics).

80 Here I make use of the meanings Bobbio proposes for political philosophy. Cf. N. Bobbio, 'Considerazioni sulla filosofia politica', *Rivista italiana di scienza politica*, I:2 (1971) p. 367.

81 No one doubts that one of the state's duties is to safeguard its citizens, a task which creates not a few domestic political problems. Why shouldn't health be protected internationally?

82 At most, the specific characteristics it is assuming today are new and original.

83 A rare gesture of sympathy with the programme I am pursuing here comes from S. Veca when, far from refuting 'the utopia of *the civil society of world citizens*' (his italics), he argues in favour of it. Cf. S. Veca, *Cittadinanza. Riflessioni filosofiche sull'idea di emancipazione* (Milan: Feltrinelli, 1990), p. 57.

84 Cf. the wealth of material collected by P. Picone and G. Sacerdoti, *Diritto internazionale dell'economia* (Milan: Angeli, 1982).

85 'Support' and 'demands', here used in their political meaning, are at the centre of D. Easton, *A System Analysis of Political Life* (New York: Wiley, 1965), esp. chs 3 and 10.

86 *Ibid.*, p. 191. The fundamental reference work on the regime problematique

is S. D. Krasner (ed.), *International Regimes* (Ithaca: Cornell University Press, 1983). For a general presentation of the problem, cf. L. Bonanate, A. Caffarena and R. Vellano, *Dopo l'anarchia. Saggi sul superamento dell'immagine anarchica delle relazioni internazionali e sul rischio di ricadervi* (Milan: Angeli, 1989).

Chapter 5   Cycle of Wars and Philosophy of History

1 Both Vico and Hegel, to cite but two names, speak of the destinies of nations, yet their thinking is devoted not to international history, but to the *historic individual,* or the *spirit of the people.* This is easily visible in affirmations such as Meinecke's, according to which the gradual development of 'the peculiar soul of men' transforms the destinies of *peoples.* Cf. F. Meinecke, *Historicism: the Rise of a New Historical Outlook* (London: Routledge and Kegan Paul, 1972), ch. 1, section 4. On Hegel's position, cf. M. Mori, *Le ragioni delle armi* (Milan: Il Saggiatore, 1984) pp. 275–81, and, in general, on the same issue, cf. the whole of ch. 6 below. Who can forget finally, that the achievement also fascinated the curate Blanès, intent upon establishing the precise epoch of the fall of the empires and revolutions which change the face of the world? Cf. Stendhal, *The Charterhouse of Parma,* tr. C. K. S. Moncrieff (London: Penguin, 1993), ch. 2.

2 The first systematic exposition of this thesis is Polybius, *Histories,* tr. W. Paton (Cambridge, Mass.: Harvard University Press), vol. VI, esp. section 9. On Vico's considerably more famous philosophy of history, cf., among others, K. Lowith, *Meaning in History: the Theological Implications of the Philosophy of History* (Chicago: University of Chicago Press, 1949), ch. 6, section 4; and also, for an overview, K. Pomian's 'Ciclo', in the *Enciclopedia Einaudi* (Turin: Einaudi, 1977), vol. II.

3 Cf. for an extremely detailed study, J. Le Goff's, 'Decadenza', in *Enciclopedia Einaudi* (Turin: Einaudi, 1977), vol. IV.

4 N. Machiavelli, *History of Florence and of the Affairs of Italy from the Earliest Times to the Death of Lorenzo the Magnificent* (London: M. Walter Dunne, 1901), p. 204.

5 *August Comte and Positivism: The Essential Writings,* ed. G. Lenzer (Chicago: University of Chicago Press, 1983), p. 285.

6 'To practice the philosophy of history is to take an event, or series of events, and pose oneself the problem of its "meaning" according to a finalistic (or teleological) conception of history (valid not only for human, but also for natural history), considering the course of history as a whole, from its origin to its completion, as directed to an end, to a *telos.*' N. Bobbio, *L'età dei diritti* (Turin: Einaudi, 1990), p. 47.

7 Observe, for example, how and how often in the work of R. Aron, most of which is dedicated to the philosophy of history and international relations, these two themes meet. Cf. ch. 7, 'L'aube de l'histoire universelle',

Dimensions de la conscience historique (Paris: Plon, 1961). See also the fundamental *Leçons sur l'histoire* (Paris: Editions de Fallois, 1988), a collection of the previously unpublished texts of two university courses on historiographical theory. What is noteworthy is that the majority of Aron's examples refer to international relations.

8 Cf. W. H. Dray, *Philosophy of History* (Englewood Cliffs: Prentice-Hall, 1964), ch. 5.

9 Albeit with the characteristics discussed in ch. 2, section 2, above.

10 Cf. especially P. Kennedy, *The Rise and Fall of the Great Powers* (London: Unwin Hyman, 1988). But the debate began almost a decade earlier: cf. R. Rosencrance (ed.), *America As An Ordinary Country* (Ithaca: Cornell University Press, 1976); G. Liska, *Career of Empire* (Baltimore: Johns Hopkins University Press, 1978); R. Gilpin, *War and Change in World Politics* (Cambridge: Cambridge University Press, 1981). Others reject the idea of US decline: cf. S. Strange, 'The Persistent Myth of Lost Hegemony', *International Organization*, XLI:4 (1987), and the bibliography discussed.

11 'For anyone who assumes this standpoint, events cease to be facts to be described, recounted, arranged chronologically, and even to be explained according to the consolidated research techniques and procedures habitually followed by historians, but become revealing *signs* of or *clues* to a not necessarily intentional process, towards a pre-established direction,' Bobbio, *L'età dei diritti*, p. 47.

12 Cf. L. Canfora's introduction to the Italian translation of Thucydides' *History of the Peloponnesian War*, *La guerra del Peloponneso* (Bari: Laterza, 1986), pp. x–xi.

13 O. Spengler, *Der Untergang des Abendlandes* (Munich: Beck, 1972), vol. I, ch. 2, section 2. Cf. also note 15 referring to the passage cited, in which the author exemplifies his point with 'the distance between the three Punic Wars, and the identically structured series of the War of the Spanish succession, of the wars of Frederick the Great, Napoleon, Bismarck and, finally, world war'. For an international reading of Spengler, and of Toynbee (referred to below), cf. J. Joll, 'Two Prophets of the Twentieth Century: Spengler and Toynbee'. *Review of International Studies*, XI:2 (1985).

14 Cf. K. Jaspers, *Vom Unsprumg und Ziel der Geschichte* (Munich: Piper, 1988), ch. 2.

15 Q. Wright, *A Study of War* (Chicago: University of Chicago Press, 1942), p. 227 and p. 229.

16 A. Toynbee, *A Study of History* (London: Oxford University Press, 1954), vol. IX, p. 239 and p. 255. Albeit totally insensitive to such programmes, P. Sorokin nonetheless devotes a great deal of attention to the 'Fluctuation of War in Inter-Group Relations': cf. part VI of his *Social and Cultural Dynamics* (Boston: Porter Sargeant, 1957). He concludes, however, that history appears neither as monotonous and devoid of imagination as supporters of compulsory periodicity, of 'iron laws' or of 'universal uniformities' believe, nor as insensitive and mechanical as a device which completes the same number of revolutions in a unit of time.

17 Cf. F. L. Klingberg, 'Historical Periods, Trends and Cycles in International Relations', *Journal of Conflict Resolution*, XIV:4 (1970). Curiously enough, this author glimpses a 50-year cycle in which each of the two phases lasts roughly 25 years.

18 Cf. L. L. Farrar Jr, 'Cycles of War: Historical Speculation on Future International Violence', *International Interactions,* III:I (1977).

19 For discussion of the sample and comparison of the choices of the diverse scholars, cf. J. S. Levy, 'General War Theories', *World Politics*, XXXVII:3 (1985).

20 For an attempt to systematically present the whole problematique, cf. J. S. Levy, *War in the Great Power System, 1495–1975* (Lexington: University Press of Kentucky, 1983); for an initial critical summing-up, cf. R. Rosencrance, 'Long Cycles Theory and International Relations', *International Organization*, XLI:2 (1987). In his most recent article, G. Modelski, 'Is World Politics Evolutionary Learning?', *International Organization*, XLIV:1 (1990), p. 15, refers to 2030 as the date for the next 'macrodecision' or 'global war'.

21 M. Small, D. J. Singer, *Resort to Arms: International and Civil Wars, 1816–1980* (Beverly Hills: Sage, 1982), p. 156.

22 I. Wallerstein, *The World-System: Capitalist Agriculture and the Rise of the World Economy in the Sixteenth Century* (New Work: Academic Press, 1974).

23 Cf. F. Braudel, *The Mediterranean and the Mediterranean World in the Age of Philip II* (London: Harper Collins, 1993), ch. 8.

24 J. S. Goldstein, *Long Cycles: Prosperity and War in the Modern Age* (New Haven: Yale University Press, 1988): the bibliography (pp. 399–426) is particularly noteworthy. What a pity, though, that, in such an outstanding, well-informed work, the author appears totally unaware that, over the centuries, the philosophy of history has already discussed – albeit in wholly different terms and with different arguments – the selfsame problematique.

25 Although the writings of this economic statistician date from the twenties, when he was criticized by Trotsky (cf. R. B. Day, 'The Theory of the Long Cycle: Kondratiev, Trotsky, Mandel', *New Left Review*, no. 99, (1976); and Goldstein, *Long Cycles*, pp. 23–31), for a lengthy period Kondratiev's only claim to notoriety was a brief citation made by J. Schumpeter in a note to vol. III of his *History of Economic Analysis* (Oxford: Oxford University Press, 1954). The recent publication of an English translation of two works under the title *The Long Wave Cycle* (New York: Richardson and Snyder, 1984) has led to a reappraisal of this author.

26 Cf. Goldstein, *Long Cycles*, pp. 15–16.

27 Ibid., p. 6.

28 Ibid., p. 352.

29 Ibid., p. 353. As I remarked above, it is not Goldstein alone who makes this prediction. This is why I have summarized his formulation for example's sake (simplifying dates slightly and narrowing the minor time lapses which the author hypothesizes).

30 Cf. E. H. Carr, *The Twenty Years' Crisis*, (London: Macmillan, 1939).
31 I proposed and discussed this system typology for the first time in the entry, 'Sistema internazionale', in L. Bonanate (ed.), *Politica internazionale, Il mondo contemporaneo*, vol. VII (Florence: La Nuova Italia, 1979).
32 Frankly, the nature of the sample available permits no serious statistical argument: the reasoning is valid impressionistically, but certain constant features appear odd – albeit insignificant – nonetheless.
33 I wonder who is brave enough to subscribe to Modelski's abrupt reply to the question 'Why cycles?' – 'we cannot but reply: because they are there!' Cf. G. Modelski, 'Long Cycles of World Leadership', in W. R. Thompson (ed.), *Contending Approaches to World-System Analysis* (Beverly Hills: Sage, 1983), p. 124.
34 Cf. Pomian, 'Ciclo', p. 191.
35 For a synthetic presentation of these postions, cf. L. Bonanate, *Guerre e pace. Dal progresso come promessa di pace al progresso come minaccia di distruzione* (Milan: Angeli, 1987).
36 Cf., for example, M. Wight, 'The Balance of Power', in H. Butterfield, M. Wight (eds), *Diplomatic Investigations* (London: Allen and Unwin, 1966). For an analytic-historiographical presentation, cf. M. Cesa, *L'equilibrio di potenza* (Milan: Angeli, 1987).
37 The balance logic ultimately resembles the cycle logic, if we think in terms of the type of movement it impresses on reality. For a strongly critical analysis of the international balance concept, cf. L. Bonanate, *Teoria politica e relazioni internazionali* (Milan: Edizioni di Comunità, 1976), ch. 4.
38 Talking of 'spontaneous order' with reference to the balance theory of Adam Smith, Buchanan observes that the principle of spontaneous order as such is completely neutral. Cf. J. M. Buchanan, *Freedom in Constitutional Contract: Perspective of a Political Economist* (Austin: Texas University Press, 1977), ch. 2.
39 Buchanan also asserts that the explanation of the results (of a set of spontaneous individual actions) made through the action of invisible hand-type responses does not necessarily imply the presence of normative criteria. Cf. Buchanan, *Freedom in Constitutional Contract*.
40 C. Tilly, 'The Formation of National States in Western Europe', in C. Tilly (ed.), *Studies in Political Development* (Princeton: Princeton University Press, 1975), p. 42. Hintze said something similar as early as 1931, when he proposed a reconstruction of the development of the modern state founded on the succession of three stages: the feudal, the bourgeois-capitalist and the socialized 'total' state. Cf. O. Hintze, *Staat und Verfassung* (Gottingen: Vandenhoeck and Ruprecht, 1962), ch. 7.
41 As is well known, J. Rawls himself attempts to describe this situation in *A Theory of Justice* (Oxford: Clarendon, 1972), but in much more idyllic tones!
42 K. N. Waltz, 'The Origins of War in Neorealist Theory', in R. L. Rotberg and T. K. Rabb (eds), *The Origins and Prevention of Major Wars* (Cambridge: Cambridge University Press, 1989), p. 43.

43   T. Mann, *Doctor Faustus* (London: Secker and Warburg, 1949), ch. 21, p. 175.

44   R. Aron referred the same concept, over 30 years later, to the last century: cf. Aron, 'L'aube de l'histoire', esp. pp. 263ff..

45   Cf. chapter 3, section 4, below.

46   Uttered by Mandeville in his poem *The Grumbling Hive*. Mandeville added the comment that common, short-sighted folk can rarely see beyond a link in the chain of causes, but those who can widen their vision and are able to observe sets of connected facts, may in a hundred places see good growing and evil germinating. Cf. B. Mandeville, *The Fable of the Bees,* ed. F. B. Kaye, 2 vols (Oxford: Oxford University Press, 1924). The idea is presented systematically by W. Wundt, *Systeme der Philosophie* (1889), vol. I, p. 326, and vol. II, pp. 221ff., and aspects of it are to be found also in the thinking of F. Tönnies, 'Community and Society'; in Meinecke, *Historicism*, or also in the so-called 'Thomas Theorem' discussed by Merton who, more generally, distinguishes 'manifest functions' from other 'latent functions' in human action: cf. R. K. Merton, *Social Theory and Social Structure* (New York: Columbia University Press, 1951): part II, ch. 7, p. 179 for the 'Thomas theorem'; part I, ch. 1, p. 21 for latent functions.

47   Cf. my argument in ch. 2, section 4, above, which is motivated by different intentions from the illustrative argument advanced here.

48   'Historical research may refer to general theories; but it must always use them as a source of interpretative hypotheses', P. Rossi, 'Sulla nozione di legge nella storia', *Rivista di filosofia*, LXXXI:1 (1990), p. 15. Also: 'Historical research does not so much "produce" as "consume" theory supplied by theoretical disciplines, especially – but not only – by the social sciences.' Ibid., p. 18.

49   One inevitably returns to *Doctor Faustus*, to the chapter in which Thomas Mann discusses the theme, observing among other things, that 'Now indeed arose, the other way round, as history continuously teaches, out of good much evil.' Mann, *Doctor Faustus*, ch. 13, p. 104.

50   Although there may be thousands of special or 'local' theories.

51   I use this verb in the strong meaning dicussed by G. von Wright, *Explanation and Understanding* (London: Routledge and Kegan Paul, 1971), ch. 1, section 3.

52   The syncretism of Kennedy, *The Rise and Fall*, pp. 438–9, thus appears excessive. Kennedy's is basically a blend of linear, cyclical and chaotic formulations: 'Perhaps the best way to comprehend what lies ahead is to look "backward" briefly at the rise and fall of the Great Powers over the past five centuries.' If we add that, just a few pages later, the author hypothesizes that in the near future we are bound to see the arms race continue (p. 601), we can appreciate the temerity of his forecasts!

53   I developed this interpretation in 'La rivoluzione francese e le relazioni internazionali. Questioni di metodo', *Teoria politica*, V:2–3 (1989).

54   Rawls, *A Theory of Justice*, p. 17.

55   Ibid., p. 378.

56 What better proof than the disappearance of the German Democratic Republic? This is one example of the *failure* of a state.

57 Cf., for example, the extremely interesting analysis by Hintze in *Staat und Verfassung*, ch. 7.

58 For further observations on the point cf. ch. 1, section 4 above.

59 H. J. Grimmelshausen, *The Adventurous Simplicissimus* (Omaha: University of Nebraska, 1962).

60 Even though the war lasted much longer, US commitment was not, except for limited periods, intensely concentrated.

61 Using the Hobbesian lesson with the true spirit of analogy, how can we forget the famous passage in ch. XIII of *Leviathan* in which Hobbes specifies that, 'It may peradventure be thought there was never such a time, nor condition of warre as this': cf. Hobbes, *Leviathan*, p. 89.

62 Cf. ch. 1, section 3 above.

63 Cf. ch. 2, section 4 above.

64 Or, in other words, of control techniques. Cf. my observations in ch. 4, section 4 above.

Chapter 6   The Future of International Justice

1 Here philosophical research has achieved highly interesting results, although it is not easy to translate them into empirical terms. Cf. the seminal J. Rawls, *A Theory of Justice* (Oxford: Clarendon Press, 1972); but also B. A. Ackerman, *Social Justice in the Liberal State* (New Haven: Yale University Press, 1980); M. J. Sandel, *Liberalism and the Limits of Justice* (Cambridge: Cambridge University Press, 1982); S. Veca, *La società giusta e altri saggi* (Milan: Il Saggiatore, 1988); B. Barry, *Theories of Justice* (London: Harvester Wheatsheaf, 1989).

2 These are the reasons, in ch. 4, for my insistent criticism of the anarchic formulation, on the basis of which international politics is ultimately a rough copy of domestic politics (section 2), and my discussion of the terms and limits of the 'individual–state' analogy (section 3).

3 Cicero, *Pro Milone*, vol. IV:10.

4 What I mean is that the two realms are both equally open to a theory of justice but, given the complexity of the subject, it is better to keep them separate. In any case, besides the traditional attempts by St Augustine, St Thomas and F. Vitoria, there has been no shortage, more recently, of efforts to formulate a theory of justice *in bello*. Cf., for example, M. Walzer, *Just and Unjust Wars* (London: Allen Lane, 1977), pp. 58–63.

5 Much of ch. 4, section 3, above is dedicated to the question.

6 It is worth citing the extremely original, courageous attempt to construct a *vertical* theory of international law to oppose the traditional *horizontal* version. Its claim is that international law only concerns the joint relations of states. But:

The horizontal approach builds international law on the political norms regulating the relationship between the individual and the relevant political institution. From the vertical perspective, a state's action outside its territory, and against non-citizens, must be evaluated in terms of the political justification that grants that state the right to operate domestically. It denies that the legitimacy of the bombing of an Iranian oil platform for national security reasons is qualitatively different from the legitimacy of the bombing ... of the headquarters of a domestic political group for national security reasons.

L. Brilmayer, *Justifying International Acts* (Ithaca: Cornell University Press, 1989), p. 2.

7   Only rarely do philosophers take this into account. For them the content does not change along with its recipients, but they fail to consider the context variable of the individual's much fuller subjective right to respect and autonomy with respect to the state. The incidence of their negligence emerges clearly in analysis of justifications for international aid.

8   Cf. ch. 1, section 2 above.

9   Suffice to think of the rich tradition which purports to found international life on the principle of non-intervention (or non-interference).

10 Whereas the problem of indemnity for the damage caused by centuries of exploitation is so complex and 'insoluble' as to be better left to one side. Cf. J. Stone, 'Approaches to the Notion of International Justice', R. A. Falk and C. E. Black (eds), *The Future of International Legal Order*, vol. I, *Trends and Patterns* (Princeton: Princeton University Press, 1969), p. 441. This problem is very often associated with another; that of the responsibility for the future as opposed to the past – for generations to come, that is. Cf., for a general overview, R. I. Sikora and B. Barry (eds), *Obligations to Future Generations* (Philadelphia: Temple University Press, 1978).

11 Here I summarize the argument presented in ch. 8 of P. Singer, *Practical Ethics* (Cambridge: Cambridge University Press, 1979), which contains most of the arguments expounded in 'Famine, Affluence and Morality' in *Philosophy and Public Affairs*, I:3 (1972). It should be added that, in ch. 8, the author stresses that his argument 'does not depend on particular values or ethical principles', almost as if it actually depended on a *pre-moral* logic.

12 Cf. J. Fishkin, 'Theories of Justice and International Relations: the Limits of Liberal Theory', in A. Ellis (ed.), *Ethics and International Relations* (Manchester: Manchester University Press, 1986), p. 9. The same author makes substantially analogous remarks in 'The Boundaries of Justice', *Journal of Conflict Resolution*, XXVII:2 (1983).

13 Jonas clarifies the complexity of this point by drawing attention to the fact that, 'aid from without ... will have to be a more voluntary, magnanimous and at the same time softer kind than an ethics under the conjunction of guilt, justice and neighborliness in one's own house.' H. Jonas, *The*

Imperative of Responsibility (Chicago: University of Chicago Press, 1984), p. 182.

14 B. Barry, 'Can States Be Moral? International Morality and the Compliance Problem', in Ellis, *Ethics and International Relations*, p. 73. The author has also won acclaim for his exhaustive, detailed analysis of the few pages devoted to the issue by Rawls, *A Theory of Justice.* Cf. ch. 12 of B. Barry, *The Liberal Theory of Justice* (Oxford: Clarendon, 1973) and ch. 5 of Barry, *Theories of Justice.*

15 This is a possibility which has often been explored in game theory – recently revitalized not without some ambiguity (after all, is *significant* collaboration really possible in an anarchic realm?). *World Politics* devoted a whole issue to the topic with an introductory essay by K. A. Oye, 'Explaining Cooperation under Anarchy: Hypotheses and Strategies', *World Politics*, XXXVIII:1 (1985).

16 Cf. Barry, *Can States Be Moral?*, p. 79.

17 Ibid., p. 81.

18 Cf. R. Tucker, *The Inequality of Nations* (New York: Basic Books, 1977). It is worth stressing that this author is one of the very few to insist on the *interstate* character of the problem, which he uses to deny that moral rules valid for individuals may also be valid for other entities such as states. Cf., for example, this judgement: 'Whereas the order we have today is an order of states, the justice which is sought by the new political sensibility is, for the most part, a justice for individuals that can be guaranteed only by the atrophy of the sovereign powers states continue to claim' (p. 137).

19 For a brilliant presentation of the 'naturalist fallacy', cf. W. K. Frankena, 'The Naturalist Fallacy', in P. Foot (ed.), *Theories of Ethics* (Oxford: Oxford University Press, 1967), esp. p. 57.

20 Tucker, *The Inequality of Nations*, p. 149.

21 Ackerman, *Social Justice*, section 56, par. 3.

22 Ibid., p. 343.

23 Except of course for the case in which it is a government which asks for external aid.

24 For a general presentation of this problem, cf. vol. XXIII of *Nomos*; J. R. Pennock and J. W. Chapman (eds), *Human Rights* (New York: New York University Press, 1981); and the recent J. Donnelly, *Universal Human Rights in Theory and Practice* (Ithaca: Cornell University Press, 1989), which contains a rich bibliography. A noteworthy analysis of the problem is A. Gewirth, *Human Rights: Essays in Justification and Applications* (Chicago: Chicago University Press, 1982). The growth in attention to standards of respect for human rights is also becoming an object for interesting assessments: cf. D. W. Gillies, 'Evaluating National Human Rights Performance: Priorities for the Developing World', *Bulletin of Peace Proposals*, XXI:1 (1990). G. Pontara, 'Interdipendenza e indivisibilità dei diritti economici, sociali, culturali e politici', in *I diritti umani a 40 anni della*

Dichiarazione universale (Padua: Cedam, 1989), makes a forceful argument for a right not only of interstate, but also of international survival. Cf. also F. Viola, *Diritti dell'uomo, diritto naturale, etica contemporanea* (Turin: Giappichelli, 1989).

25 I would not wish this example to be considered marginal or interpreted simplistically. The collective sensibility of today regards as absolutely unacceptable types of conduct which for centuries were extremely commonplace, and which, according to some, have still not fallen completely into disuse. The history of the secret services cannot, by definition, be well known, but traces of it are to be found in political history, nonetheless!

26 As I argued in chapter 1, section 3, above.

27 Thus going one step further than Nozick's minimalist conception, which obviously cannot contemplate the hypothesis that the state has duties externally, arguing that it has too many domestic duties to start with. Yet consider the paradox whereby the state cannot even envisage the existence of a plurality of states: in this way, it risks dying of a disease which is said to be non-existent. Cf. R. Nozick, *Anarchy, State and Utopia* (New York: Basic Books, 1974).

28 Brilmayer, *Justifying International Acts*, p. 11.

29 Which is not to underestimate its complexity, in view of the difficulties involved in achieving forms of redistribution inside the state. On this issue, which goes beyond my argument, cf. A. Sen, *Choice, Welfare and Measurement* (Oxford: Blackwell, 1982).

30 A simple, cogent demonstration of this is provided by Cotta, who makes the distinction between the ethics of justice and the ethics of love, and concludes that, in any case, 'aid is a (universal) duty, implying the correlative (universal) right to receive aid, when it satisfies the prerequisite of universalisable reciprocity.' S. Cotta, *Diritto persona mondo umano* (Turin: Giappichelli, 1986), p. 247.

31 Cf., for example, G. Pontara, *Filosofia pratica* (Milan: Il Saggiatore, 1988), p. 179.

32 It seems to me no coincidence that most external aid theories (with their accompanying difficulties) are utilitarian in nature. They cannot found a duty of moral conduct on the state itself, unless they do so to increase the social wellbeing of citizens. But it is extremely hard to argue that the reasons why children must not die of starvation in the Third World reside simply in the duty to increase the wellbeing or moral sense of citizens of rich countries.

33 Jonas, *The Imperative of Responsibility*, p. 182 (my italics).

34 Wasn't the Carter administration's emphasis on its 'human rights policy' aimed precisely at the domestic situation of many foreign countries?

35 Unlike the Hegelian ethical state, recognition of the 'morality' of the state refers neither to a nation's mission nor to its destiny, and entails nothing other than the awareness that the state may be judged, both in terms of its domestic policy and its role on the international scene. As the interpreter

of a national interest, as the artificial representative of a community, the state cannot be removed from a moral context.

36 In other words, 'the whole within which the individual is reunited with others as a member (i.e., the state) is a whole amongst other wholes, i.e., a state among other states. At the level of international affairs the state is an individual *vis-à-vis* other states, and its individuality is reciprocally bound up with the individuality of its citizens.' M. Frost, *Towards a Normative Theory of International Relations* (Cambridge: Cambridge University Press, 1986), p. 178.

37 An example which clarifies this point well is, in the realm of the relationship between domestic and international law, the solution advanced by Kelsen, who considered that, in general systematic terms, international law ought – *logically* – to precede the various domestic laws. Cf. H. Kelsen, 'Der Wandel der Souveranitatsbegriffes'. in *Studi Filosofico-Giuridici dedicati a Giorgio del Vecchio*, vol. II (Modena: Società Tipografica Modenese, 1931), chs 6–8, and *General Theory of Law and State* (Cambridge, Mass.: Harvard University Press, 1945), part VI.

38 The problem of the 'domestic–external' relationship is normally analysed in an entirely different way in terms of the ability of either level to influence the other, without reference to the *coherence* of a single states's domestic and external behaviour. In other words, analysis is only systematic and never subjective. Cf., for example, A. R. Zolberg, 'L'influence des facteurs "externes" sur l'ordre politique interne', in M. Grawitz and J. Leca, eds, *Traité de science politique* (Paris: Presses Universitaires de France, 1985), vol. I, ch. 9. In short, not only philosophers but also political scientists neglect this vital nexus.

39 Cf. my observations in ch. 1, section 2.

40 The implications of the position defended here become clearer if we compare them with M. Walzer's diametrically opposed position. Walzer, in fact, argues that the situation is a different one altogether since the international realm cannot be given a political arena connotation (but for a confutation of this type of argument, cf. ch. 3, section 3 above):

> Rights are only enforceable within political communities where they have been collectively recognized, and the process by which they come to be recognized is a political process which requires a political arena. The globe is not, or not yet, such an arena. Or rather, the only global community is pluralist in character, a community of nations not of humanity, and the rights recognized within it have been minimal and largely negative, designed to protect the integrity of nations and to regulate their commercial and military transactions.

M. Walzer, 'The Moral Standing of States: A Response to Four Critics', *Philosophy and Public Affairs*, IX:3 (1980), pp. 234–5.

41 I realize that my argument may ultimately appear anti-international, as if

domestic political components were the only ones relevant to the development of international politics. Yet the same argument might be reversed, if we remember that what I am searching for in this context is the foundation for moral judgement on the effective conduct of states: this cannot be attributed to statesmen or governments, which have an intense external activity, and the results of whose actions often affect millions of people.

42 Cf. yet another reformulation in N. Elias, *Die Gesellschaft der Individuen* (Frankfurt: Suhrkamp, 1987), ch. 3, section 15; in English as *Society of Individuals*, tr. E. Jephcott (Oxford: Blackwell, 1991).

43 In purely statistical terms, it would be impossible to explain the grand transformation of eastern Europe, the 1989 revolution!

44 Discussing the limits of patriotism and the support we owe to our own state, if need be to the detriment of others, Hare concludes that, 'we are not allowed to give priority to the interests of any state, its inhabitants, just because it is our state.' M. Hare, 'Philosophy and Practice: Some Issues about War and Peace', *Essays on Political Morality* (Oxford: Clarendon, 1989), pp. 72–3.

45 Acceptance of this formula implies nothing short of a complete review of the borderlines which divide political science, international relations and political philosophy. In my formulation here the three are confused. Yet perhaps in the past there has been too much insistence on differences as opposed to affinities. Without treading on one another's toes, a certain fusion might serve to uncover the existence of macro-problems which cannot be perceived, let alone resolved, by the single disciplines.

46 Whether we are speaking about statesmen, for example, or of public opinion.

47 H. Bull also singles out three levels, which he calls: 'international', with reference to national rights, 'interstate', with reference to the state, and 'cosmopolitan', with reference to individuals as a whole: cf. H. Bull, *The Anarchical Society* (London: Macmillan, 1977), pp. 81–4. The levels are exclusively horizontal (among equal subjects) and comprise neither crossovers nor transversal relations.

48 This many-sidedness in no way changes the idea which has inspired this book from the outset. The principal object of my analysis is 'international relations'; the relations of states as permanent, solid structures upon which the content of the *justice* or *injustice* which individuals experience in their own and other states depend.

49 T. Nardin, *Law, Morality and the Relations of States* (Princeton: Princeton University Press, 1983), p. 259.

50 Ibid., p. 269, p. 271.

51 Ibid., p. 275.

52 Albeit extremely sympathetic towards programmes of this type, R. B. Douglass, 'International Economic Justice', *The Review of Politics*, XLIV:1 (1982), stresses the absence at present of this necessary prerequisite.

53 A good example of this type of attitude is that of the Good Samaritan used

by M. Walzer to argue that it is not possible to go any further, simply because there must be some limit to an otherwise 'indefinite drainage. The very phrase "communal wealth" would lose meaning if all resources and all products were globally common.' Cf. M. Walzer, 'The Distribution of Membership', in P. G. Brown and H. Shue (eds), *Boundaries: National Autonomy and Its Limits* (Totowa: Rowman and Littlefield, 1981), p. 19.

54 Cf. G. Hardin, 'Lifeboat Ethics: the Case Against Helping the Poor', in W. Aiken and H. La Follette (eds), *World Hunger and Moral Obligation* (Englewood Cliffs: Prentice-Hall, 1977), an essay first published in 1974 in *Bioscience*; O. O'Neill, 'Lifeboat Earth', *Philosophy and Public Affairs*, IV:3 (1975); Ackerman, *Social Justice*, section 20, par. 1.

55 So that, at a certain point, there will be so many more poor than rich that they really will invade their possessions! Cf. Hardin, *Lifeboat Ethics*, p. 17.

56 Ackerman does not take into account the plurality of states. This position prevents him from progressing beyond denouncement of the injustice of the present situation: 'the party challenged (the rich) cannot respond by asserting the moral inferiority of the challenger (the poor).' Ackerman, *Social Justice*, section 20, par. 1.

57 Cf. O'Neill, 'Lifeboat Earth', p. 281.

58 Singer, *Practical Ethics*, ch. 8. The 'conditional' which Singer used 15 or so years ago has now, alas, become an 'indicative'!

59 The rise and fall of oil prices is emblematic. The attempts of oil-producing nations to determine the price of oil per barrel autonomously from 1973 – which effectively created difficulties for the developed countries for some years afterwards – was followed by a 50 per cent drop in prices between 1980 and 1989, thanks to the superior bargaining power of the buyer nations.

60 An initial, nascent example is the exceptional increase in emigration from poor to rich countries. Aren't the non-EC citizens who are currently invading western Europe simply trying to jump into the lifeboat before it is too late?

61 It is rather odd that, after at least 30 years of talk of interdependence, the fundamental and dramatic problems of equality among individuals have led to a revival of sophisticated distinctions and separations.

62 Ecological problems are typical of our time only in terms of the way they manifest themselves. Actually, they are at least as old as industrial development itself.

63 The 'international ecological question' is now a central one, and has aroused intense interest among scholars: cf. O. R. Young, *International Cooperation. Building Regimes for Natural Resources and the Environment* (Ithaca: Cornell University Press, 1989); cf. also F. Armao and W. Coralluzzo, 'Ecologia internazionale', *Teoria Politica*, VI:1 (1989), which includes many bibliographical references, and A. Caffarena, 'Regimi per l'ambiente', ibid.. The question of fishing rights is turned into a fascinating apologue by H.

Fain, *Normative Politics and the Community of Nations* (Philadelphia: Temple University Press, 1987), pp. 64ff..

64 D. W. Pearce and R. K. Turner, *Economics of Natural Resources and the Environment* (London: Harvester Wheatsheaf, 1990), ch. 15, seek to include ethics in the environment debate, contrasting utilitarian consequential ethics with deontological ethics, and expressing a preference for neither. They simply argue that our duty to future generations is to conserve renewable goods to compensate them for the limited access they will have to resources. Cf. p. 238.

65 By way of a banal example: at the end of World War II, the USA and Great Britain had substantially different ideas about the future of Italy. Whereas the USA opted in favour of the Christian Democratic Party almost immediately, the British tried at first to support the monarchy. The fact is that, in the case discussed here, formulations of this kind are *by nature* unpresentable.

66 The fact that this awareness is emerging clearly only today does not mean that the nature of the problem was different in the past.

67 Totally analogous justifications have prompted widespread reflection on international democracy.

68 M. Serres, *Le contrat naturel* (Paris: Bourin, 1990), p. 72. Despite his at times monotonous style, this author manages to convey the great existential originality of the new situation, when he observes that 'history enters nature; nature in its globality enters history' (p. 18), or that 'we have lived for some time in a contractual relationship with the earth' (p. 171). Much less optimistic and much more 'panic' are the considerations of Jonas, for whom, 'the humanization of nature' is taking place 'more or less along the same lines as the "ennoblement" of the serf, the slave of the feudal nobility', hence 'humanization' is 'a hypocritical euphemism which designates man's total subordination to total exploitation as a means of satisfying his needs.' Cf. H. Jonas, *Das Prinzip Verantwortung* (Frankfurt: Insel Verlag, 1979), ch. 6, B, section 4, the original German text of which *The Imperative* is an abridged translation.

69 The specific problematique of which is discussed in detail by J. F. Paradise, 'International Social Justice: Philosophical and Political-Economic Considerations', *Millennium: Journal of International Studies*, XIV:1 (1985).

70 On the contemporary debate on utilitarianism, cf. A. Sen and B. Williams (eds), *Utilitarianism and Beyond* (Cambridge: Cambridge University Press, 1982), and C. A. Viano, 'L'utilitarismo', in C. A. Viano (ed.), *Teorie etiche contemporanee* (Turin: Bollati Boringhieri, 1990).

71 Rawls, *A Theory of Justice*.

72 C. R. Beitz, *Political Theory and International Relations* (Princeton: Princeton University Press, 1979), p. 128.

73 Ibid., p. 180. A. Walter, 'La giustizia distributiva nella teoria delle relazioni internazionali', *Politica internazionale*, XII:6 (1984), is sympathetic to Beitz's argument, although he does have a few objections to make.

74   I. Kant, *Universal Natural History and Theory of the Heavens*, tr. (with introduction and notes) S. L. Jaki (Edinburgh: Scottish Academic Press, 1981).

75   Cf. S. Hoffman, *Duties Beyond Borders* (New York: Syracuse University Press, 1981), p. 156. Cf. Hoffman's critique of Beitz in the preceding pages.

76   Ibid., p. 198.

77   Nardin, *Law, Morality*, p. 274.

78   For the special meaning I have attributed to this word, cf. ch. 2, section 4, above.

79   Who can deny that the redistribution which ensued from World War II was preferable to what might have come about if Nazi Germany had won?

80   There is no doubt that the use of such a sad reality for an example does not attempt to hide the responsibilities (not that it addresses them) of western countries in which drugs are most widely consumed. If there were no demand, the supply would drop and drug producers would have to change jobs! For an internationally-oriented analysis, cf. P. D. Scott and J. Marshall, *Cocaine Politics, Drugs, Armies and the CIA in Central America* (Berkeley: University of California Press, 1991).

81   As long as there are no forms of unification, reunification and fusion.

82   Cf. Walzer, *Just and Unjust Wars*, pp. 90–2.

83   Cf. K. N. Waltz, *Man, the State and War* (New York: Columbia University Press, 1959). The problem is normally defined in international language as one of analytic levels, the best known presentation of which is J. D. Singer, 'The Level of Analysis Problems in International Relations', in K. Knorr and Sydney Verba (eds), *The International System: Theoretical Essays* (Princeton: Princeton University Press, 1961).

84   Some of my 23 readers (Manzoni joked about the number of his readers, but I am being serious: there are even fewer than 23 official international relations specialists in Italy!) may be surprised to find me contradicting well nigh 20 years spent arguing in favour of the study of international relations founded on the exclusiveness of their special viewpoint. I must stress, though, that, in the first place, the problematique addressed here is situated at a much higher and broader level of conceptualization than the specialized level (which it incorporates), and secondly, that this innovation seems to me absolutely in order in as much as international relations are now entering into a totally new phase. Now that the subject has won the battle for the recognition of its autonomy, there is no longer any point in its retreating into specialization and purity: the time has now come to address the problems which reality creates with an open methodological spirit. We now need to improve and diversify our theoretical and philosophical baggage. If we do, this may enable our discipline to make a step forward in quality.

85   I use the expression 'international society' simply because we still lack a name for this organizational level of reality. Or is it because only now has it become possible to conceptualize states as an effective whole?

Chapter 7   Conclusion

1   Albeit somewhat rough and ready, cf. the catalogue drawn up by G. C. Kohn, *Dictionary of Wars* (New York: Facts on File, 1986).

2   Cf. the remarks made in his 'Conclusions' by N. Elias, *The Civilizing Process: Power and Civilization* (New York: Pantheon Books, 1982); also in one-vol. edn, *The Civilizing Process* (Oxford: Blackwell, 1994).

3   Cf. M. W. Doyle, 'Liberal Institutions and International Ethics', in K. Kipnis and D. T. Meyers (eds), *Political Realism and International Morality* (Boulder: Westview, 1987), pp. 185–211; N. Bobbio, 'Democrazia e sistema internazionale' and L. Bonanate, 'Dalla pace alla democrazia internazionale', both in L. Cortesi (ed.), *Democrazia, rischio nucleare, movimenti per la pace* (Naples: Liguori, 1988), pp. 37–52 and pp. 53–68 respectively.

4   All I am doing here is applying the principles discussed in ch. 1, section 2 and in ch. 4, section 4.

5   Just how dramatic the consequences of this lack of control may be has emerged in the affair of the exploitation of the Iraqi market (a sort of haven for gun runners) over the last few years.

6   Cf. *Gazzetta ufficiale della repubblica italiana*, III:3 (1990), pp. 4–5.

7   Although one does of course wonder exactly how many other countries need similar aid. G. Pontara, *Filosofia pratica* (Milan: Il Saggiatore, 1988), esp. ch. 5, devotes particular attention to the justification of the duty of rich states to help poor ones. In his conclusion to ch. 6, he adds that no theory of rights is needed to justify humanitarian measures, since the utilitarian theory is sufficient in itself. Cf. esp. p. 209.

8   One of the most recent studies on the topic is C. Allègre, *Economiser la planète* (Paris: Fayard, 1990).

9   'Far-sighted interest would here be twofold: the (in the long run) better return effect of a healthy world economy upon one's own, and the fear of a pent-up need exploding into international violence.' H. Jonas, *The Imperative of Responsibility* (Chicago: Chicago University Press, 1984), p. 183.

10   Or, better still, they have to adapt their culture to the changed conditions of world reality.

11   R. Caillois, 'La vertige de la guerre', in *Quatre essais de sociologie contemporaine* (Paris: Olivier Perrina Editeur, 1980).

12   Of course I refer here exclusively to those relevant from the ethical-political point of view, not to political-strategic ones (although the latter are by no means insignificant in the case in point). I make more specific remarks on this point in 'La rivoluzione internazionale', *Teoria politica*, VIII:2 (1991).

13   Cf. ch. 6, section 4 above.

14   I would never be as ingenuous as to think that this order is *just* simply because it exists.

15   Although it was precisely in these terms that extremists on both sides lived the war.

16 The same principle is now determining one of the most dramatic challenges to the Soviet Union, as the programmes of independence or separatist programmes in the different republics of the Union demonstrate.

17 That is, perhaps we have entered the phase of 'an increase in war' surmised in the cyclical hypothesis discussed in ch. 5, section 2, above.

18 Just as then there was discussion of the 'Better dead than red – better red than dead' dilemma, shouldn't we ask ourselves today whether it is better to be Islamic and alive or dead and free? For a synthetic reconstruction of the controversy, see L. Bonanante (ed.), *La guerra nella società contemporanea* (Milan: Principato, 1972).

19 I use the conditional to stress that what we have here is a possibility, not an obligation.

20 In these applications of principles to a specific case, I deliberately omit the position of Iraq. The circumstances applied to Iraq are (with much greater justification) those which it imposed on its enemies. It thus seems totally superfluous to me in this context to argue the moral unjustifiability of Iraq's invasion of Kuwait, or its conduct towards the country's inhabitants or its goods.

21 On the determination of these conditions, cf. N. Bobbio, 'Diritto e guerra' (1965), now in *Il problema della guerra e le vie della pace* (Bologna: Il Mulino, 1984), p. 104. For the classical formulation of this problem, cf. the passages from Grotius included in L. Bonanate (ed.), *Diritto naturale e relazioni tra gli stati* (Turin: Loescher, 1976).

22 Of course the theme of the justification of war might be addressed from a religious point of view as well: cf. W. L. LaCroix, *War and International Ethics: Tradition and Today* (Boston: University Press of America, 1988); *La conscience juive face à la guerre* (Paris: Presses universitaires de France), 1976; K. Barth, *Dogmatica ecclesiastica* (Zurich: TVZ Verlag, 1951), vol. III, part 4.

23 However 'upright' the intentions which led western states into war, however sincere their desire to restore legitimate government to Kuwait, however great their legal authority (the three principal conditions of *jus ad bellum*), their handling of operations seemed neither 'proportional' nor capable of 'discriminating' combatants from civilians (the universally acknowledged principles of *jus in bello*). If we apply the same five considerations to Iraq, the result is all the more depressing. All these arguments were applied by N. Bobbio in his press articles during the Gulf war and put into perspective in the introduction to the collection, N. Bobbio, *Una guerra giusta? Sul conflitto del Golfo* (Venice: Marsilio, 1991).

24 As I argued in ch. 2, sections 2 and 3 above, not even the surrogate of practical deterrence is an exception to respect for principles.

25 C. von Clausewitz, *On War*, tr. Michael Howard and Peter Paret (Princeton: Princeton University Press, 1984), vol. I, 7, p. 78.

26 In ch. 3, sections 2–3, for example, I highlighted the unjustifiability of *non*violent reciprocal deterrence politics.

27 Hence, entirely different from 'international law'.

28 The 'second state' in this ingenuous metaphor would be the few states which lived off the reflection of their protectors' privileges.

29 J. Lee Ray, 'The Abolition of Slavery and the End of International War', *International Organisation*, XLIII:3 (1989), p. 423.

30 Ibid., p. 425.

31 I am only too well aware that a great many other formulations might be used against mine. One is that of N. Elias, 'War seems the eternal heritage of humanity', cf. N. Elias, *Humana Conditio. Beobachtungen zur Entwicklung der Menscheit am 40* (Frankfurt: Suhrkamp, 1985), section 13.

32 As he himself was to tell in his *Experiment in Autobiography* (London: Gollancz, 1934), vol. II, p. 667.

Index